PHENOMENOLOGY, INTERPRETATION, AND COMMUNITY

Selected Studies in
Phenomenology and Existential Philosophy   19

PHENOMENOLOGY, INTERPRETATION, AND COMMUNITY

Edited by
Lenore Langsdorf and Stephen H. Watson
with E. Marya Bower

STATE UNIVERSITY OF NEW YORK PRESS

Published by
State University of New York Press, Albany

Printed in the United States of America

For information, address State University of New York
Press, State University Plaza, Albany, N.Y., 12246

Production by Cathleen Collins
Marketing by Dana Yanulavich

Library of Congress Cataloging-in-Publication Data

Phenomenology, interpretation, and community / edited by Lenore
    Langsdorf and Stephen H. Watson with E. Marya Bower.
        p.   cm. — (Selected studies in phenomenology and existential
    philosophy : 19)
        Includes bibliographical references and index.
        ISBN 0–7914–2865–6 (alk. paper). — ISBN 0–7914–2866–4 (pbk. :
    alk. paper)
        1. Phenomenology.   2. Hermeneutics.   I. Langsdorf, Lenore, 1943–
    II. Watson, Stephen H., 1951–   .   III. Bower, E. Marya, 1959–
    IV. Series.
    B829.5.P485   1996
    142′ .7—dc20   95–19602
                                                                                               CIP

10 9 8 7 6 5 4 3 2 1

Contents

Introduction

In his influential text of 1936, "The Origin of Geometry," Edmund Husserl
began to articulate the transcendental background of *Wissenschaftstheorie*
by denying that objectivity could be reduced to the epistemic capacity for
repetition of self-evident truths.[1] Although this statement may at first appear
to be paradoxical, granted not only many of his commentators, but equally
the axioms of his own position, he immediately added: "It does arise, however—in a preliminary stage—in understandable fashion as soon as we take
into consideration the function of empathy and fellow mankind as a community of empathy and language" (OG 360). The typical complexity of
Husserl's position is as evident here as it is elsewhere. Following Bolzano,
Husserl had been committed throughout to truth as a system of determinate
repeatables. From Brentano he had learned the significance of intentional
inexistence not only as a distinguishing mark of the mental, but as an epistemic source of evidence, of "judgment with insight." As his correspondence with Frege makes evident, Husserl had joined Frege in rebelling
against the attempts of intuitionists or conventionalists to reduce the symbolic matrices of geometry to syntactic play, that is, to what he had con-
demned from the outset as mere *Spielbedeutung*.[2]

That the "Origin" added the criterion of empathy to the features of *objectivität* may, nonetheless, even from the distance of time, seem strange. None
of the above thinkers had, after all, joined him in this. Husserl's extension of
the concept of objectivity, however, was neither new in his thought in 1936
nor new to the phenomenological "movement" in general, as it came to be
called. On the one hand, the problem of empathy extends before Husserl not
only to his idealist predecessors (for example, Fichte and Hegel), but
beyond them to the reception of treatises on the passions in philosophical
modernity (for example, in Hobbes, Shaftesbury, Adam Smith, and
Rousseau). On the other hand, the problem of empathy had equally formed a
critical part of the itinerary of phenomenology. This can be witnessed in the
great treatises on this topic, such as the writings of Scheler, Stein, Husserl's
fifth Cartesian Meditation[3] (all bearing in turn the effect of Lipps), as well
as, in a quite different genre, in the writings of Levinas, Lacan, or even

Lyotard and Habermas. But this was perhaps the point. As Husserl well knew, at stake at the center of his foundational claims were a number of traditional metaphysical operators as paradoxical as the set paradoxes he had attempted to solve in Russell's aftermath.[4] Thus, it would be no accident that the fifth Meditation would center on the problem of appresentation by means of the category of analogy, nor that in the "Origin" itself the community of empathy and language would be immediately glossed as a community of "reciprocal linguistic understanding," nor finally that this "differential" itself would be glossed as an exchange between the determinate and the indeterminate, sign and symbol, the univocal and the equivocal. Such, after all, would be the remnant of abstract or propositional objectivity, as the *Formal and Transcendental Logic* had already realized in ultimately criticizing the misguided presupposition of truth in itself.[5] Now, as the latter declared, all truth would be involved in "relativities" and, as "The Origin of Geometry" stated, everywhere the problems are historical (OG 368).

In one sense, all this seemed new, granted Husserl's earlier arguments on behalf of what he once termed the "mighty forces of objectified strict science" that were levied against the claims concerning decadence common to historicism.[6] And yet, at the same time, these developments only made explicit the analysis of a certain history that had accompanied phenomenology from the outset. In the "Origin," as in other writings of this period, the effect of this history would be referred to by Husserl in terms of the constant, indeed unavoidable, "danger" attending the reciprocal linguistic understanding that underlies the "community of communication," namely, that the origins of evidence in the "living truth" revealed in intentional analyses might succumb to a certain forgetfulness (FTL 279).

It would take perhaps a Heidegger to see the conflict between formalists, logicists, and phenomenologists as a conflict between the ancients and the moderns, specifically between Aristotle and Hobbes. It was all of that and more. Surely this was true of the problems of empathy or sympathy, where at stake were not only links to Kant's account of pure feeling in the third *Critique*, but a whole archive that could be traced back, for example, to the Augustinian *ordo amoris* or beyond to Aristotle's *Nichomachean Ethics*.[7] It perhaps was even more straightforwardly true of the philosophy of mind and epistemology at stake in phenomenology. Husserl (like Heidegger after him) had begun by attempting to deepen Brentano's retrieval of neo-Thomist and Aristotelian accounts of intentionality and the evidence of "daily life" upon which they relied. They realized and indeed tacitly affirmed the intransigence of their differences with respect to the ancients (FTL 199). Indeed,

Husserl and Heidegger were in agreement, at least in this respect, that these differences now involved a failure in memory, a failure in the retrieval of origins, a certain forgetfulness regarding authentic beginnings. In addition, they agreed that, as a consequence of this failure, communities were in principle—to use Husserl's term—dangerous.

> Now one will say that in the sphere that interests us here—that of science, of thinking directed toward the attainment of truths and the avoidance of falsehood—one is obviously greatly concerned from the start to put a stop to the free play of associative constructives. In view of the unavoidable sedimentation of mental products in the form of linguistic acquisition, which can be taken over by anyone else, such constructions remain a constant danger. (OG 362)

For Husserl, the preeminent danger in question was the danger of passivity, the unconscious entanglement of free association, a domain the *Formal and Transcendental Logic* had described as an "anonymous" one of unfulfilled "symbolic rhythmics" (FTL 369–70). Notwithstanding his reliance upon the fecundity of passive synthesis for extending the foundations of static intentional analysis, Husserl turned steadfastly against the problem of passivity, against, to use Fichte's staunchly non-Aristotlian terms, a certain *vis inertia* of habit.[8] At stake, to use Husserl's terms, was a history in which "[g]reater and greater segments of this life lapse into a kind of talking and reading that is dominated purely by association" (OG 362). And, despite all his commitments to historicity and tradition, Heidegger was equally troubled by this same failure in his critique of the inauthenticity of the everyday. Indeed both were even "Nietzschean," to the extent that they both claimed that the foundations of science required a critique of the traditions of the everyday. As Nietzsche had put it, "we philosophers need to be spared one thing above all: everything to do with 'today' [*Das Heute*]."[9] If tradition was a source or origin, "tradition" was equally, both Husserl and Heidegger agreed, a source of illusion.

The position was Hobbesian twice over perhaps, consistent with what Husserl had recognized as Hobbes's generalization (and subjectivization) of Galileo's revolution.[10] In the first place, the protocols of the position articulated tradition as being haunted by the failure of false authority. Second, they articulated the domain of the political not only as a domain of "living truth" and its *arete*, but equally as a domain regulated by the economics of stray desire and its danger, and, in the extreme, by the possibilities of death. But, against Hobbes, the copula could not be reduced to calculability. For

Husserl, and it should be recalled that it was equally his argument against Frege, such reductions were "onesided," that is, lacking an account of the adjudicative acts that underlie intentional contents. Moreover, the point was not that the position was simply abstract, but that, in the extreme, such onesidedness was falsifying. In his later works Husserl becomes more extreme in his characterization of such reductions, their omissions, and their exclusions; indeed, he claims in "The Vienna Lecture" of 1935 that "a one-sided rationality can certainly become an evil."[11] But this perhaps indicates as well the status of Husserl's modernism. As Leo Strauss put it, Hobbes was always concerned with the extreme case.[12]

Perhaps at no time would Husserl become closer to those like Horkheimer and Adorno in their critique of instrumental rationality and what Husserl called elsewhere the "unquestioned tradition" of *Technisierung*.[13] But we should also recall what instigates this danger for Husserl in the text of the "Origin" itself: precisely that point at which the science of infinite tasks constituting philosophy *de jure* collides with philosophical claims *de facto* (OG 291), that is, the distinction between the regulative, the underdetermined task of historical judgment, and the ideal of objectivity that regulates such judgment. Even Foucault would affirm the result: the claim to ideology and objectivity need not conflict—nor, as he also would point out, would increasing rigor or the return to origins dissipate the role of ideology.[14] But, of course, that just is the problem of judgment, especially granted Husserl's immediate claim that "no line of knowledge, no single truth may be absolutized and isolated" (OG 291).

To add that "the community of communication" would require the community of empathy as a condition of *objectivität* is not only to raise the problem of its permanence (its iterability or documentability), it is also to recognize that the community of rational agents is likewise a community of passions, with both its constitutions and its "dangers" implicitly linking knowledge to power. This recognition reappears in Husserl's call for vigilance of conscience over against submission to unconscious effect that gives rise to the possibility of fulfillment and to the hope that we might be able "to transform the logical chains of centuries" into a "lasting traditionalization" (OG 367). Still, if Bolzano's account of truths-in-themselves had required a certain intentional modification to grasp the phenomenological iterability that underlay scientific identity (Husserl had worried about their mythic status from the beginning), the famous analyses of empathy by Theodor Lipps, founded on the concept of inner imitation and self-projection, would need to be similarly altered and perhaps even detached from the notion of mimesis and self-projection. The task of overcoming the limitations of the latter had been begun quite early by Max Scheler and Edith Stein, both of whom had noted the egoistic distortions of modern philosophy in its formulations.[15] Their analyses also provided theoretical links with Aristotle, particularly in the notions of understanding [*synesis*] and sympathetic judgment [*syngnome*]. It is not accidental, then, that the problem of community and nature would reemerge in this guise, as the later books of the *Ideen* would initially reveal, but as would equally be demonstrated by the continuing presence of the genre of *Naturrecht* in its discourses. Moreover, that phenomenology had concerned itself from the outset with these problems is evident as early as Reinach's contributions to the first volume of Husserl's phenomenological *Jahrbuch* in 1913.[16]

At the same time, however, granted the history (not to speak of the histrionics) that accompanied this development, it would be naive—indeed perhaps ideological—to claim that such retrievals might occur forthwith and without regard to the history that governs both the concept of community and the concept of nature. Here too the problems are not only historical, but often enough Hobbesian as well. If phenomenological narratives were originally (or often enough) Aristotlian in inspiration, they inevitably ran into a Hobbesian challenge, as is shown implicitly in Husserl's criticism of modern philosophy. This also is made explicit in Heidegger's criticism of the *commercium* of *Das Man* and the demand for a hermeneutics of empathy that would not only overcome the abstractness of previous theoretical formulations, but also articulate "the unsociability [*Das Unumganglichkeit*] of the dominant modes of Being-with" in which empathy is first constituted. These no doubt complicated his own "dangerous" attempts "to gain the mastery over the everyday."[17] The various analyses of the Other that took place in Heidegger's wake—epistemically, ontologically, and ethically—and that accompanied the descent of phenomenology (surely troubled by Husserl's and Heidegger's shortfalls here) only truncated the obvious concerning this failure of traditions and the historical embeddedness of their own analyses.

The problem perhaps had already received its protocols from Hobbes's own transformation of the "vain and fabulous" tradition,[18] a transformation that was poised between certainty and the threat of oblivion. As Hobbes put it, recalling both the ancient "virtue" of friendship and the principle of charity: "The affection wherewith men many times bestow their benefits on strangers is not to be called charity, but either contract, whereby they seek to purchase friendship, or fear, which maketh them purchase peace."[19] The problems affecting community would be infinitely complicated by this analysis, estranged in the distinction between theory and object, self and other, power and knowledge. Hegel also would affirm the breach between nature and institution that it entailed. Although (like the initial phenomeno-logical glosses on the pure feeling of empathy) Hegel affirmed the Romantic's retrievals—that is, he could affirm that "everything begins with the heart"—it is equally true too, he claimed, that "feeling and heart is not the form by which anything is legitimated as religious, moral, true, just, etc."[20]

To raise the issue of contract is indeed to raise the question of legitima-tion and the problem of the law itself. It is to raise again the distinction between 'positive' law and 'natural' law, the issue of constitutions both political and transcendental—and to do so throughout a domain that, *qua* theoretical, remains struck with the vagaries of theory, that is, underdeter-mined. It is just here, of course, that the problem of interpretation emerges, complicating both the explication of experience and the language of the-ory.[21] Indeed, as Spinoza recognized in raising the problem of interpreta-tion, the models for such laws were not only political, but theological and scientific, a matter analogical through and through.[22] Or, as Hobbes himself put it, "All Laws, written and unwritten, have need of interpretation"—and this is especially true of the natural law that has "the greater need of able Interpreters."[23] Insofar as neither Hobbes nor Spinoza had simply acceded to the Nietzschean "new infinity of interpretation," both had encountered its problem. The recognition of the underdeterminacy at stake, that the Babel of language has become theoretical, underwrote both the Hobbesian preoccupation with certainty as well as the Hobbesian investment in sover-eignty. Surely Hobbes's theoretical concern with the problem of translation is of a piece with his search for certainty in the *polis*, a concern already con-fronted with the disruption of the natural language of theory and practice, and the problem of recognition and the transfers, both theoretical and polit-ical, it entailed. Indeed, in one sense, still hopeful for an eidetic resolution, Scheler had not argued otherwise insofar as he claimed of moral theory that its concern with criteria for evaluation was already a sign of a certain deca-dence: "its origin is always connected with processes of disintegration in an existing *ethos*."[24]

The same rupture attends not only the problem of *ethos*, but the problem of community operative in all "phenomenological" discourses associated with it: the problem of tradition and lifeworld, the inherited and the invented, the given and the constituted, nature and culture. And if Husserl's turn to empathy as a condition of objectivity seems from a particular vantage point surprising, the final account of empathy—perhaps even from his own standpoint—becomes startling. First, Husserl's commitments to the significance of temporality surely becomes tensed within his historical turn. Empathy, as *Experience and Judgment* puts it, thus becomes the opening of "intersubjectively common time"—still providing thereby a commonality of one and the same objective world.[25] But, additionally, the latter, taken in the most comprehensive sense, becomes understood as "our earth," articulating a "matrix" from which the philosophemes of origin, naissance, and the lived world would ultimately achieve a certain founding determination.[26]

    Gadamer had claimed in his own account of the post-Kantian archive of hermeneutics that neither empathy nor sympathy could be reduced to a condition of knowledge; yet neither could either of them be reduced to simple emotion. This was indicative of the complex interplay constitutive of traditionality in general (TM 233). In this way, tradition should be seen as a "multifariousness of voices" (TM 284). What was important here was not simply an internal relation of intentional "transfer," to use Hobbes's term, but an "I and Thou" relation, that is, a matter of dialogue. And here the point concerned not cognitive iterability or agreement, but interpretability. Gadamer, however, like Foucault, would not deny the epistemological project. Instead he would demand its extension: "objectivity" would be the working out and application of such possibilities through dialogue (TM 267).

    Still, the implications of the latter remain perhaps inevitably unclear. It is just this problem that haunts the move from the bonds of nature, constitution, and cognitive agreement to interpretability. The complicated remainder such a move imparts regarding judgment and legitimation once again underscores the underdeterminability that divides claims *de facto* and claims *de jure*. Gadamer glossed dialogue as an event that summons its participants "to come *with* one to 'judgment'" (TM 261n). Thus the account remained evidential, if always articulated through a historical context, still "ordered to the object, a *mensuratio ad rem*" (TM 261). Moreover, Gadamer had distinguished what he had called his own "revival" of hermeneutics and its account of rationality of traditions from commitment to the past *simpliciter*, that is, from "traditionalism."[27] Even simple reiteration would require legitimation. Here again there is no perspective (and doubtless no tradition) "in itself."

    Yet the complicated remainder these developments impart with respect to problems once readily invested in the problem of empathy (and the dangers accompanying it) are apparent, bequeathing a domain divided between action and passion, self and other, the individual and the universal, experience and judgment. In one sense, this division is the division of judgment [*Urteilung*] itself, as Hegel had learned from Hölderlin.[28] Bolzano would stop the logical progression of his own *Wissenschaftslehre* to criticize explicitly this division, its complication, and its threat.[29] But as Hölderlin's original rendering claimed, what is also at stake in the equivocity of signification—to use Husserl's terms, its 'symbolic rhythmics'—is the question of its reduction and the possibility of a certain counter-rhythm or caesura, that is, a content irreducible to presentation.[30] Here the phenomenological quest for adequacy and cognitive agreement, an event in which "everyone is equal to everyone else" (FTL 226), encounters its limit in the problem of difference, alterity, and incommensurability. Indeed, as Jean Hyppolite once put it, in a text that explicated the *Logic* of Hegel, judgment here becomes "the precarious abode of understanding which oscillates between the subjective and the objective, the empirical and the transcendental, the judgment of perception and the judgment of experience."[31] And, it should be added, consciousness and the unconscious, as Hegel already had seen.[32] Hyppolite's text is one that many saw as a *parcours* to the issues of "poststructuralism." Thought would remain, as Foucault would put it, a "perilous" act whose "identity" is always articulated through difference, thus divided between self and other, sign and symbol, conscious and unconscious—and ultimately between those who possess community (*communitas*) and those who do not. It is at this point that phenomenological experience and its account of the community of rational agents encounters its Hobbesian ancestry in its midst, confronting there the agonistics of reason and power and the rupture of traditions anew. This would result in a complex legacy for phenomenology, the narratives and the evidence it invokes, and the communities from which it sought assurance and sought in turn to sustain.

If none of this simply dissolves the evidence that the phenomenologist seeks to interrogate or the judgments that result from this interrogation—indeed, if it still must be claimed that there are instances in which it would be irrational to judge otherwise and that we are morally obligated at times to so judge—then likewise it is true that justification and obligation equally confront both the complexity of their limits, the summons of their responsibility, and the heterogeneous interface between interpretation and community. Indeed, in many ways, as has been seen, the problem of this interface has accompanied the itinerary of phenomenology itself—one that doubtless bears thinking and rethinking.

It is just to this task of thinking and rethinking to which our authors in this volume turn. In the first part of the volume, entitled "Origin, Insight, and Explication," John Brough begins this task by offering a careful and interesting examination of Husserl's inquiry into the experience of time-consciousness. Focusing on Husserl's responses to two common but opposed conceptions of time-consciousness, namely, that one can never perceive the present and that one can only perceive what is present, Brough provides the reader with an opportunity to perceive the richness of the notions of presence and absence as they appear in Husserl's thought. Husserl's understanding of the experiences of retention and recollection also are discussed, as well as his notion of the absolute flow of consciousness.

The chapter written by Dieter Lohmar provides an opportunity for the reader to see how Husserl's consideration of the concept of the Life-world contributed to his critique of idealizations. Drawing upon a broad array of his works, Lohmar examines the different ways in which Husserl attempted to determine the basic and shared experience that grounds or makes meaningful the idealizations that we invoke. In addition to providing insight into the problem of idealizations in general, this chapter also explores what the implications might be of the "seeping in" of scientific concepts and perspectives into our everyday Life-world.

The question of the origin of *Being and Time* is the focus of the chapter by Theodore Kisiel. Going back beyond the opening pages of that work, and further back than the Introduction to the Aristotle book of 1922, Kisiel directs us to the *Kriegsnotsemester* of 1919. In this semester, Heidegger explored the possibility of a radicalized phenomenology and laid the groundwork for his future inquiries into the experience of Being. Combining an analysis of the major themes of that semester with an inquiry into the hints that appeared in Heidegger's habilitation work of 1915, Kisiel provides a far-reaching and thought-provoking chapter in which the multiple directions in which Heidegger's paths of thinking would take him become clearer.

The last chapter in this part is cast in terms of an inquiry into the cleverness that is required to do phenomenology. Here, Dominique Janicaud seeks to explore what he identifies as phenomenology's "unavoidable tension between method and project." He clearly identifies the dilemma inherent in the need for method, namely, that establishing rules or procedures might render phenomenology ultimately reductivist and formal, while not establishing rules might leave phenomenology so vague and flexible that it ceases to be a coherent discipline. To solve this dilemma, Janicaud suggests that phenomenology should establish its own notion of rigor, one that is coupled with a particular openness to phenomena. This openness is characterized as a type of aesthetic sense. Taken together, this openness and this sense of rigor should render phenomenology "too clever to be science, not clever enough to be art."

The second part of this volume moves from exploring the broader questions of origins and interpretation that undergird these investigations and turns to consider more directly the implications of an inquiry into the boundaries of the individual and the state. To this end, Anthony Steinbock's chapter explores the possibility of creating a nonfoundational, yet transcendental, theory of intersubjectivity. After sketching out some of the difficulties inherent in Husserl's Cartesian, and hence foundational, account of intersubjectivity, Steinbock proceeds to discuss three variant phenomenological methods: the static, the genetic, and the generative methods. The generative method, with its concentration on cultural, historical, and normative phenomena, appears to be most fruitful for this project. An examination of the notions of homeworld and alienworld within the context of this method leads Steinbock to suggest that phenomenology and the phenomenologist have a dual responsibility to be "ethically 'critical' of the home and ethically 'responsible' towards the alien."

The chapter by H. Peter Steeves begins by investigating how Husserl's explication of the experiences of apperception and pairing enable one not only to recognize the Other, but also to recognize multiple Others, that is, to recognize one's own community. Steeves acknowledges the criticism that Husserl's theory can be said to lead to a version of relativism in which intercultural understanding is impossible. In order to respond to this criticism, Steeves builds upon the analyses explored earlier to show not only that it is possible to understand various cultures, but also that one necessarily participates in a transcendent community, a community that is itself greater than the sum of its elements. In his closing section, Steeves provides some provocative suggestions for further reflection on the implications of the existence of this transcendent community.

David Kolb's chapter explores the differing views of Heidegger and Hegel with regard to the nature and structure of the state and its role in shaping the circulation of goods and identities within it. He contrasts Hegel's perspective—in which fixed anchors of meaning and substantiality such as the agricultural class and the craft corporation develop and hence limit circulation so that there is space for the rational exercise of political freedom—with Heidegger's notion of *das Gestell*, in which there is a depthless circulation of identities and goods that may nevertheless be mediated by one's own finitude. In addition, Kolb examines the possible criteria that each thinker (and his or her successors) has available for making a critical judgment between the forms that civil society may take.

In the next chapter, Shaun Gallagher focuses on Habermas's critique of Hegel's political philosophy. Gallagher first shows how Hegel's theory indicates that the particular historical reality of a nation and of its citizens limits the universality of a state. This results in a nationalism that is based upon trust and a lack of critique; a possible consequence of this nationalism is the emergence of totalitarianism. He then explores Habermas's attempt to develop a theory of postconventional patriotism that is less trusting and that includes an element of vigorous critique and a commitment to universal, consistent values that are not shaped by the realities of a particular nation, but by a commitment to internationalism and consensus. After exposing some of the limitations in Habermas's theory, Gallagher proposes that these limitations can be overcome by a retrieval of the concept of *phronesis* that mediates the ambiguity between the universal and the particular.

James Hart's essay completes this part. In it he challenges the reader to reflect upon what it means to live as an authentic member of a political community. Drawing upon a wide array of resources, including the writings of Husserl, Thoreau, Arendt, and Dewey, Hart moves the reader beyond mere theoretical reflection to a consideration of the implications of our current practical, everyday actions. By means of an examination of the limitations of representational democracy and the commitments that we implicitly make when we pay taxes, Hart focuses our attention upon the ethical responsibility that we bear for the immoral military actions undertaken by our nation.

The third part of this volume includes three chapters that focus upon Gadamer's experience of truth in tradition. Holly L. Wilson begins this threefold exploration by taking up the question of Gadamer's conservatism. After summarizing how several thinkers have responded to the charge that Gadamer's commitment to tradition makes his work irreducibly conservative, and the weaknesses that she sees in these defenses, Wilson proposes a new strategy by which this charge might be answered. This strategy builds upon what she identifies as Gadamer's conception of the multifariousness of traditions, a perspective that is not committed to a view of tradition as a monolithic or unitary phenomenon. Wilson's proposal is supplemented by an analysis of Gadamer's view of language and its relationship to the Socratic and Hegelian notions of dialectic and the Christian understanding of the power of the spoken Word.

The chapter by James Risser invites the reader to reflect upon the presence of truth in the hermeneutic experience. He presents an overview of Gadamer's analysis of the beautiful and the concept of mimesis and examines the relationship between both a copy and an image of a picture and the original picture itself. An image, Risser suggests, becomes an event of self-presentation or shining forth of what is beautiful. Proceeding from the analysis of the beautiful, Risser goes on to propose that there is an imaging of truth, an image-play in language and conversation, that is akin to a performance. Invoking the concept of "thick images" in which we become entangled, Risser suggests that this performance does not refer back to something that is more true or more real, that is, it does not represent something that must be dis-entangled. Rather, this performance is itself a site in which truth comes to fullness in the act of saying what is meant.

Lawrence Schmidt provides the final discussion of the notion of hermeneutic truth in this section. He suggests that a key concept that has not been explored fully is Gadamer's notion of the *Einleuchtende*, that is, the enlightening. By examining how this concept is both similar to and different from Aristotle's notion of *phronesis* and Husserl's notion of evidence, Schmidt is led to characterize the experience of enlightening as one in which there is a shining forth of the probable truth of the thing itself. This shining forth, which can overtake one without warning, provides the ground for the judgment that distinguishes between more and less legitimate prejudices that one might have regarding what one encounters. Using the concept of enlightening to ground the notion of hermeneutic truth, Schmidt suggests some responses to several contemporary critics of Gadamer, including Rorty, Bernstein, and Caputo.

The last part in this volume includes a number of papers that explore the issue of how justice arises within a community and the question of how a community itself is defined. The first chapter is written by James Hatley. It explores the responses made by Levinas and Arendt to what is characterized as Hegel's conception of impersonal historical judgment. In order to clarify the notion of heterogenous judgment, which is offered as a response to Hegel and which is said to form the foundation of justice, Hatley investigates Levinas's notion of ethical judgment. Ethical judgment, grounded in an experience of an other who cannot be reduced to one's own plans and purposes, results ultimately in an acknowledgment of one's responsibility to the other and an offering of one's apology. Hatley then contrasts this Levinasian notion of apology with Arendt's conception of conscience, a critical perspective that one directs toward one's own thinking. By illuminating the tensions and areas of agreement that exist between these two thinkers in their shared project, Hatley enables the reader to reflect profitably on the question of the ground and limitations of ethical and political judgment.

Steven Hendley's chapter inquires into the implications of the loss of both a notion of universal emancipation and, hence, a stable and justifiable notion of one's self and of one's community. Drawing upon the work of Lyotard, Hendley suggests that two possible responses to this loss, the first, to adopt a "secondary narcissism" and to use it as a foundation for justifying one's own behavior and for judging the behavior of others; and the second, to determine what it means to be a community within the particular, shared context in which we find ourselves, should be rejected. In order to develop an alternative response, Hendley explores Lyotard's insight that questions concerning the "we" and the context in which the "we" emerges are always problematic and remain open to discussion by competing genres of discourse. It is suggested that a shared commitment to renewed and continued questioning concerning the nature of the "we" may be the only form of consensus or dissensus that can endure and enable a community to be.

The chapter by John Protevi examines the relationship of force, law, and justice in Derrida's thought. Protevi begins with an overview of Derrida's debt to and dialogue with Hegel and his analysis of force in nature. He then examines Derrida's contention that the general text itself is a site in which there is a play and an overflow of both force and signification. Finally, concentrating on Derrida's essay "Force of Law," Protevi considers how an interplay of forces concurrently grounds and threatens to rupture political and legal institutions, both in terms of their ability to dispense justice and in terms of our understanding of their meaning.

Max Pensky's essay takes up the question of the relationship between remembrance and justice. Weaving together a reflection on Derrida's image of the haunting, ghostlike trace of memory (which whispers of violence and responsibility) with an account of Habermas's objection to the instrumentalization of memory (which enables the actions of the past to become mere history), Pensky explores the strengths and the weaknesses in the thought of both of these philosophers. More important, in so doing, Pensky bids the reader to engage in the struggle to comprehend the impossible possibility of the event of justice arising in the shadow of the Holocaust.

The chapter by Steven Vogel explores two elements of an antinomy of Western Marxism and the implications that this antinomy has for thinking about the environment. The first element, discussed by Lukács, suggests that the solution to our social crisis requires a recognition that nature and the surrounding world are socially constructed and, in addition, an acknowledgment of our responsibility for its condition. The other element, discussed by Adorno, suggests that such "identity-thinking" must be replaced by a recognition of the radical otherness of all that lies beyond one's thought. Vogel bridges this antinomy by suggesting that the reality of our practice, that is, our always already being involved with our surrounding world despite its otherness, provides a ground for a respectful recognition of our responsibilities for and to a nature and world that is other, yet not totally independent.

Ute Guzzoni's essay provides the final chapter for this volume. Her essay commences by asking whether and in what way, in our current age, nature can present itself as an appropriate theme for philosophical inquiry. By reflecting on a portion of a poem by Rilke, and drawing on the insights of both Heidegger and Adorno, among others, Guzzoni leads the reader to consider what type of thinking is appropriate for thinking about nature. She suggests that philosophy must take up finite thinking, that is, thinking grounded in our experience of the world, sensual thinking, aesthetic thinking, indeed, thinking that is fundamentally *Gelassenheit*, as its proper mode. This thinking can be directed not only toward nature as it has been conceived classically, but also toward that "second nature" that appears to be particularly problematic and challenging. This second nature includes those technological processes and artifacts that, although made by human hands, have slipped from our grasp and control. Guzzoni challenges us to consider whether finite thinking, directed toward those features of our technological world that elude us and appear as emancipated, might empower us to enter into a fruitful relationship of free mutuality with these elements.

In closing, it should be noted that the papers collected in this volume derive from the annual conferences held at Villanova University and the University of Memphis. The local coordinators for these meetings were Walter Brogan and John Doody of Villanova University and Robert Bernasconi, Len Lawler, and Tom Nenon of the University of Memphis. The members of the Executive Committee for these meetings were John D. Caputo, Drucilla Cornell, Arleen B. Dallery, Lenore Langsdorf, Dennis Schmidt, and Stephen H. Watson. Our thanks are offered to all of these people who helped to make those meetings successful and who thereby helped this volume to be produced.

NOTES

1. Edmund Husserl, "The Origin of Geometry," in *The Crisis of European Sciences and Transcendental Phenomenology*, trans. David Carr (Evanston: Northwestern University Press, 1970). Henceforth all references to this text will use the abbreviation OG.

2. See the correspondence between Husserl and Frege. "Frege-Husserl Correspondence," in *Southwest Journal of Philosophy* 5 (1974): 83–96.

3. Edmund Husserl, *Cartesian Meditations*, trans. Dorion Cairns (The Hague: Martinus Nijhoff, 1960).

4. Husserl's treatment of the paradoxes of set theory remains unpublished at this time.

5. Edmund Husserl, *Formal and Transcendental Logic*, trans. Dorion Cairns (The Hague: Martinus Nijhoff, 1978). Henceforth all references to this text will use the abbreviation FTL.

6. Edmund Husserl, "Philosophy As Rigorous Science," in *Phenomenology and the Crisis of Philosophy*, trans. Quentin Lauer (New York: Harper & Row, 1965), 135.

7. This history, as Scheler noted, had been undertaken quite early by Dietrich von Hildebrand. See his "Die Idee der Sittlichen Handung," *Jahrbuch fur philosophie und phänomenologische Forschung*, vol. III. See also Max Scheler, *Formalism in Ethics and Non-Formal Ethics of Values*, trans. Manfred S. Frings and Roger L. Funk (Evanston: Northwestern University Press, 1973), 262. Moreover, much of Gadamer's *Truth and Method* is devoted to its further elaboration. See *Truth and Method*, second revised edition, trans. Joel Weinsheimer and Donald G. Marshall (New York: Crossroads, 1989). Henceforth all references to this text will use the abbreviation TM.

8. See J. G. Fichte, *The Science of Ethics*, trans. A. E. Kroeger (New York: Harper & Row, 1970), 258.

9. Friedrich Nietzsche, *On the Genealogy of Morals*, trans. Walter Kaufmann and R. J. Hollingdale (New York: Random House, 1967), 109.

10. Edmund Husserl, *The Crisis of European Sciences and Transcendental Phenomenology*, trans. David Carr (Evanston: Northwestern University Press, 1970), 54.

11. Husserl, "The Vienna Lecture," in *The Crisis*, 291.

12. Leo Strauss, *Natural Right and History* (Chicago: University of Chicago Press, 1953), 196ff. On Strauss's view of phenomenology, and especially of Husserl and Heidegger, see "Philosophy as Rigorous Science and

Political Philosophy," in *Studies in Platonic Political Philosophy* (Chicago: University of Chicago Press, 1983).

13. The locus classicus of Horkheimer and Adorno's position is *Dialectic of Enlightenment*, trans. John Cumming (New York: Continuum, 1975). Compare Husserl's *Crisis*, 46–47.

14. Michel Foucault, *The Archaeology of Knowledge*, trans. A. M. Sheridan Smith (New York: Pantheon, 1972), 184ff.

15. See Max Scheler, *The Nature of Sympathy*, trans. Peter Heath (New Haven: Yale University Press, 1954) and Edith Stein, *The Problem of Empathy*, trans. Waltraut Stein (Washington, D.C.: ICS Publications, 1989). To these should be added Husserl's own criticisms of Lipps to be found in the investigations on intersubjectivity. See Edmund Husserl, *Zur Phänomenologie der Intersubjektivität*, vol. I and II, ed. Iso Kern (The Hague: Martinus Nijhoff, 1973). To this should be added the critique of psychologism in the "Prolegomena to Pure Logic." See *Logical Investigations*, trans. J. N. Findlay (New York: Humanities Press, 1970), 91–94, 146, 155.

16. See Adolf Reinach, "Uber die apriorischen Grundlagen des buergerlichen Rechts," *Jahrbuch fur Philosophie und phänomenologischean Forschung*, vol. I (1913). Husserl provided a synopsis of this work and characterized it as both a masterpiece and a classic in the history of the philosophy of law in his 1918 "Adolf Reinach: In Memoriam" (trans. Frederick Elliston and Theodore Plantinga in *Husserl's Shorter Works*, ed. Frederick Elliston and Peter McCormick [Notre Dame: University of Notre Dame Press, 1981]). Reinach is credited with demonstrating that in this domain there are "a priori truths in exactly the same sense in which primitive arithmetical or logical axioms are a priori" (p. 355)—a claim that will become more complex as writings in this volume will attest.

17. Martin Heidegger, *Being and Time*, trans. John Macquarrie and Edward Robinson (New York: Harper & Row, 1962), 162–63, 422.

18. Thomas Hobbes, *Leviathan*, ed. C. B. MacPherson (Baltimore: Penguin 1968), 687.

19. Thomas Hobbes, "Human Nature," in *The English Works of Thomas Hobbes*, ed. Sir William Molesworth (London: John Bohn, 1840), IV: 49.

20. G. W. F. Hegel, *Philosophy of Mind*, part three of *The Encyclopedia of the Philosophical Science*, trans. A. V. Miller (Oxford: Oxford University Press, 1971), §400, p. 74.

21. That Husserl recognized the link between the problem of interpretation and the problem of intersubjectivity, that moreover both were complicated problems of the 'empathy' at stake in the appeal of the "Origin of

Geometry" to the latter as a sufficient condition of objectivity, is evident from fragments collected on the phenomenology of intersubjectivity in Husserliana volumes thirteen and fourteen (for example, Beilage LXVI of the latter). See Edmund Husserl, *Zur Phänomenologie der Intersubjektivität*, vol. II (The Hague: Martinus Nijhoff, 1973).

22. Benedict de Spinoza, *A Theological-Political Treatise*, trans. R. H. M. Elwes (New York: Dover, 1951), chapter IV.

23. Thomas Hobbes, *Leviathan* I, p. 26 (322).

24. Scheler, *Formalism*, 306.

25. Edmund Husserl, *Experience and Judgment*, rev. and ed. Ludwig Landgrebe, trans. James S. Churchill and Karl Ameriks (Evanston: Northwestern University Press, 1973), 165.

26. Husserl, *Experience and Judgment*, 163.

27. TM 281. Gadamer's texts actually manifest a great amount of ambiguity on these matters. Immediately before distancing himself from a revival of tradition, and against the Enlightenment, he apparently endorsed Romanticism at least this much: "The real force of morals, for example, is based on tradition. They are freely taken over but by no means created by a free insight or grounded on reasons" (TM 280).

28. See Friedrich Hölderlin, "Judgment and Being," in *Essays and Letters on Theory*, trans. Thomas Pfau (Albany: SUNY Press, 1988).

29. See Bernard Bolzano, *Theory of Science*, trans. Rolf George (Berkeley: University of California Press, 1972), §22.

30. Friedrich Hölderlin, "Remarks on Oedipus," in *Essays and Letters on Theory*, trans. Thomas Pfau (Albany: SUNY Press, 1988).

31. Jean Hyppolite, *Logique et existence* (Paris: Presses Universités de France, 1952), 173.

32. The text in question derives from Hegel's *Faith and Knowledge*, where, commenting upon Kant's accounts of judgment, Hegel already had raised the problem of the copula as an identity in opposition to difference, and an identity that exceeds consciousness. See G. W. F. Hegel, *Faith and Knowledge*, trans. Walter Cerf and H. S. Harris (Albany: SUNY Press, 1977), 72. This same text and Hyppolite's commentary upon it would return in both Foucault's and Derrida's works, and reappears again in recent attempts to account for the heterogeneity of judgment.

Part I

Origin, Insight, and Explication

CHAPTER 1

Presence and Absence in Husserl's Phenomenology of Time-Consciousness

JOHN B. BROUGH

This will be a rather old-fashioned essay: modern rather than postmodern, constructive rather than deconstructive, and mainly expository. It may, however, supply some ammunition both to those inclined to criticize Husserl from a deconstructive point of view and to those bold enough to defend him, particularly his phenomenology of time and the consciousness of time.

Husserl's consideration of the different ways in which presence and absence enter into our temporal experience is subtle and nuanced. He draws delicate distinctions and points to continuities and discontinuities that deserve the philosopher's careful and sympathetic attention. I will focus on a few of these, hoping that they will suggest something of the rich resources for reflection on this topic present in Husserl's texts.

Since the focus of the essay is on some aspects of presence and absence in Husserl's phenomenology of time-consciousness, I will take presence, for the most part, to mean temporal presence. More specifically, I will take it to mean temporal presence in the sense of the now. It seems natural to take the now as presence in its most vivid and original sense. Absence will refer to temporal absence in the sense of past and future. But other senses of the terms will intrude from time to time.

There is a cleavage in views about the now, or better, a pull in two directions, that Husserl struggled with and finally overcame. On the one hand, there is the conviction that one *only* can be aware of what is present, of what is there itself in the sense of the now. On the other hand, there is the conviction that one can be aware of anything *except* the present. The now—if one can speak of it at all—will have vanished before consciousness can even register it.

THE NOW AS TEMPORAL WAY OF APPEARING

Consider first the view that one cannot experience what is now, that one cannot experience what is present in its presence. *"Consciousness,"* Husserl writes, *"is a perpetual Heraclitean flux."*[1] One could take this to mean that one can intend something as now, but that it will immediately pass away and then be retained in continuously changing modes of the past. But the view that one cannot experience what is now goes further than that. It understands the term "flux" to imply that one cannot be conscious of what is now in any significant sense at all: it is always gone before it can be fixed by consciousness.

One might argue in defense of this position that, although one is indeed aware of what the casual observer or incautious philosopher thinks one is aware of, for example, the first part of a melody, the awareness that one enjoys is not the presumed awareness of the object as now. Rather, one is aware of it as past. In an interesting text in which Husserl directly confronts this argument, he takes as his example the internal consciousness one has of a present act of consciousness. The hearing of the melody mentioned above would be a case in point. (It is worth noting that what he says about the presence of the act would also be true, with a few qualifications, of its object.) Now one might be inclined to say that one is conscious of the initial phase of the act as now. But according to the view that Husserl desires to reject, one would never be aware of the initial phase of the act as now, although the phase would in fact occur. *After* its original occurrence, of which one would not be aware, it would come to be given, but "only on the basis of retention" (Hua X: 119/123). It would never cross the threshold of consciousness if retention did not make it conscious.

Husserl responds that it is indeed true that the initial phase of the act can become an *object*—as opposed to something experienced "nonobjectively," as one's acts always are when one is not reflecting on them—only by means of retention and reflection (or reproduction). "But if it were intended *only* by retention, then what confers on it the label 'now' would remain incomprehensible" (Hua X: 119/123). Retention confers the label "just past" on what it intends. Furthermore, if it were intended only in retention, the initial phase in its first occurrence would not appear at all: it would be unconscious. But, Husserl claims, "it is just nonsense to talk about an 'unconscious' content that would only subsequently become conscious" (Hua X: 119/123). The nonsense Husserl has in mind is double-barreled. It is nonsense, first, because "retention of an unconscious content is impossible" (Hua X: 119/123). Retention's role is to retain, in the mode of the past, what has just appeared in the mode of the now. If the content never appeared in its presence, there would be no content for retention to intend in its absence. And, second, it is nonsense to deny that one experiences things, whether immanent acts or their transcendent objects, as now: "the primal datum is already intended—specifically, in the original form of the 'now'" (Hua X: 119/123). This is a matter of experiential fact.

One cannot help but notice how adamant Husserl is in maintaining this position. He simply affirms that some things appear as now. At a moment in philosophy's history when the willingness to deny that one ever experiences anything as present is seen by some to be a test of one's philosophic mettle, Husserl's claim may seem naive or even dogmatic. A brief glance at experience, however, suggests that something might be said for it. Husserl, of course, thinks that one is always conscious of something as now, whether the experience is pedestrian and ordinary, as it usually is, or whether it is dramatic and exceptional. Perhaps experiences of the latter sort—the extraordinary ones—supply the most striking evidence that one can be aware of something as now. Imagine a perfectly still morning, for example, Thanksgiving Day at seven o'clock. Imagine that no sound disturbs the stillness as you lie in bed. Then imagine that a tremendous boom rends the silence. To deny that the sound is there in full and startling presence seems plainly and perversely false. The sound, it is true, will immediately sink into the past; it will be retained, and you will almost surely direct a natural reflection toward the retained sound and ask, "What was that?" But this presumes that it did stand before you as now. Consider another example. You are coming to a rapid stop in a line of cars on a bridge. Your concentration is focused on the car in front of you and on bringing your vehicle to a halt. You succeed, and at that very moment there occurs a massive blow emanating from the rear that throws you violently forward against your shoulder harness. Someone in the car shouts, "We've been hit!" The statement is a report and depends again on a natural reflection on a retained complex of experience. It also will strike everyone in the car as a statement of the obvious because the blow was experienced, alarmingly so, in the mode of the now.

If someone persists in denying that anything is actually experienced as now in these cases, there is not much that one can do. As Husserl says about

the experience of both now and past: "Here, in the unity of the consciousness that gives us something itself, the past pretends to be given itself only
as past; the now, only as now. We state this honestly, just as we see it and
have it" (Hua X: 344/355).

I suspect that one reason the possibility of experiencing what is now as
now might be questioned is that one has surreptitiously imported the model
of reflection into the experience. There is no more reason to claim that all
presence is reflective presence, however, than there is to claim that all consciousness is reflective consciousness. Husserl asserts neither and denies
both.

It remains true, of course, that what is experienced as now is fleeting; it is
caught up in the Heraclitean flux of consciousness. As we have seen, this
might supply another reason for denying that what is present is ever experienced in its presence. It could instead be something that dissolves into
absence before even announcing its presence; only its trace would be left
behind in retention. Husserl, however, never suggests that what appears in
the now is anything but fleeting. Any attempt to capture and to fix what is
now in its immediate presence is indeed doomed. One experiences what is
now precisely as flowing: its presence ceaselessly giving way to absence. It
is that character that the phenomenologist must "state . . . honestly, just as
we see it and have it." The very character of the now that some philosophers
find so frustrating is precisely the character on which they, as philosophers,
should reflect.

But what is the now, as Husserl understands it? It is not a thing or a part of
a thing; it is not *what* is present. Nor is it a "time-point" in the sense of a
place or a location in a series of points forming "time," whether subjective
time or objective time. It is not part of an object's duration or part of an
objective succession. The now, or presence, is a mode of appearance (Hua
X: 24/25): the mode of appearance of that which is present.[2]

This means that the now itself does not appear outside a peculiar kind of
reflection. The now—"presence" in its preeminent and original form—is,
one might say, "absent." But what appears in the mode of the now is not
absent: it is there as present, as present "itself," "in person" (Hua X: 60/62),
in its fullness, just as the explosive sound shattering the morning stillness
was present. Not itself a temporal position, "the now . . . is the givenness of
the present of the temporal position" (Hua X: 66/68). "Now" is the name or
the "label" (Hua X: 119/123) for this irreducible way of appearing. If one
reflects in the appropriate way (Hua X: 275/285), which will not be a natural
reflection, then one will be able to point philosophically to the difference

between the object appearing, that which is present, and its temporal way of appearing, its presence, just as one can point to the difference between the spatial object and the spatial perspective in which it is given. What is said of the now is also true of past and future: they too are modes of appearance and are not identical to what appears in them, which is why the same object can appear as future and then as now and then as past.

To say that the now is "absent" is to say that it is not a thing or a part of a thing: it is not the type of thing that appears in a temporal perspective. It is not absence in an absolute sense, but only absence of a particular sort of being. As mode of appearing, or as a mode in which something is given to consciousness, it is as transparent and yet as real as any spatial perspective.

That the now is absent in the sense of not being a thing or a part of a thing accounts for two of its essential features: its oneness and its hospitality. The now is one in the sense that everything that I am conscious of as present in a given moment has the same now (Hua X: 71/73, 207/214), that is, the same form or mode of appearance (Hua X: 77/81). Simultaneity is, originally, "same nowness" [*Gleichjetzigkeit*] (Hua X: 117/120). The sounds I am now hearing, the colored shapes I am now seeing, the memory I am presently entertaining do not each possess their own individual nows (Hua X: 207–8/214–15); rather, they share a common now: they all appear in the same temporal way. This in turn points to the hospitality of the now. If the now were a thing in some sense, it could not play host simultaneously to such a rich and varied range of experience. Its presence as a mode and its absence as a thing enable it to accommodate whatever is compatible in a single moment. That does not mean that the now is infinitely hospitable; certain experiences cannot exist simultaneously with others. Beyond that restraint, however, the fact that the now is a kind of absence grants it a hospitality unmatched by, for example, the spatial perspective, which can accommodate only what is spatial. The temporal perspective embraces what is spatial, including the spatial perspective, but it also includes many other things. It is the "one" in which the "many" of experience first appear.

That the now is one and open suggests two of the reasons why Husserl speaks of the "privilege" of the now (Hua X: 35/37). There are other reasons as well. One of these is connected with the now as absence in the sense of its not being a thing, not even a present thing. The now, Husserl claims, is the source of the new. The now's absence as a thing is to consciousness as the window's absence as something opaque is to the wall of a house. The now is consciousness's aperture to the new. Indeed, the Husserlian monad not only has its window, but is downright drafty with the new. The now, he writes, is "the living source-point of being" in which "ever new primal being . . . wells up" (Hua X: 69/71). What appears in the now is something "new" and "original," something "deposited 'from without,' 'alien to consciousness'" (Hua X: 88/93). It is in this mode that I hear sounds that I have never heard before, read new texts about old texts, and wonder whether I ever experience anything as present. It is also—to turn from what fills time to time itself—the place in which time-points first appear: the now is "the source-point of all temporal positions whatsoever" (Hua X: 72/74). What is present is what is new, and the now is its mode of appearance.

Once the new has announced itself in the now, it slips away into the past; having become present in that peculiar absence that is the now and that lets new things and events become present for the first time, the new becomes absent in the mode of the past. The new becomes "old"; it no longer appears in temporal presence, but in temporal absence. This suggests a further aspect of the privileged status of the now, an aspect that involves past and future.

The now, Husserl claims, is the point of reference for consciousness, the point of orientation in terms of which what appears as absent in our temporal experience organizes itself. Any temporal object is originally given in the now; it then immediately slips into the past. "Past" here is not to be understood in terms of an objective 'before' and 'after.' This would be a relative sense of past in which something could be past in relation to one thing and future in relation to another. The past that we are considering here is a past always "oriented towards the actually present now" (Hua X: 106/111), that is, the now understood as an absolute standard determining the degree of pastness in which something appears. Moreover, what is past in this sense continually sinks further and further into the past in relation to the actual now; its mode of the past continuously changes. Thus the past has a "shifting orientation in relation to the living now" (Hua X: 55/57). The now is therefore "one" in a new sense. Not only is it the common form of appearance for everything that appears in it, it is also the single point of orientation for all of my temporal experience. Husserl, it is true, does sometimes speak of ever new nows replacing those that have become old (Hua X: 275/285), but the emphasis in such statements is on the element of the new, on what appears in the now: the now itself is the abiding and formal mode of appearance that is always freshly filled in one way or another while preserving its identity as absolute point of reference. Here again it can be said that if it enjoyed the presence appropriate to something given in perception, the now would not be able to fulfill its task. It too would recede into the past and could not be the orientation point in terms of which one talks of something receding in the first place.

Retention is one of the ways in which I experience something appearing as past in relation to the now. Recollection or secondary memory is another. In recalling the past object, the recollection always gives it a position in relation to the actually present now (Hua X: 51/53). Indeed, authentic memory is distinguished from "mere" phantasy because the former posits its object in relation to the now while the latter does not (Hua X: 104/110). The now is the mode in which the act of memory itself is experienced, and the present memory relates the past of which it is aware to its own position. It would not be memory otherwise. To fulfill such a memory, Husserl suggests, means to fulfill the nexus of intentions running from the remembered past perception up to the now (Hua X: 301/313). The now's privilege, then, consists in its hospitality, its openness to the new, and its position as an absolute point of orientation for the life of consciousness. It is the mode of appearing according to which what is present can be experienced as present and in relation to which the absent can appear as absent.

THE PREJUDICE OF THE NOW

The suggestion that one never really experiences the present surely has more currency in our philosophical world than it did in Husserl's. It was the other conviction—that all one ever really experiences is the present or what is in the now—that seemed most seductive and formidable to Husserl. It appears in many guises in his texts on time. And in at least one way and at one time in his career, he fell victim to its charms. Husserl's task, in struggling against this second conviction, is not to salvage some vestige of presence from the threat of universal absence. Rather, it is to admit real absence into a realm of presence from which it seems to have been excluded.

Any temporal object that one experiences certainly seems to appear both in presence and in absence. Consider a succession of tones: first tone A appears as now and tones B and C as yet to come, then B appears as now and A as just past and C as yet to come, then C as now and B as just past and A as still further past. The tones that no longer appear as now have sunk into the past, but not into "the abyss of the . . . past" (Hua X: 349/360) in the sense of disappearing from consciousness altogether. This sort of "abysmal absence" may well occur, but not in cases such as this. What is past here—or what is future—is not simply absent. One is aware of the tones that are past in their absence, as one must be if one is to be aware of their succession at all. One might be tempted to say that the absent tones are somehow still present. I think, however, that it would be safer and more accurate to say that they appear in appropriate modes of absence. In Husserl's language, the elapsed tone phases "are *still* intended, they still *appear*, but in a *modified* way" (Hua X: 275/285).

Now none of the theories that Husserl argues against in his writings on time deny that one experiences enduring or successive objects—temporal objects—and that they appear in something like the way I have described. The differences arise regarding how the consciousness of such temporal objects is constituted. It is here that what I would call the "prejudice of the now" asserts itself. This prejudice takes somewhat different forms.

As Husserl presents it, Brentano's view would represent one version of the prejudice, specifically, the version based on the conviction that one can be conscious of something only if it is in some sense present or now. From this perspective, Brentano's theory offers a double difficulty with respect to presence and absence. First, Brentano thinks that in the actual perceiving of a temporal object one is aware of the object's just-past phases in the same way as one might be aware of an object that one perceived in the more distant past. Thus the elapsed phases of a passage of music that one is now hearing on the radio would be intended in the same way as a concert that one remembers attending last week. In both cases, one is conscious of what has become absent. Husserl, however, wants to insist that one is aware of them in their absence in quite different ways. The difference is the difference between retention and recollection. These are species, respectively, of impression and re-presentation [*Vergegenwärtigung*], the two distinct modes of consciousness that, according to Husserl, divide the whole of conscious life. In retention, "the past object is 'given' as past" (Hua X: 311/322); it is presented (Hua X: 97/102) or "*perceived*" (Hua X: 39/41). In recollection, the past is not presented, but re-presented. It is not there "in person," but intended as if "seen through a veil" (Hua X: 48/50). In both cases, the mode of absence is that of the past. The modes, however, let their objects appear in fundamentally different ways. Thanks to retention and its mode, one can be said to perceive a melody and not just those tones that appear as now. In more general terms, one can be said to perceive a succession or duration. That Brentano cannot account for such perception, that he restricts perception to what appears as now and leaves to recollection the consciousness of what is past, suggests one of the ways in which he is subject to the prejudice of the now.

The second respect in which Brentano is subject to this prejudice is revealed in his account of the way in which the consciousness of past or future phases of the perceived object is constituted. Brentano holds that one can be conscious of a past phase of a temporal object only on the basis of a present content *now* in consciousness. What this means is that one can really experience only what is now. The tone that one seems to be conscious of as past is really present.

Husserl argues against this position by insisting that past and now exclude one another (Hua X: 318/330), that what is past is really past (Hua X: 152/156). What appears as past is neither covertly nor overtly present in the sense of the now. If it were, it could not appear as past, and Husserl insists that it does appear as past: "the past pretends to be given only as past; the now, only as now" (Hua X: 344/355).

The view that the consciousness of something that is not now can be had only on the basis of some content that is now appears in at least two other forms in Husserl's texts. One of these is the image-theory of secondary memory. The image-theory that Husserl criticizes assimilates recollection to pictorial consciousness, that is, to the representation of something absent by means of a present painting, sculpture, or other kind of image (Hua X: 59/61, 309/321). Husserl does not deny that pictorial consciousness occurs. His point is simply that it is not the same kind of consciousness as recollection. Indeed, pictorial consciousness is an attractive candidate for the task of explaining the intentionality of memory only if one is convinced that one cannot be directly conscious of what is past itself. Its appeal rests on the assumption that the consciousness of what is past, precisely because what is past is absent, must depend on a present surrogate, on something like a pictorial image.

The suggestion that memory might be an instance of pictorial consciousness raises a question about whether one is aware of the past itself in secondary memory. In some texts, Husserl suggests that forms of re-presentation, including recollection or secondary memory, do not give that past object "itself" (Hua X: 41/43, 45/47). In other texts, however, he indicates that re-presentation does give the object itself (Hua X: 59/61) and that the difference between re-presentation and retention or other impressional forms of awareness rests in the way in which the object itself is intended. The latter, I believe, is clearly Husserl's settled view. Thus when one remembers the illuminated theater that one experienced yesterday, it is the past, the absent theater itself, that one remembers. One intends something absent in the manner appropriate to it, that is, in the manner of recollection as opposed to retention. No present content stands between one and the past object one intends. The past object itself stands before one in its absence.

The prejudice of the now also appeared in Husserl's interpretation of the constitution of time-consciousness before about 1908. During this period, Husserl thought that the retention of just-elapsed phases of the perceived object and the protention of phases yet to come depended on the presence in the "now of consciousness" (Hua X: 321/333) of appropriate contents and appropriate temporal apprehensions. This would mean, for example, that the retention of elapsed tone A would be constituted by the animation of an "A" content now present in consciousness by the appropriate apprehension of the past. That the prejudice of the now is at work in this interpretation should be clear enough. The awareness of the not-now must, in effect, be the consciousness of something that is now, based upon the underlying assumption that one cannot be directly conscious of what is absent. Husserl eventually came to criticize this interpretation of the constitution of time-consciousness on the grounds that a content that is actually present in consciousness must appear in its presence, as now, and could not also be apprehended as past (Hua X: 322–23/334–35). If the consciousness of the past is made to depend upon the consciousness of what is now, then one will never be conscious of the past at all. One will have no experience of time or of temporal objects—or even of the now, since now and past are relative to one another (Hua X: 68/70).

When Husserl rejects this interpretation, he comes to understand retention, primal impression, and protention as intentional moments that transcend the actually present phase of consciousness to which they belong. Retention, for example, simply *is* the consciousness of what is just past and does not include in itself any present content, not even an echo of what is past (Hua X: 31/33, 311–12/323–24). In its retentional and protentional moments, consciousness transcends the present toward the absent. And in so doing, it makes no attempt to transmute the absent into the present, the not-now into the now. Time-consciousness is no alchemist. It lets what is absent appear as what it is. Husserl thus comes to conceive of consciousness as self-transcending intentionality and not as a kind of bag (Hua X: 279/289) stuffed with really present contents that are supposed to stand in for things now abysmally and irrecoverably absent: "*retention*, which is an act now living . . . transcends itself and *posits* something as being—namely, as being past—that does not really inhere in it" (Hua X: 344/355–56).

Husserl, as noted above, insists that consciousness must reach out beyond the now to what is not-now in the sense of what is past and what is future. Time-consciousness, then, is always the awareness both of what is present and of what is absent. There is a further dimension of this awareness that deserves attention. It may be seen against the background of yet another version of the prejudice of the now.

Husserl reports that it is a common conviction that the perception of a temporal object, for example, of a succession, must occur in a single now of consciousness. The consciousness of succession would not itself be successive. The consciousness of a duration would not itself endure. Husserl finds this "dogma of the momentariness of a whole of consciousness" in Lotze and Herbart (Hua X: 20/21–22 the phrase is William Stern's), but one suspects that it applies equally to his own rejected interpretation of time-consciousness in terms of contents and apprehensions. The prejudice of the now shapes this view in the sense that the view assumes that only in the immediate present could consciousness do its constitutional work. Past phases of consciousness are gone, absent, and so could play no role in constitution. Consciousness is shrunk to its immediate now-phase. The succession of consciousness *cannot* be the consciousness of succession.

Husserl, on the other hand, argues that consciousness reaches out beyond the now to the past and future phases of the temporal object precisely through its own succeeding phases and, therefore, through its absent phases as well as its actual phase. On this view, the succession of consciousness is the consciousness of succession; the two are inseparable. Absence, then, is not only an ingredient of the temporal object, but also of the consciousness of the object.

It is only with the maturing of the notion of the "absolute time-constituting flow of consciousness" (Hua X: 73/77) and its double intentionality that Husserl is able to give a satisfactory account of the sense in which the succession of consciousness is, or makes possible, the consciousness of succession. What Husserl means by the absolute flow is notoriously difficult. I only want to make a few comments here about how the theme of presence and absence enters into it.

Husserl acknowledges that he employs a metaphor when he calls the absolute consciousness a flow (Hua X: 75/79, 371/382). Like all good metaphors, however, it conveys a number of important truths. In this case, the metaphor points to the continuous character of time-consciousness. Time-consciousness is continuous in the sense that its phases ceaselessly well up and pass away, and it is continuous in the sense that its phases dovetail with one another. There are no beginnings and endings in the flow. Through its phases, one becomes conscious of acts as immanent temporal objects. If the acts have transcendent objects, then one becomes conscious of those transcendent objects as well. The absolute consciousness, there-fore, is a continuous flow in which objects as well as the flow itself are intended in presence and in absence.

There are at least two ways in which the flow is involved with presence and absence. The first echoes the peculiar absence we saw earlier in the case of the now as mode of appearance—or of past and future as modes. Considered in itself, the actual phase of the absolute flow, with its primal impressional, retentional, and protentional moments, is the absence of any-thing except sheer experiential consciousness. Just as the now is absence in the sense of not being any particular thing, but only a mode of appearing, so the primal impression of the flow is not an act or content, but only the con-sciousness of acts and contents as now. The primal impression is the inten-tional source-point (Hua X: 133/136) for what appears as now and as new in the life of consciousness. Thanks to it, one can experience "all at once" sound and color contents, kinesthetic experiences, a feeling of anxiety, and the judgment that $2 + 2 = 4$. As the absence of anything except experiential presenting, the actual phase of the flow makes possible the great variety of experiences one lives through at each moment. It is an absence in the center of conscious life that, through its moment of primal impression, allows us to have acts and contents in their presence and, through its moments of reten-tion and protention, in their absence. As the source of the temporal modes, the flow itself is beyond them. We have no names for the absolute flow (Hua X: 75/79, 371/382), Husserl says, by which he means no temporal names.

The second way in which presence and absence are involved in the flow is through what Husserl called the *"Längsintentionalität"* (Hua X: 81/85, 379/391) of the flow, the flow's intending of itself. The actual phase of the flow will elapse and be replaced by a new actual phase. This will happen continuously. One will be conscious of this "succession" of phases of the absolute flow not through another flow, but through that very succession of phases of the flow. Furthermore, it is through the flow's consciousness of its own elapsing phases that it is conscious of the immanent temporal objects that endure and succeed one another. It is in this sense that the succession of the flow is the consciousness of succession, both of its own succession and of the succession of immanent objects. The flow lets itself go, but recaptures itself. It becomes absent, but overcomes its absence intentionally. Each actual phase of the flow intends retentionally the just-past—the "just-absent"—phase of the flow and is open protentionally to phases yet to come. The flow recaptures itself not by making its own absent phases present, but by intending them (retentionally) in their absence. The retained phase is also preserved with its reference to the now-absent moment of the immanent object originally given in it. The immanent object is therefore constituted in its temporal extension. This "double" intending (Hua X: 81/85, 379/390)— of phase of the flow by phase of the flow, and thereby of phases of the immanent object—goes on until retention fades. The temporal object and the flow itself are thus woven out of presences and absences. The consciousness of object and flow is equally a complex process of presenting, of letting go, of letting become absent, and also of intending what has become absent in its very absence.

NOTES

1. Edmund Husserl, *Zur Phänomenologie des inneren Zeitbewusstseins (1893–1917)*, herausgegeben von Rudolf Boehm, Husserliana X (The Hague: Martinus Nijhoff, 1966), 349; *On the Phenomenology of the Consciousness of Internal Time (1893–1917)*, trans. John Barnett Brough (Dordrecht: Kluwer Academic Publishers, 1991), 360. Page references to Husserliana X will be placed in parentheses in the text preceded by "Hua X" and followed by the corresponding page numbers in the translation.

2. See Thomas Prufer's discussion of the difference between presence and that-which-is-present in "Heidegger, Early and Late, and Aquinas," in *Edmund Husserl and the Phenomenological Tradition*, ed. Robert Sokolowski (Washington, D.C.: Catholic University of America Press, 1988).

CHAPTER 2

The Role of Life-world in Husserl's Critique of Idealizations

DIETER LOHMAR

In this paper I will examine Husserl's concept of Life-world [*Lebenswelt*] against the background of his attempted critique of idealizations. First, I will outline several possibilities for determining a kind of frontier between the idealizations and the 'ground' [*Boden*] that should motivate them. Then I will consider Husserl's efforts at drawing such a border. We will see that the "critique of idealizations" is a unique topic in his thinking, one that runs through all periods of his phenomenology. I also want to consider several early stages of the development of the concept of Life-world in some manuscripts of the years 1931–32. By this means, it will be possible to show the solution of an irritating double sense of the concept of Life-world in Husserl's *The Crisis of European Sciences and Transcendental Phenomenology* (Hua VI).[1]

TWO ASPECTS OF A UNIFIED ATTEMPT: THE SEARCH FOR IDEALIZATIONS AND FOR THE MOTIVATING BASIC LEVEL OF EXPERIENCE

In the second part of *Formal and Transcendental Logic* (Hua XVII),[2] Husserl outlines the task of revealing the constitution of idealized concepts in logic and mathematics. I will extend this attempt to the idealizations that are present in our everyday-understanding of the world. Even the explicit idealizations of physics and mathematics can be dissolved into and be intermingled with the everyday-understanding. In the *Crisis*, Husserl named this process *seeping-in* [*Einströmen*]. To give an example, Husserl focuses on the concept of the *infinite world*, but not to ponder arguments for and against it. He tries to make clear if and how such a concept is *reasonably motivated*. His idea is to go back to the basic level of experience that—in Kantian terms—can give the justification of this posing of a certain meaning [*Sinn-Setzung*] We use the Kantian term of justification in a Husserlian sense when we are searching for the intuition from which the idealization could possibly spring. Therefore, what we and Husserl have to search for is a usually unthematized basic level of experience that is independent from cultural and historical facts.

Our search must be oriented in a twofold manner. On the one hand, Husserl tried to find a basic level of experience from which all idealizations could receive their motivation. On the other hand, we can become aware of idealizations as such only by means of contrast, that is, only against a non-idealized background. In the *Crisis*, Husserl calls this universal fundament of justified motivation and validity "Life-world." Earlier stages of this concept are to be found in the rich material published in *Husserliana XV*. The different concepts of *Heimwelt, Fremdwelt, Alltagswelt, Kulturwelt*, and so on, which are used freely in these manuscripts, have something in common with the Life-world of the *Crisis*, that is, the idea that immediate sensual perception is the first and deepest level of experience. But the extent of our everyday-beliefs is not limited in such a way. The broader framework of motivation is the usual mode of life with its periodic needs and personal relations. In addition to this, the knowledge that we get through others oversteps the borders of what is intuitively given. This kind of stratified analysis of the motivating basis of experience is a standard Husserlian method. For my own purposes, I will call the motivating basic level of experience *Grundschicht*.

Concerning a concrete idealization, Husserl's question is whether there is a motivating element in everyday-life that initiates the idealized concept. That is, is there something that makes the idealization meaningful, justified, and reasonable? In order to perform this function we cannot use our own Life-world that is merged with scientific beliefs. The basic level of experience that we are looking for has to be independent of culturally fixed beliefs. *Grundschicht*, therefore, cannot mean a concrete conception of the world. It is a *function* that has to be filled as a necessary condition if the speech of idealization is to be meaningful. The search for idealities is practically inseparable from the search for the *Grundschicht*.

HUSSERLIAN WAYS TO DETERMINE THE *GRUNDSCHICHT*

In the *Logical Investigations*,[3] Husserl takes a similar approach toward simple acts of perception. He makes the distinction between immanent compounds [*reeller Bestand*] and intentional compounds [*intentionale Charaktere*] (Hua XIX.1: 355–61). Although these are connected intimately, Husserl's descriptive approach in the *Logical Investigations* is built upon the belief that drawing such a separating line is possible even within elements that are inseparably interwoven like a fabric or intermingled like an alloy. The immanent compounds are not thought of as a kind of sense-data, as in empiricist philosophy. They are not conceived of as separate and independent from my intuitive grasp of them. Rather they are abstract parts of the acts that fulfill them. Nevertheless, they are inseparably connected with objectifying apperception. I never hear tone-sensations and I never see color-data: I always hear melodies and see colors (Hua XIX.1: 374).

Husserl's second attempt to determine the basic level of experience that can be used for justifying idealizations might be best characterized as a careful *expansion* of the sensuously intuitive given field. His enlargement of the concept of intuition to include categorical objects can be seen as a first step in this direction (Hua XIX.2: 657–93). This careful enlargement of the field of intuition is more than a single addition of an element. In his analysis of the simplest cases, Husserl points out that sensuous experience founds categorical intuition. Moving to more complex examples, we see that the field of contents that are apperceived has to be enlarged also: categorical intuition is founded in nearly every case by both sensual and non-sensual contents. Husserl points out that these non-sensual contents are primarily syntheses of coincidence [*Deckungssynthesen*]. They appear between the articulating [*gliedernde*] acts that belong to the process of categorical intuition. They are apperceived in the last step of the categorical process and fulfill the categorical thesis.

In the *Ideas I* (Hua III.1),[4] Husserl introduces the theme of horizon-intentionality [*Horizontintentionalität*]. This is an attempt to describe more explicitly what we really mean when we are thinking of a single perceptual object. Thus we see that in a certain way even the world is present in every single intention. The presence of the world as horizon reveals the difficulty of placing an upper limit on the further extensions of the *Grundschicht*.

This attempt to determine the *Grundschicht* by *extending* the most basic level of experience leads to the more complex possibility of its determination by a process of *shrinking* (that is, contracting) beginning with the whole of our everyday-beliefs. The starting point of this new way of determining the realm of the *Grundschicht* is our natural belief concerning the world. We carefully try to contract the field of beliefs with the aim of separating the more or less obvious idealizations from the residuum that should be the *Grundschicht*. We have to draw a borderline. On one side of this frontier there are those elements of the totality of our beliefs that we are able to identify as idealizations. We can probably use a kind of "historical" or "cultural" differentiating method to decide this question. The different opinions concerning morals, religion, and the sciences—especially their early forms—seem to be such elements.

A historical method for isolating idealizations could proceed by a very simple pattern: what was seen anywhere in history in a different way than we see it could be suspected to be only a historical, and therefore arbitrarily idealized, conception. Husserl speaks of these propositions as *founding* [primal establishment, *Stiftung*]. For example, it would be possible to think of the ancient idea of the finitude of the cosmos in contrast to the idea of an infinite world that stems from the creators of modern physics.

We can also take a second, *synchronic* version of the *contracting method* that is oriented toward the culturally different ways in which we form our beliefs concerning the world. The pattern of judgment of this method is similar to the one noted above: what other cultures conceive of in a different way could be linked to factual history and thus suspected of not being motivated by the universal *Grundschicht*.

Taking into account the two versions of the contracting-method of determining the *Grundschicht*, we could characterize this method as a search for a historically and culturally indifferent core of human apperception of the world. This method would enable the modern natural sciences to appear in clear contrast to a neutral background. They offer themselves as elements of our modern worldview that seem to be lasting and worthwhile. We can make the "new" scientific idealizations appear against the background by contrasting the view of the world "before"and "after" their discovery.

We cannot use the historical method with idealities that do not have a written history. We have to ask: Are the idealities of geometry solely motivated in the *Grundschicht* for which we search or did they stem from a founding that we cannot affix to a certain historical point or person? Therefore, to a degree, the synchronical method of differentiating is a complementary supplement of the historical (that is, diachronical) heuristics. A culturally differentiating heuristic does not only regard changes in one politically, territorially, or traditionally limited world. It also has to regard the differences between such limited cultures.

One limitation of this method is that even the thoroughgoing existence of a special "thesis" in all cultures cannot assure us that it is motivated exclusively in the universally equal *Grundschicht*. It could be an idea that is very useful in certain widespread political contexts. For example, think of the divine right of kings. The culturally differentiating heuristic strives to find not only elements that are in fact equal in some cultures, but also those that are essentially equal in the universal *Grundschicht*.

HUSSERL'S CASE-STUDY OF THE "INFINITUDE" OF THE WORLD

In several manuscripts of 1931–32 Husserl considers in an experimental way the concept of the *generative Home-world* [*generative Heimwelt*] in the function of a *Grundschicht*. His special interest here is in the idea of the *infinite world* in the dimensions of space and time. This approach involves a methodological complexity. The attempt to determine the *Grundschicht* aims at specifying the *method of research*, yet at the same time this method has to be employed in any particular idealization. Thus we must begin with a provisional determination of the *Grundschicht*, here the attempt of a *generative Home-world*. Husserl tries to find common, invariant structures in different concrete surroundings such as a modern scientific world, a prescientific world, or even a mythological world. The concept of *Home-world* for Husserl seems to be capable of filling the function of a *Grundschicht*. He uses it together with a counterpart, *foreign world* [*Fremdwelt*], to describe a common structure in different concrete world concepts.

The most important characteristics of the Home-world are that it is cognitively *well-known* and affectively *familiar*. Both suggest a very concrete, typical knowledge of the *use of things* and of the *aim of deeds* (Hua XV: 430ff.). The characteristics of the Home-world are the common language (perhaps even the dialect), the familiar gestures, and the shared traditions, customs, and ethos (Hua XV: 205, 627ff.). The Home-world is closely connected with the community in which we live every day.

When we come into contact with people of a foreign world, our expectations may be fulfilled without conflict. We always expect unknown things to be a certain modification of well-known things (Hua XV: 430). When this occurs, it is "as expected." It may also happen, however, that the concrete expectations are disappointed and the concrete analogy is broken. Then our concrete expectations are modified to very general expectation of things, human persons, trees, wood, grassland, and so on.

By calling the Home-world generative, Husserl wants to stress that every human being is born and educated in a family that consists of different generations. It also indicates that we have periodic needs for food, sleep, and so on (Hua XV: 413, 433). In one manuscript,[5] Husserl tries to employ the generative Home-world in the function of a motivating *Grundschicht*. As if carrying out a chemical experiment, he adds more and more "legitimating elements" of the Home-world to the test-tube to see which reaction will follow. Thus he attempts to see which elements will be able to motivate justifiably the belief that the world is infinite.

At first, beginning with a very elementary level of experience, this seems not to be very exciting. The world of experience as the well-known and familiar surrounding has a style of *relative finitude* (Hua XV: 198). Our factual knowledge of the surrounding is always limited, but nevertheless always enlargeable. This means that we are able to extend it "again and again." Although we can overstep every factual reached limit, the Home-world remains *finite*.

When we consider the elements that arise through communication, we find an analogous extension in an iterative style (Hua XV: 200). The knowledge attained through communication can stem from other persons I don't know and so forth. As in the fifth Cartesian Meditation (Hua II),[6] it is in this complex interchange of my intuitive knowledge with the knowledge of others that the *one* world is constituted (Hua XV: 202–5). Nevertheless, this world remains finite.

Husserl next takes into account the interwovenness of every person with a series of ancestors. He "adds" this to the field of legitimating elements. Suddenly the chemical reagent changes its color. Husserl says: "Für die Zeitlichkeit haben wir die Generationen" (Hua XV: 206). That is, the idea of an infinite time is reasonably motivated through our interwovenness in a chain of ancestors. A kind of *empirical prelineation [empirische Vorzeichnung]* lies in the intuitive fact that every human being has parents and so on. It allows us to progress by idealization to the idea of an infinite past.

With respect to infinite space, however, Husserl points out that we cannot find a comparable reason for it in the elements of the Home-world. Neither the limited Home-world itself, nor the extensions of it, nor contact with foreigners and their world could motivate this idea. We can, of course, *think* of ourselves as moving onward in space without limit, but this is no empirical prelineation for infinite space (Hua XV: 207).

There are several objections to Husserl's method of searching for the motivating elements of idealizations. First, we cannot be sure that there is *no* successful way of motivation. Perhaps it is just by accident that we do not see it. We can hardly reach a definite negative result. Second, the whole method appears to be very vague and not well worked out. Thus we fear being persuaded by an argumentative trick and find nearly everything reasonably motivated. Only very careful scrutiny of the basic demands of the *Grundschicht*, that is, historical and cultural indifference, can provide protection.

Husserl also can take a nonpractical "world of sensuous perception" as a universal *Grundschicht*. This "world" might be equally present for every human being and also be free from traditional elements. But, for Husserl, this can only be a *dependent* basic level of the *Grundschicht*. In the implicit intentions that belong even to every simple perception of a real thing there is an indissoluble connection to the respective Home-world and its concrete beliefs. We are able to recognize this in irritating encounters with people from a foreign world. The foreigners even "see"—metaphorically speaking—the things of their world in a completely different way than we see them. Seeing a cow, a Hindu may have the immediate impression of dignity that we are not used to seeing in a cow. With regard to the respective Home-world, each object is connected with a certain sense that could be different from the connections that we have in mind (*geistiger Sinn*, Hua XV: 433ff.). We get used to a certain set of connections by living in this Home-world. The level of purely sensuous perception is an abstract and dependent layer in the horizon that we call the Home-world. The "world of perception" is not yet a world.

EIDETIC VARIATION AS A METHOD FOR DETERMINING THE *GRUNDSCHICHT*, AND THE DOUBLE SENSE OF LIFE-WORLD IN THE *CRISIS*

Husserl also tries to use his phenomenological method of eidetic variation to work out the universal invariant *Grundschicht*. The eidetic variation leads us to a historically and culturally invariant level of the world that remains the same in all possible *concrete surroundings* (Hua VI: 142, 380). Following Husserl, the concrete, respective surroundings in Europe, Africa, India, and China have a common nonrelative structure (Hua VI: 142).

In the context of the *Crisis*, Husserl aims at the clarification of nonhistoric elements in two different, but closely connected, directions. First, Husserl wants to gain clarity about the omnitemporality of ideal mathematical objects. In *Experience and Judgment*,[7] he points out that even these elements are constituted in time. Yet they are not individualized by the concrete act of their constitution in consciousness (EJ §64). Husserl becomes aware that the question of whether idealities in common are justified or not can only be handled properly on the basis of an invariant common core of all possible concrete surroundings [*Umwelten*], that is, the *Grundschicht*.

In determining the *Grundschicht*, one may not be bound to a factual, historically and culturally limited surrounding (Hua VI: 386). Still, our concrete Life-world [*Lebensumwelt*] or the similar surroundings of others have to be the starting point for the eidetic variation. The imaginative variation should lead us to all possible forms of concrete surroundings (Hua VI: 106, 123, 158). This methodical abstracting process shows us the common invariant structures that Husserl calls *the* Life-world. As an abstraction, one can never live in *the* Life-world as we do in a concrete Life-world. Although we do not, in fact, live in a *foreign world*, we could. Husserl employs a subtle difference in the terms he uses. "*Lebensumwelt*" (singular) and "*Lebenswelten*" (plural) mean several concrete Life-worlds of which "*die Lebenswelt*" (singular) is an abstract common structure (Hua VI: 142, 176, 363, 383).

By means of eidetic variation, this abstract structure reveals itself as an invariant *function* in every possible concrete Life-world. From this abstract, functional point of view I also view the persons and animals that I meet as concrete instantiations of variables for functions (Hua IX: 91ff.). This close bond between the eidetic abstracting process and the process of formalization allows Husserl to speak of a common formal structure of concrete Life-worlds (*das Formal-Allgemeine der Lebenswelt*, Hua VI: 145; IX: 92). Thus, we see the reason for an irritating double sense of the term Life-world. The use of modifiers like "the immediate intuitive" Life-world is a reconcretizing use of the word that originally means an abstract structure. For example, the abstract function of "sensuous perceptional thing" is not itself to be perceived immediately. Only a reconcretizing use of the concept makes it possible to speak of the "immediate intuitive" Life-world.

The paradoxical-sounding expression "non- and pre-scientific" Life-world (Hua VI: 77, 106, 125, 127, 150) and the connected problem of the seeping-in [*Einströmen*] of scientific concepts into our concrete Life-world (Hua VI: 134) can be understood within the framework of our interpretation. In the invariant functions that are common to every concrete Life-world, the exact natural sciences could not be found. To this extent, we could call the

Life-world "non- and pre-scientific." But our own concrete Life-world is stained with scientific beliefs. We recognize a paradox when we identify the reconcretizing use of "prescientific Life-world" (oriented to the abstract common functions of all concrete Life-worlds) with our concrete and factually scientific Life-world. Our immediately intuitive, concrete Life-world that is mixed up with scientific insights and views cannot be the ultimate founding instance [*Geltungsboden*] for science. This founding could only be performed by a common function called "the immediately given," which we nevertheless could not use outside the context of a concrete Life-world.

By being attentive to this irritating double sense of Life-world, we also avoid a crucial difficulty for our own interest in justifying idealities. A *Grundschicht* in which idealized elements of science continuously "seep in" [*einströmen*] would be of no use for a critique of just these idealizations. We could not even distinguish them from the neutral, nonidealized background. Such a *Grundschicht* would contain exact determinate things just as the sciences want us to see them.

THREE UTILIZATIONS OF IDEALITIES

The eidetic variation leads us to common invariant functions as "raw material" for idealizations (*Material der Idealisierungen*, Hua VI: 383). There are persons, things, qualities of objects, and so on. Moreover, there is a practical life attuned to our needs and technical practices that aims at manufacturing and gradually improving its products. Straight planes and straight lines are possible aims of such a praxis (Hua VI: 384). In addition, the just distribution of commonly earned goods and profits demands reliable counting and measurement. The fictive original founder of geometrical idealities ("Arch-Euclid") had to found his idealizations on these functions. Husserl's theses concerning the "Origin of Geometry" claim that there are reasonable ways to conceptualize, for example, the idea of a straight line out of this "raw material" (Hua VI: 131f., 361, Anm l).

I will try to delineate this briefly. In manufacturing special artifacts, for example, tables, there arises the concept of a standard. This could be a judgment made by the naked eye or with a ruler. Reflection on the possibility of manufacturing such standards gives rise to the insight that it is not possible to create an absolutely correct standard. It remains an unreachable and unreal ideal. Nevertheless, we can think of our progress toward this goal as unlimited. In this way, we idealize our possibility for acting, that is, to try "again and again" [*immer wieder*] to improve our standard. This also is empirically prelineated by some details of the process of straightening some-thing. We always detect a series of uneven points that we could straighten one after the other. We carry the next step protentionally in mind. The common sense attitude encourages us to think of this unreal standard as a real prod-uct, that is, as flawless. The idea of a straight line is a craftsman-idea.

This way of tracing back to the motivating elements could be transferred to other idealities that indicate an *idealizing foundation* [*Urstiftung*]. Husserl also mentions the idea of a constantly identical object as being the same in infinitely many perceptions (Hua VI: 359). In his first attempt to find the *Grundschicht* in the *immanent contents*, Husserl finds intentional objects that are not fulfilled by sensuous perception alone. In the fifth Logical Investigation, he mentions the "objective evenness of the red color of this globe" (Hua XIX.1: 359). This could only be present in adumbrations [*Abschattungen*], that is, the apperception of the *even* red color transcends the given sensation, which is only partly red and not evenly colored because of highlights and shadows.

This difference between the intended "overall and evenly" red and the given immanent contents shows that there is a surplus that exceeds the sen-suously given. In the objectivity of an *object* there is implicitly intended an unlimited series of perceptions of the same. In the *Ideas I* (1913), Husserl searches for the legitimate, reasonable motivation of such infinite elements in original intuition [*originäre Selbstgebung*]. Thinking of an object as "really being" is legitimated, that is, reasonably motivated, if we have it intuitively given (Hua III.1: 314ff.).

It is impossible, however, to have all of the perspectives of a real object intuitively given. Nevertheless, the way to further givenness is empirically delineated. In protentional consciousness we are able to have "again and again" new perspectives of the same. This does not presuppose a sensuous approximation of the object. With every new perspective there are new details intuitively present, but also others that vanish. To think of this unlimited process as complete is therefore reasonably motivated. The "stay-ing" object demands a certain style of nonconflicting, continuous fulfilling intuitions.

In the well-known addendum to the *Crisis—The Origin of Geometry* (Hua VI: 357–64)[8]—Husserl points out that the *exact objectivity* of scientific knowledge is a result of an idealizing process. He reveals that and how exact objectivity goes beyond vague, *everyday objectivity*. In prescientific, every-day life we have objective things that are thought to be the constantly identi-cal pole of several attributes and possible perceptions. But the cognition of the attributes and even of the identity remains at a vague, half-distinct level that is limited by practical demands and their time-pressure. This does not disturb everyday life. Here it is sufficient for our knowledge of a thing to be "practically complete" (Hua VI: 358; see also Hua XXVII: 231ff.).

This "normal," everyday objectivity consists only of the idealized possibility of following the style of intuition "on and on" [*immer wieder*]. It does not imply the element of an approximation to a maximum of vividness or precision, such as the exact objectivity of the sciences that are absolutely exact (*absolut exakt*, Hua VI: 358). The connected idealization means not only the vague constancy of the object in this concrete situation, but an object that is determinable in an exact way, that is, as an always and absolutely identical point of measurement and calculation. It is always possible to determine its attributes in a more precise way (Hua VI: 359). Husserl does not want to reject this idealization as unjustified. He tries to distinguish exact objectivity as a more complex idealization from everyday objectivity.

Husserl also wants to hint at a certain danger that is connected with all idealizations. Once they are founded, they can flow unregarded and uncontrollable from the sphere of exact science into the concrete everyday Lifeworld (Hua VI: 134). If they become an unreflected element of the simple apperception of things and of myself, they might be an obstacle to an unobstructed view of both.

NOTES

1. Edmund Husserl, *The Crisis of European Sciences and Transcendental Phenomenology*, trans. D. Carr (Evanston: Northwestern University Press, 1970). I will refer to Husserl's works following the Husserliana edition (The Hague: Martinus Nijhoff, 1950–) using the convention Hua vol.: page).

I would like to mention gratefully the help of Dr. Philip Buckley, Marya Bower, and Paul Crowe on the English text. I have also to thank the Alexander von Humbolt Stiftung, to which I owe a research fellowship during 1991–1993, and the kind support of Dr. Lenore Langsdorf, Dr. Thomas Nenon, Dr. C. Steel, Dr. R. Bernet, and Dr. S. IJusseling.

2. E. Husserl, *Formal and Transcendental Logic*, trans. Dorion Cairns (The Hague: Martinus Nijhoff, 1969).

3. E. Husserl, *Logical Investigations*, 2 vols., trans. J. N. Findlay (New York: Humanities Press, 1970).

4. E. Husserl, *Ideas Pertaining to a Pure Phenomenology and to a Phenomenological Philosophy, First Book*, trans. F. Kersten (The Hague: Martinus Nijhoff, 1982).

5. For the following passages, compare Text NR. 14, *"Die vorgegebene Welt in anschaulicher Enthullung—die Systematik der Erweiterung (Mitte August 1931),"* in E. Husserl, *Zur Phänomenologie der Intersubjektivitat. Dritter Teil: 1929–1935*, Husserliana, vol. XV (The Hague: Martinus Nijhoff, 1973), S. 196–214.

6. E. Husserl, *Cartesian Meditations*, trans. D. Cairns (The Hague: Martinus Nijhoff, 1973).

7. I will refer to E. Husserl, *Experience and Judgment*, trans. K. Ameriks and J. S. Churchill (Evanston: Northwestern University Press, 1973) using the key EJ.

8. E. Husserl, "The Origin of Geometry," appendix VI in *The Crisis*, 353–78.

Chapter 3

The Genesis of *Being and Time*
The Primal Leap

THEODORE KISIEL

Where, in fact, does Heidegger begin his masterwork, *Being and Time*? For decades, this question could only be answered in the obvious way, by beginning with its opening pages, and so with the abstruse classical question of being that is raised in Plato's *Sophist* and Aristotle's *Metaphysics*. We all know what can come of this starting point: decades of ontophobia among countless students alienated by the very nebulosity of the word "being," which seems so curiously out of tune with our times. This alienation persists to the present day in the onslaught of ontoentropy within a postmod squad revolted by the disgustingly "cloying piety of the House of Being."[1] It only serves to prove Nietzsche's point that this "highest concept" names the gigantic and fateful fallacy of the Occident: "Being" has long become but a hollow word-idol that "dissolves like a tatter of cloud" when exposed to the sunlight and that disappears like "the last streak of evaporating reality."[2]

It is only recently that we know better how to go Greek with the early Heidegger and yet remain firmly footed in the concrete. We must flip the pages of *Being and Time* even further back than its frontispiece quote from Plato's *Sophist*, back thousands of pages in the doxographical record to October 1922, when Heidegger spells out his own hermeneutic situation for a projected book on Aristotle and discusses for the first time the text of *Nicomachean Ethics* Z on the five ways "in which the soul trues and is true," οἷς ἀληθεύει ἡ ψυχή (1139b15). From these, Heidegger selects, in opposition to theoretical truing in its orientation toward the ever-being of constant presence, the two pretheoretical or practical ways of human making and human doing, whose orientation toward "that which also can be otherwise," τό ἐνδεχόμενον ἄλλως ἔχειν, yields a particularly appropriate paradigm for a new, more temporal sense of being.

Let us therefore repeat our opening question: Where does Heidegger himself actually, in fact, factically, out of his own factic situation, begin *Being and Time*? To hear the old Heidegger tell it in his "Dialogue on Language with the Japanese," one might think that it simply occurred to him sometime in summer semester 1923 to start jotting down notes for a book that would bear the title "Being and Time."[3] But our allusion to Heidegger's Greek beginnings already points to a far more complex context that places this matter-of-fact anecdotal simplification in a far richer trajectory of biographical and historical precedents and tendencies. Months before summer semester 1923, *Being and Time* in its overall program had its birth in October 1922 in that Introduction to a book on Aristotle.

But now that we have begun to backtrack into the factic doxographic record, back before the actual drafting of *Being and Time* to its first programmatic outlines in October 1922, why stop there? Can we go back even further to the initial stirrings, to the secret beginnings of *Being and Time* in its motivating question and the situational setting that prompted that question? To put it in Heidegger's own interpretive terms, how far back can we go to expose the hermeneutic situation of prepossession, prevision, and preconception in which the topic of *Being and Time* came into being? Where in fact does *Being and Time* begin, before the fact of *Being and Time* itself, in its very first stirrings in the facticity of the young Heidegger's interrogative situation? Herbert Spiegelberg once called *Being and Time* itself "this astonishing torso," referring especially to its aft-structure, the absence of its third division and its second part. But this also aptly describes its initial "before-structure" as well, referring to the long-standing fact that Heidegger published absolutely nothing in the decade preceding *Being and Time*. Without the aid of prior publications, for a half-century the reader of *Being and Time* has been forced to regard this complex work as something that sprang full-grown, as the saying goes about Athena, from the head of Zeus. That situation is now rapidly changing. The most glaring gap in the doxographical record of Heidegger's development, the decade of publication silence between Heidegger's habilitation work of 1916 and his masterwork of 1927, is about to become a dense thicket of documents made up mainly of Heidegger's hitherto unpublished lecture courses of that period.

Out of the surfeit of documents now surfacing sporadically from the archives, however, it is only in the last five years that the three most pivotal documents that mark the three giant leaps forward, the three *Ur-sprünge* (primal leaps), toward *Being and Time* have in fact come out into the open. The long-standing "missing link" in the early Heidegger's development, for example, the *Einleitung* to the Aristotle book of October 1922, was first discovered in its entirety in 1989 in a Göttingen archive.[4] The Book of Genesis of perhaps the single most important book of twentieth-century philosophy can now be written. It is finally possible to follow the genesis of *Being and Time* virtually from beginning to end through its most crucial articulations into three major phases. These three critical junctures, where the development takes a leap forward, in fact mark three different geneses of *Being and Time*, ranging from the remote to the proximate, and so give us three different magnifying lenses or prisms through which this still opaque systematic masterwork can be viewed along its historical trajectory. In the language of the maxim that the dying Heidegger affixed to his *Gesamtausgabe, Being and Time* can now be viewed in three different ways, not as a work, but as a way. These three different ways are marked by three increasingly articulated beginnings or geneses. In brief, the three geneses are: (I) *Being and Time* as a topic; (II) *Being and Time* as a program; (III) *Being and Time* as a text.

Let us therefore begin at the very beginning and (all too briefly) mark the development forward to *Being and Time* itself by way of the three major events of breakthrough in the early Heidegger's academic career:

I. It all begins with Heidegger's "primal leap" out of the historical problem of naming the identity of being and tracing its differentiation into regions, called the "category problem" in Heidegger's habilitation, in the tradition of Aristotelian scholasticism and neo-Kantianism. The breakthrough occurs in *Kriegsnotsemester* 1919, the extraordinary "war-emergency semester," when the returned "war-veteran" becomes Edmund Husserl's assistant and advocates a radicalized phenomenology understood as a *pretheoretical primal science of origins* differing from any other, that is, theoretical, science. For, according to Heidegger, phenomenology's original subject matter is not an object at all, but the already meaningful "stream" and encompassing whole of life in which each of us is already caught up and underway. But how does one approach this topic without "stilling the stream"? And how does one—Paul Natorp's second objection to phenomenology—articulate this nonobjectifiable "something" [*Es*] that contextualizes [*Es weltet*] and properly temporalizes each of us [*Es er-eignet sich*]? With his response to the double objection against the accessibility and express-

ibility of the immediate situation of the individual, traditionally regarded as
ineffable, Heidegger has named not only the topic of *Being and Time*, vari-
ously called life, the historical I, the situated I, the factic experience of life,
facticity, and finally Dasein, but also his lifetime topic, "being in and
through life," the *Sein* of *Da-sein, das Ereignis*. *Das Ereignis*, the event of
"properizing," for example, will become the old Heidegger's very last word
for Being. The courses of 1919–21 constitute an initial phenomenological
elaboration of this topic in the hermeneutic language of life-philosophy and
in continuity with the young Heidegger's project of a phenomenology of religious experience.

II. *Die Aristoteles-Einleitung*, October 1922: This version of an
Introduction to a projected book on Aristotle, written to secure a chair at the
University of Marburg, brings together for the first time the double-pronged
program familiar to us in *Being and Time* of (1) a fundamental ontology
based on a hermeneutic analysis of the "human situation" [Dasein] and (2) a
destruction of the history of ontology. More explicitly, the document (1) jux-
taposes for the very first time the original seizure of my certain death,
through which the very movement of being human becomes visible, with the
countermovement of falling through absorption in the averageness of the
public "one." This polarity between life's movement and its countermovement will become the nucleus around which the very first draft of *Being and
Time* is composed two years later, in order to develop two basically different
ways in which the human situation is temporal. (2) For the very first time,
with Aristotle understood as an original fount of the Western tradition,
Heidegger poses the task of an original retrieval of our still very Greek conceptions of that situation rooted in λόγος, φύσις (especially its κίνησις)
and ἀλήθεια. The project of *Being and Time* thus takes shape in 1922–24
against the backdrop of an unrelenting exegesis of Aristotle's texts, especially *Nicomachean Ethics* Z, from which the manifestly *pre*theoretical models for the two divisions of *Being and Time*, the τέχνη of ποίησις (the art of
making and using things) for the first and the φρόνησις of πρᾶξις (the pru-
dence of properly human, that is, self-referential, action) for the second, are
derived. (The νοῦς of these two more practical dia-noetic virtues—as well
as of the two theoretical virtues—is in *Being and Time* replaced by the
"lighted clearing" [*Lichtung*] of ecstatic temporality, in marked contrast to
the "eternal" νοῦς in Greek philosophy.)

III. "Der Begriff der Zeit," July 1924: the talk to the Marburg theologians
entitled "The Concept of Time" inaugurates the writing of the three drafts of
Being and Time:

1. The hermeneutic draft of November 1924, the 75-page article like-wise entitled "The Concept of Time" and rejected by a budding young journal, seeks to found the problem of historicality raised in the Dilthey–Yorck correspondence. This first draft could thus be called the "Dilthey draft," reflecting the tacit dedication of *Being and Time* to a figure just as important as Husserl in Heidegger's initial breakthrough to his topic.

2. The phenomenological-ontological draft, the course of summer 1925 on the "History of the Concept of Time," is introduced by an extensive exegesis of Husserl's sixth Logical Investigation. In its ontological move, this draft for the very first time analyzes Dasein as the being that questions being itself. This penultimate "Husserl draft" is thus equally the "ontoeroteric" draft.

3. The final draft, *Being and Time* itself, turns out to be more the Kantian draft rather than the "existentialist" draft that it is taken to be, reflecting the last-minute introduction and development of the temporal apriori of being understood as an ecstatic schematization of horizons.

Despite the previous two drafts, *Being and Time* itself, composed in its major lines in a single month, in March 1926, constitutes a massive step forward in its innovations. Perhaps too far forward, as Heidegger will eventually conclude when he later observes that "perhaps the fundamental flaw of the book *Being and Time* is that I ventured forward too far too soon" (US 93/7). The course of winter semester 1925–26 graphically records Heidegger's sudden and unexpected burst of enthusiasm for Kant's schematism, that obscure "art hidden deep within the human soul," which emboldens Heidegger in *Being and Time* into his own existentialized schematization of the horizons of time. But why an existentialized "ec-static" schematization, which is just as novel to this last draft? For, contrary to the appearances given by chronologically distorted editions of the *Gesamtausgabe* through the posthumous introduction of the principle of an *Ausgabe letzter Hand*, all the drafts of *Being and Time* except the very last diligently avoid the terminology of *Existenz* and the talk of *Existenzialien*, a terminology that literally inundates the draft we have had in print for over a half-century. Why this sudden and just as unexpected turn toward an existentialistic draft, toward a terminology that Heidegger was hitherto loathe to use in public?

The question cannot be answered doxographically, since only the last half of the working manuscript of *Sein und Zeit* drafted in March 1926, beginning with the second division of the first part, is to be found. The first half of the manuscript, in particular that of the first twelve paragraphs of *Sein und Zeit* in which these terminological decisions were first made, thus constitutes our new "missing link" in the early Heidegger's development. The question is, how did Heidegger overcome his manifest resistance to the popular jargon of Kierkegaardian existentialism that was in vogue, much to his disgust, during his early Marburg years? The reason appears to be more ontological than existential. It is tied to his last-minute discovery of the appropriateness of the Greek term ἐκστατικόν to describe the character of temporality as "*out*side-of-itself,"[5] thereby allowing time to be connected etymologically with "*ex*-sistence." One suggestion is that Heidegger got this connection from a reading of Aristotle's treatise on time in the *Physics*: here he came upon a discussion of a kind of change called ἐξίστημι that involves a radical displacement [ἔκστασις] and manifests itself in a manifold determination [ὁρίζειν].[6]

Another is hidden in the folds of winter semester 1925–26, where he singles out the "being-*out*-for its own can-be" as the element in the formal structure of care that overrides the ousiological element of always already being-in-the-world, thus "having" the world and clinging to it. Being-outfor, by contrast, suggests the never ending "out" of always being underway, never being finished, never at an end or entelechy, always "having to be" in a distinctly non-ousiological sense. The interminable insecurity of "being-*out*-for its own can-be" beyond the world finds its apogee in the *out*ermost possibility of death. This consciously Christian meditation on a nevertheless formal gramma-ontology is what now prompts Heidegger to make *ex*-sistence (out-standingness) the overriding element in the structure of care, just in time for the final draft of *Being and Time*.[7]

Postponing this Aristotelian-Christian version of "existentialism" until 1926 also implies a *caveat lector*, prompting us to read the published *Ausgaben letzter Hand*, the "editions of the dead hand," with greater reserve. The extant course transcripts from the students who attended winter semester 1921–22, for example, are essentially free of existentialist jargon, contrary to the published volume 61 in the *Gesamtausgabe*. To keep the chronological and doxographical record of Heidegger's development straight, therefore, when one reads the *Gesamtausgabe* version of this course on "Phenomenological Interpretations to Aristotle," the 35 instances in it of "existentiell" (and similarly for "*Existenz*" [15] and "*Existenzial*" [3]) must be placed "under erasure" or crossed out, "deferred" for at least a year or two, if not until 1926.

The bold claims induced by the spell of the Kantian schematism apparently led Heidegger to believe that something like a schematism of human existence is capable of definitively articulating the evasive immediacy of the human situation, that is, of "saying the unsayable." This confidence first becomes fully transparent in the extreme statements made in the course of summer semester 1927, which coincides with the appearance of *Sein und Zeit*. After vacillating since *Kriegsnotsemester* 1919 over whether the *pretheoretical* venture of phenomenology is anything at all like a "strict science," Heidegger in summer semester 1927 unequivocally responds in the affirmative. For, just as the particular sciences must objectify their entities against the horizon of their Being, so philosophy, if it too is to become a science, must "objectify Being itself" (!) against the horizon of time.[8] It is only with the "Turn" of two years later that Heidegger will finally undo this very unHeideggerian way of speaking! Ever since *Kriegsnotsemester*, when Heidegger first discovered and named the unique subject matter of his thought, he had frequent occasion to observe the almost contradictory nature of philosophy; as the primal science seeking to articulate the pretheoretical subject matter of all the sciences, philosophy is like no other science, for it is a nontheoretical science, forcing us to the very limits of science. In view of its ambition to overtake and to keep to our vital origins, this original science is not really a science in the usual sense of the word, but "more." Thus, in early 1929, when Heidegger definitively abandons the project of making philosophy into a strict science, he observes that philosophy is not a science not out of lack, but rather out of excess, since it springs from the ever superabundant and ebullient "happening of Dasein" itself.

With the Turn, the exaggerated claims for the scientific character of philosophy give way to the judgment that the book *Being and Time* was an aberrant way to the one topic of philosophy and thought. When Heidegger first realizes that *Being and Time* was a failed project, he then re-turns to earlier insights left unpursued in order to begin again. This Re-turn is the real meaning of his self-professed and much discussed "Turn." Thus the theme of *es weltet* first sounded in 1919 resounds again in 1929; *das Ereignis* reappears in the following decade with an ever increasing insistence. The Book of Genesis of *Being and Time* must therefore conclude by following the same trajectory, going beyond *Being and Time* by going back to its most incipient beginning in *Kriegsnotsemester* 1919. Could it be that the hermeneutic breakthrough of 1919 already contains *in ovo* everything essential that came to light in the later Heidegger's thought? Could it be that there is nothing essentially new in the later Heidegger after the Turn that is not already to be found at least incipiently in that initial breakthrough of the early Heidegger? Could it be that not only *Being and Time*, but all of Heidegger can be reduced to this First Genesis, the hermeneutic breakthrough to the topic in

Kriegsnotsemester 1919? Heidegger seems to suggest as much by using Hölderlin's line, "For as you began, so will you remain" (US 93/7), to place his entire career of thought under a single "guiding star." Such questions obviously call for a closer look at the very first genesis of *Being and Time*, at how Heidegger first found his lifetime topic and the initial terms in which it was discussed. Accordingly, we shall now concentrate on the very first of the "primal leaps" toward *Being and Time*, the most remote of the magnifying lenses or prisms through which we can now view not only *Being and Time* itself, but the entire stretch of Heidegger's *Denkweg*. With the first emergence of "*Being and Time* as a topic" in the remote but still fertile seedbed of the ever so traditional and prosaic concepts in 1915–19, we shall find impulses that not only telegraph the structures of *Being and Time*, but travel far beyond, into even the most poetic moments of the later Heidegger.

BACK TO THE PRIMAL LEAP

Where exactly does *Being and Time* begin? It all began in *Kriegsnotsemester* 1919. Heidegger is two semesters too late when he observes in a footnote in *Being and Time* (SZ 72n) that it was in winter semester 1919–20 that he first developed an analysis of the environing world in the larger context of a hermeneutics of facticity. It all really began in *Kriegsnotsemester* 1919, when facticity, and the hermeneutics indigenous to it, is first brought into sharp focus and concentration. Heidegger's slip of memory seven years later—there is no environmental analysis to speak of in winter semester 1919–20—served to plunge the revolutionary course of the extraordinary postwar semester into oblivion even in the archives. As a result, it was virtually unknown until extant transcripts of it were first publicly discussed in a symposium on "Facticity and Historicity" in Bochum in 1985.[9] Not even listed in the publisher's prospectus where the decision to publish the Early Freiburg Lecture Courses was first announced in 1984, *Kriegsnotsemester* 1919 itself first abruptly appeared virtually unannounced in the *Gesamtausgabe* (vol. 56/57: the double number is an indication of a slip in planning) three years later, in 1987.

1915–16

It all began in *Kriegsnotsemester* 1919. This main thesis acquires historical sustenance from its auxiliary precursor thesis: it all began in the habilitation work of 1915. Against the historical thickness of the intervening (and obscure) four years, intersected by tendencies working at cross purposes, one can then appreciate the full measure of the breakthrough made in 1919. Regarding the Scotus dissertation as a precursor brings out the elements of a hermeneutics of facticity already operating in filigree within what Scotus might have called his "speculative formal grammar of thisness [*haecceitas*]." It is simply a matter of staring at the dense jungle of the tired old habilitation, dormant now for over seven decades, long enough and in the right places until a gestalt switch occurs to bring its overgrown hermeneutics of facticity out into the open. The effort is guaranteed to succeed. For Heidegger himself, in a letter to Karl Löwith in 1927, dates the very beginnings of *Being and Time* back to certain tendencies already operative in his Scotus dissertation, in which "I first had to go all out after the factic in order to make facticity into a problem at all."[10] What wins out in 1919 out of the dense polyglot jungle of the habilitation, which fuses scholasticism, neo-Kantianism, and phenomenology, is the phenomenological voice: "Back to the matters themselves," in this context, "Back to the facticities, back to *haecceitas*."

The habilitation also records Heidegger's early interest in the more formal structural resources contained in a living language, as in medieval speech theory's concern for privations, fictions, nonentities beginning with Nothing itself, and other such *entia rationis*. Finally, there are the extremities to which univocity and equivocity, absolute indifference and absolute difference, can be taken, of which the analogy of being is the middle ground. It is more to such empty and indeterminate speech significations, rather than to empirical metaphors, that Heidegger will turn for his peculiarly structuralist approach to facticity, which he soon will call a formally indicative hermeneutics. The formal indication is Heidegger's real method, too little discussed even by Heidegger himself, who instead dwells on its division into reduction, destruction, and inductive construction. The formally indicative goal of a schematism of existence is thus already taking shape, even at this early date, in such structuralist parameters to be found within an a priori logical grammar. It sets the stage for the grammatical transformation that we find in *Being and Time*, where the pivotal nouns are not the traditional substantives, but rather prepositional phrases (being-in-the-world, being-with-others, etc.), and where the adverbials of the verb "being" (being authentically, concerned, falling, etc.) replace the traditional adjectives modifying noun-substances.

The same grammatical transformation applies to the peculiarly receding structure of a hermeneutics of facticity, where the apparently double theme is really only one topic. For the "of" in "hermeneutics *of* facticity" is a double genitive and thus no genitive at all. This ultimate degenetivization is not a de-generation but, on the contrary, the way to the very heart of generation, the genesis of sense in human experience. Life's facticity is hermeneutical because life in its self-sufficiency articulates itself, so to speak, in its own language, which the later Heidegger will discuss in the equally double-genitive terms of the language *of* being. This self-articulation, like Kant's art of schematism "hidden deep within the human soul," will in the next semesters be described in terms of a triple-sensed structuration of intentionality, the senses of relation, containing content, and actualization in act. All such schematizing approaches receive their justification and basis in what the early Heidegger called the strategies of formal indication. But why does a seemingly natural hermeneutics stemming from the very burgeoning of life's facticity include a seemingly artificial moment of schematic formality? Heidegger's first answer stems from Husserl's doctrine of the natural attitude. A phenomenological hermeneutics seeking access to life in its very facticity must work counter to the natural and theoretical tendency to objectify and to reify our experience. The structuralist approach of formal indication seeks to provide such a nonsubstantifying framework.

This yields a phenomenological hermeneutics of the highest schematic formality, a phenomenological facticity that is literally matter itself, the matter of life, which takes the maxim, "Back to the matters themselves!," *literally*; a phenomenological hermeneutics stemming from Husserl, whose subject matter is the facticity of the whole of life as articulated in Dilthey's life-philosophy. It is often asked, exactly how does Heidegger transform Husserl's phenomenology into a hermeneutic phenomenology, that is, in what sense are Husserlian structures like intentionality and categorial intuition taken in a hermeneutic direction? The usual approach is to begin with the Husserl draft of *Being and Time* in summer semester 1925, with its detailed gloss of the sixth Logical Investigation. Such an approach is ten years too late, since we find this hermeneutic transformation already in full swing in the habilitation work on Duns Scotus. Already in 1915 we find that the categorial structures of real domains are not so much seen or intuited as they are drawn out and read off directly from the facticity of these domains. Such domains are accordingly not a brute facticity, an irrational and chaotic flux of sensations as the neo-Kantians would have it, but are themselves already meaningfully structured both intentionally and categorially. If that is the case, then there must be a prior tacit experience of the categorial from which we then more overtly explicate, draw out, and read off the categories phenomenologically. We first live in categories as in contexts or "worlds," through which we interpretively know the things embraced by them.

Unfortunately, there is no Emil Lask draft of *Being and Time*, but the help of this neo-Kantian proto-phenomenologist was crucial in this hermeneutic transformation of the immediate categorial experience. For example, Lask uses the nonvisual and nonreflexive term *Hingabe* to describe such an immediate experience. We already find ourselves surrendered or submitted to the meaningful structures of immediate experience, given over to them, and it is this experience of immersive surrender and total absorption, rather than inspection and reflection, that the working phenomenologist must repeat and intensify. Explicating or reading off the basic structures of immediate experience is not achieved by looking at them [*Hinsehen*], but by giving oneself over to them [*Hingeben*]. The immediacy sought by the working phenomenologist at this point begins to approach the oneness sought by the mystic. Meister Eckhart, that proto-phenomenologist, had already found the *epoché* of *Abgeschiedenheit* [detachment] as the way to the active heart and core of human experience, to the place where the Logos is born. The young Heidegger himself, in the habilitation, already makes note of Eckhart's pithy description of the central activity at this ineffable still-point of fusion of the soul with God: *Es west*, it essences, it makes sense.[11] There is an analogy of ineffabilities upon which the phenomenologist Heidegger will draw here: as the mystic is related to the influx of the Divine Life, so am I immediately related to my own life in its unfathomable nearness and inaccessibility. Heidegger knew well that Schleiermacher regarded this commonplace, albeit overlooked, immediate experience of the whole of life, upon which one feels absolutely dependent, as a religious experience. Thus Heidegger's pretheoretical paradigm for intentionality and categorial intuition at this early stage was religious experience and not practical experience, as it will be in *Being and Time*, although even at that late date the "call of conscience" still provides some of the old religious overtones.

Let us leave this all too brief glance at the habilitation with a curt summary that simply posits the three ways in which it already betrays its backtracking phenomenological proclivity toward a hermeneutics of facticity: (1) In the shift in the locus of truth from validity to intelligibility, from the truth of judgment to that of simple apprehension where, in Lask's phrase, we already "live in truth" (that is, in intelligibility and meaning) prior to the conforming judgments. Simple apprehension is not just an empirical, but more basically a categorial, intuition, or better, a categorial immersion or absorption. (2) In the shift from intentional consciousness to intentional life, from intentionality as a mode of knowing to a mode of being. The scholastics sometimes called this *modus essendi activus* (FS 260ff.), correlative to the more passive givenness of reality. For them it is the *intellectus principiorum*, an immediate understanding of the primary intelligibles of being, one, true, and good. It is the noetizing of eternal νοῦς in temporal life itself, operating here as a precursor to Dasein's preontological understanding of being. (3) In the shift in primacy from form to matter, in what the young Heidegger calls the "principle of the material determination of form." This is clearly an outgrowth of Lask's "doctrine of the differentiation of meaning," according to which the ultimate articulation of meaning is not form, which gives timeless validity, but the contingent facticity of matter. This principle leads to a hyletic specification of the maxim of phenomenology: "Away with forms, back to the matters themselves." All of phenomenology, rightly understood, is hyletic phenomenology. What forms? What matters? The answers are to be found three years later in the opening hours of *Kriegsnotsemester* 1919, which opens with a critique of neo-Kantian value philosophy.

Kriegsnotsemester 1919

Neo-Kantianism is oriented teleologically toward the ideal forms and norms of thought and of life, in the values of the true, the good, and the beautiful. But why just these three axiological domains of the theoretical, the ethical, and the aesthetic? Where does this differentiation of forms come from? The answer to this archeological question lies in the psychic matter studied by empirical psychology. As Rickert put it, philosophy must borrow from empirical psychology the material distinction of psychic functions into thinking, willing, and feeling as the material basis for its three normative domains of the true, the good, and the beautiful. But the real arena of value formation, as Heidegger in 1916 is already pointing out, is not the psyche, but history. But what exactly is historical matter? Rickert describes the material continuum of history as a heterogeneous continuum, an absolute heterogeneity of unceasing flux that receives significance only from above, from the forms granted by a value-laden *Ereignis*, like the birth of Christ or the founding of Rome. If historical matter is but an indifferently unstructured heterogeneity, then it has absolutely no power to differentiate from out of itself, from below, as it were. A chaos of sensations is absolutely impotent. Such a matter of itself yields nothing, does nothing, does not differentiate and therefore has absolutely no organizing power, no λόγος. The anarchy of multiplicity can start absolutely nothing, and so it is not an ἀρχή at all, except in the most passive sense of that pregnant term.

Reification Experiment

At the pivot of the course in *Kriegsnotsemester*, in the transition from the first (neo-Kantian) part to the second (phenomenological) part, the young Heidegger turns the anarchic fluidity of the psychic flux around into the empiricist tendency to atomize and so solidify the flux into psychic facts through scientific analysis. Heidegger's move here toward the reification of experience approximates Husserl's thought experiment of the annihilation of the world. The result of psychologism's reduction of the psychic subject to the factual series of sensations and representations amounts to a reification of the psychic flux into atomic facts. With this reification, with this absolutizing of thingness, everything is reduced to the level of the sheer and naked "there it is . . . and nothing else," to the level of brute facticity. But can we even speak of things when there are only things? Heidegger concludes: "There is in fact no thing, not even *nothing*, for with the total domination of the thing itself there is not even a 'there is'. Is there the 'there is'? [*Gibt es das 'es gibt'?*]."[12] What is left after the naturalistic devastation of totally objectifying experience into an absolute thingness? There is still the interrogative movement itself, "Is there . . . ?" And this is not a psychic process, "a mere entitative occurrence," something objectifiable and reifiable, but rather a living experience. Moreover, this particular experiencing turns out to be not only non-objective, but also impersonal. For is it really I myself, in full personal involvement, who asks an abstract contentless question like "Is there something?" The noetic correlate here is *an* I but not *my* I, a "no matter who" characteristic of the theoretical I, which is "utterly I-remote." The restoration of experience in a thoroughly reified world thus gives us the most minimal structure of the intentional relation, the bare-bones skeletal structure of a bare and naked subject standing over against an equally barren realm of objects reduced to the homogeneity of the sheer "there it is," sheer givenness. This homogeneous extreme surfaces time and again in *Being and Time* as the sheer "indifference of the present-at-hand" and finds its medieval counterpart in the *ens commune*, about which one can indifferently say, "it is." And although total indifference and homogeneity spell structurelessness and destructuration, the reinstitution of the minimal structure and potency of intentionality has saved us from total destruction or destructuration. The thought experiment has taken us to the very threshold of the structured and the unstructured, to the moment of destructuration that precedes any structuration from origins, to the place of incipience of structure from the unstructured, along with the power to transcend that level.

In fact, the indifferent identity of being, thought to its extreme limit, still suggests a moment that precedes objectification. Something in general, the "object" pure and simple, is not an object at all, but rather is a homogeneous continuum of being. The very first of the reflexive categories of thought in Lask is *Es gibt* or *Bestand*, the persistent being of permanent presence. It is only out of this absolutely indifferent identity that identity-and/with-difference first arises, by which an object first clearly becomes *an* object. "Why is the something a something, *one* something? Because it is not an other. It is a something and in being-something it is not-the-other" (FS 160). This is Rickert's "heterothesis thesis." In short, being identical with itself and being different from something else are "equally primordial." This very first use of this all-important methodological term in Heidegger's thought, already in 1915, thus occurs in the course of bringing out the inescapable heterology that belongs to the apparent tautology of the transcendental *unum*. This likewise gives rise to an initial version of the ontological difference and, with it, a contextualist thesis: in the apparently tautologous sentence *ens est*, there is an ontological difference between the noun *ens* and the verb *esse*, between the object in general and its state of affairs or nexus (its *Bewandtnis*), where *esse* implies at least the minimal context of the heterology of *ens*, namely, identity with itself and difference from another (FS 323).

But beyond this static analysis, it is important to note that the ontological difference does something. In this context, it *is* the power to differentiate and to identify, thereby to contextualize entities, the δύναμις of dif-ferring, bearing apart. But it is not Derridean *différance*, if *différance* is absolute difference and entropic deferral. Absolute difference is just as impotent as absolute sameness. Homogeneous uniformity and heterogeneous multiplicity, absolute presence and absolute absence, are equally indeterminate and impotent in their lack of any order or in their state of total disorder. Parmenides and Heraclitus are the same. Each extreme equally spells entropy. Sartre will later reenact both extremes in his novel *Nausea*, with the same results: the absurdity of being. The early Heidegger, in rehearsing these moves of early Greek philosophy, therefore takes the Middle Way of Aristotle. Heideggerian difference is always the equiprimordiality of identity and difference, that middle ground of potency between the impotent extremes of an absolutely indifferent identity and a hopelessly heterogeneous *différance*. This differentiable and differentiating indifference abounding in potency is the prime matter of phenomenology. It is at once the terminus of phenomenological formalizing, which is not the same as logical formality, that ends in the dualism of subject and object. Phenomenological formalizing is destructurization down to sheer indifference and the incipient restructuring initiated by the primal heterology and its ensuing contextualization. This formally schematic deconstruction is still too little noticed in all of the discussion over historical destruction. The prolific central role in *Being and Time* of the reduction to such a formal indifference is thus likewise largely unnoticed: for example, the indifferent leveling of average everyday absorption in the world, the everyone-self, the indeterminacy of the When of death and of the Nothing of angst. Each of these is related to an equiprimordial heterologous structure: the No-thingness of world, death as the possibility of the impossibility of being-in-the-world, being-like-everyone coupled with being-with-another, the leveling of everydayness versus the temporal particularity of a unique lifetime.

All of these multiple moments are to be regarded as equally primordial structures in the articulated *field* of experience that we call simply Dasein, which the later Heidegger will describe in terms of the spread and leeway of a "temporal playing field" [*Zeit-Spiel-Raum*]. The Being of the experience that is "in each instance mine" refers to the concrete unity of a distributive universal and not to the dispersive scatter of individual atoms in random flux. But such a unity is hardly "phallocentric," since it is the "matrix" of a distributed field. The differentiating potency of matter is mater-nal. The phenomenological return to the very genesis and generation of sense is feminine in gender, the primal parting is the primeval vagina [*Urscheide*], the under-part [*Unter-Schied*] that in-folds, in-vaginates in concealment back into the womb of time. The maternal proportions of this chthonian matrix of generation are abundantly clear in the later Heidegger's gloss on Trakl's images on the "intimacy of the under-part," the labor of dif-ference and the "pain of the threshold," the birth-, love-, and deathpangs of parturition and parting, the pain of entry and exit, coming and going, *genesis* and *phthora*, in short, the ins and outs of life, love and death (US 17–33). Being for Heidegger is hardly an Archimedean point, like Descartes's *cogito*, but rather an enveloping whole out of which we emerge as out of an empowering element in which and by which we live, move, and are. The abyss of being is a black hole, a chthonic indifference that differentiates in concealment in the *womb* and not the tomb of time, as Bataille would have it.[13]

The Environmental Experience

After the reification experiment and its highly formalized results, Heidegger rather abruptly introduces an entirely different experience, the environmental experience, that by contrast is far richer in content than the formal schematic of an impersonal theoretical I standing over against a something in general. The experience of looking around [*Umsehen*] and seeing my desk is very much my individual seeing and not at all a depersonalized experience. It is not an experience of bare general things but of things like desks, books, and pens that give themselves directly out of the immediate content-rich context of meaning that encompasses us and that we tend to call the world. But if we take the primacy of this signifying milieu seriously, if things receive their significance from that meaning-giving context that encompasses us, then the true locus of our experience is this meaning-yielding milieu, this signifying element itself, this "It" that "worlds" (ZBP 73). Could it be that this experience of *es weltet* is as impersonal as the abstractive experiment of *es gibt*? True, the I here is not the "I-remote" theoretical subject; my own and temporally particular I is in some way wholly present "with" the worlding experience. But that is the point: in the seeing involved here, my I goes out of itself completely and immerses itself in the world in total absorption. Even though this impersonal experience of the historical I wholly given over to its world is the very opposite of the theoretical I almost totally remote from its objectified *es gibt*, it is likewise ensconced in a milieu of homogeneous indifference. But now, however, it is not a totally empty indifference, but the indifference of meaning, intelligibility, and truth. We are back to the baseline of homogeneous indifference with its potential for differentiation: It worlds, It contextualizes. And, contrary to theoretical remoteness, I find myself deeply involved, in tune and in total harmony with this experience, I literally "live through" [*er-lebe*] It. It is my life; my full historical I is there in a peculiar way where the personal borders on the impersonal (Bergson's and Merleau-Ponty's terse formulation is apt here: *j'en suis*, "I am of it," "I belong to it"). *It* is an experience proper to me, *It* in fact appropriates me and I, in accord, appropriate It. *Es er-eignet sich*: It properizes (ZBP 75).

Es weltet, es ereignet sich: with this double It, Heidegger has in fact named his lifelong topic already in *Kriegsnotsemester*, a pretheoretical and preworldly "primal something" that is the proper topic of the pretheoretical science of origins, the *Ur-sprung* [primal leap] out of which phenomenology springs. More fundamental than the psychic matter uncovered by the neo-Kantians, this It is the historical matter that manifests the full facticity of the differentiating power of the undifferentiated. This pretheoretical It that worlds and that properizes replaces the wholly theoretical neo-Kantian *es gilt* [it holds, it validates], the It that empowers theoretical judgments in their truth, in the sequence of impersonals through which the course of *Kriegsnotsemester* unfolds. From the beginning to the end of his career of thought, Heidegger never loses his fascination with the impersonal sentence that proliferates in the German language, this peculiarly German infection that he picked up in his early neo-Kantian years. It is his primary way to say what has traditionally been regarded as unsayable, namely, our most immediate and original experience, the experience of finding ourselves already caught up in the nonobjectifiable stream of life, already underway in existence, so that we are always too late in our attempts to return to our origins. This unsayable original experience nevertheless persists as the constant background experience of all of our more specific experiences.

What is this empowering It of being and life that takes place, happens to me, like a Big Bang or sudden onslaught? *Es blitzt,* "It flashes like lightning," Heidegger says already in 1914 (FS 126). The It first refers to this sheer happening of the temporally particular I in the overwhelming moment of worlding. It is therefore not to be regarded as a reifying substantive It. *It* refers simply to the sheer upsurge and movement of life. The original something is an original movement, our facticity is an Event, the facticity of time and being. And the most effective way that Heidegger finds to name this It that happens to us, to point to this sheer Event, is the impersonal sentence. The It is thus demonstrative, it points outs, it indicates. What the It as a neuter 'it' conveys is (1) the anonymous, unnamed, and ultimately unnameable character of the Event; and (2) the impersonal character of this happening vis-à-vis the personal I. Life befalls me. At first blush, life is not a gift that implies a personal giver. Throughout his long career, Heidegger will never seek to surpass this central insight giving priority to the impersonal Event enveloping the personal I that takes place within that Event. Ultimately, however, the impersonal sentence is to be understood more in terms of the intransitive verb without the It at all, thus as a sheer action that is both subjectless and objectless. Understood in this way, the impersonal sentence at once expresses the ontological difference between being and beings, whether these be subjects or objects. Being itself, both subjectless and objectless, can only be directly indicated as an empowering action and δύναμις through the intransitive verb. But, in view of being's generative relationship to beings, the grammatical term "intransitive" is a misnomer, at least in sentences like "it worlds" and "it properizes."

Inaccessible/inexpressible?

Having emasculated experience in the reification experiment and recharged it again with the enveloping environmental experience, Heidegger now moves to a third and final climactic moment in the dramatic last hour of the course of *Kriegsnotsemester* that draws the empty and full back together. The context is Paul Natorp's double objection against phenomenology's ambition either (1) to *intuit* or (2) to *express* the immediacy of experience. (1) In reflection, life-experience is no longer lived but looked at. And looking objectifies. The gaze of intuition stills the stream of life, dissects that stream by theoretically inflicting an extractive objectification upon it. (2) Expression likewise objectifies. For description is always circumscription into general concepts, a subsumption under abstractions that objectify by generalizing (ZBP 100f., 111).

In response to the first objection, Heidegger will point to a nonintuitive form of access that hermeneutics calls understanding, a certain familiarity that life already has of itself and that phenomenology needs only to repeat. This spontaneous experience of experience, this doubling of experience, this streaming return of experiencing life upon already experienced life is the immanent historicity of life. Instead of objectifying con-cepts that seize life and so still its stream, this spontaneous access that life has to itself provides the possibility of finding less intrusive pre-cepts or pre-concepts that at once reach back into life's motivation and forward into its tendency. Such a pre-cursory pre-conception or provisional indication that at once repeats and foreruns life's course accordingly stretches itself unitively and indifferently along the whole of the lifestream without disrupting it. Thus, the response to the question of accessibility is at once an answer to the objection against the expressibility of immediate experience: *Verstehen*. Instead of the abstractive objectifying universal that is not only extractive, but also subsumptive in character, thus subject to the schema of form subsuming matter, Heidegger points to the nonobjective option of a more concrete indicative and intentional universal stemming directly from the very temporal, intentional movement of finding oneself experiencing experience. In *Being and Time*, this is developed into the authenticating holistic movement that foreruns the limit of my death and retrieves the limit of my birth in the irreplaceable present moment of opportunity (ZBP 115ff.).

This more temporal universal is the "formal indication." "Formal" here is ultimately misleading, for it is the very opposite of the highest forms superimposed from above upon matter, as abstract genera subsuming lower species. The distinction we need is between such content-laden generalizations developed in an increasing hierarchy and formalization developed in one fell swoop directly from below, from the primal something of immediate experience. The formally empty "something in general" thus achieved takes us to a realm prior to the distinctions form/matter and subject/object. All such metaphysical dualities are wiped clean from the field of experience. We are thus left with the irreducible ultimate of formless immediacy, an undifferentiated "is," a *tabula rasa* of reality, as it were, with the opportunity to start all over in experientially differentiating this field of indifferent being, finding new ways in which this field differentiates itself, and incidentally coming to understand how the old differentiations came to be as they are. Of the two, the latter is the better-known conceptual genealogy, namely, the method of destruction applied to the history of philosophy that in its positive mode seeks "to demonstrate the origin of our basic ontological concepts by an investigation which exhibits their 'birth certificate'" (SZ 22).

But Heidegger clearly does not wish to restrict himself to old paths long traversed in the field of being. He is first interested in bringing out as yet uncharted paths emerging in filigree out of this fallow field of paths [*Wegfeld*], such that one can begin again anew. How? By pointing to the incipient upsurge of being in its very origin, its primal leap, and by sketching out the direction this leap is taking: in short, by pointing to both the "out of" and the "out toward" of being. The double-edged but single movement of being is coincident with the movement of the human being who is intimate with being. For we are already there with being, having direct access to its originating movements. The upsurge of *Sein* is at once the "happening of Dasein." Thus the ultimate formal indication, which first points to the opaque boundary of our origins and then to the precursory primal leap out of these origins, is the "vital impetus" of intentionality itself in its motivated tendency, its directedness out and toward a particular world, its "outworlding" tendency. Intentionality thus makes the first stir in the opaque wall of being or, as Dilthey often observes, 'behind which thought can proceed no further'. Thought can only proceed forward out of being, following its lead through precursory indications, thus going along with life wherever it leads. This is what Aristotle really meant when he spoke of leads in terms of an ἐπαγωγή τῶν ἀρχῶν, usually translated as the induction of first principles, but which Heidegger takes to be the pointing indications that lead us to our beginnings. After the Turn, the formal indication resurfaces in the leading words of the history of philosophy or in the hints and traces found in poetry. They are called way-words, trace words, hinting words. They might also be called *Zug-Worte*, words that draft the basic structures of our language in terms of the pull and draw of life, as it withdraws into concealment and so draws on us to respond.

The key word, the leading indicator, the indication of indications is, accordingly, intentionality itself, which was already the central schematism in the habilitation of 1915 and which assumes various names in the course of Heidegger's long career of thought: caring, understanding being, *Zu-sein*, ex-sistence, transcendence, comportive *Verhalten*, the tractive tractions of *Be-Zug*, the hermeneutic relation of *Brauch* [usage], and *das Ereignis*. Since intentionality is a sheer "out toward," an object is no longer regarded as "standing over against" [*Entgegenstehendes*] but out of this dynamic relation itself as a "toward which" [*Worauf*], which is moreover to be understood as the directive "sense" or meaning [*Sinn*] of that relation. *Das Woraufhin* resurfaces in *Being and Time* as "the toward-which according-to-which of the primary project," the very "sense" of Dasein, the circle of temporality itself. This early conceptual decision on how to articulate even the "object" of the self-motion of original experience is Heidegger's ultimate response to Natorp's objection that phenomenological intuition inevitably destroys immediate experience by objectively "stilling the stream." The same trajectory persists in the later kinetics of the "give and take" of *das Ereignis*: in its "give," it "sends" being and "extends" the expanse of time . . . and yet it itself always takes itself back, which therefore reverses the exoteric intentional movement from which we began.

Because of the dynamic core of intentionality, which transcends the subject-object distinction and in fact demolishes all traditional dualisms, philosophy itself is not theory, since it always outstrips any theory or conceptual system that it may develop. Philosophy is always underway in its task of approaching and approximating, without ever really comprehending, the immediate experience it wishes to articulate. Its formulations are but pointers that orient us toward the pretheoretical origin that is its matter for thought. Formal indications are but inducive leads to our beginnings, which smooth the way toward intensifying the sense of the immediate in which we always find ourselves. Philosophy is, accordingly, an orienting, "pointing" comportment, a form of life on the edge of expression, rather than an articulated science. Insofar as *Being and Time* was understood to be more than that, it failed. But it was only after his Re-turn to his first beginnings that Heidegger saw the conceptual excesses of *Being and Time* and sought to restore it back to its first beginnings, taking it as a way rather than a work by taking it back to the first moments of the emergence of our being. For this is really where *Being and Time* begins, back at the pretheoretical, prelinguistic beginnings of our being, at the threshold of the articulation of being itself. But if Heidegger begins at the very threshold between language and being, then his lifelong question as a philosopher is really the metaphilosophical problem of the genesis of our most basic philosophical concepts, not just the "question of being," but that of the language *of* being. The genesis of *Being and Time* coincides with the radical ambition of phenomenology to come to the very genesis of the sense of human experience, tempered by the sense of the impossibility of mere mortals ever to fulfill that goal. But this is where *Kriegsnotsemester* began, where *Being and Time* in fact begins, back at the beginnings of our being, the "primal leap" [*Ur-sprung*] of being itself. Such a beginning seeks to transform us into incessant beginners and made the beginning itself endlessly disruptive and unspeakable in its yield of being.

NOTES

1. David Farrell Krell, *Intimations of Mortality: Time, Truth, and Finitude in Heidegger's Thinking of Being* (University Park: Pennsylvania State University Press, 1986), 151. See also my review of this book in *Journal of the British Society for Phenomenology* 19 (1988): 93–96.

2. Martin Heidegger, *Einführung in die Metaphysik* (Tübingen: Niemeyer, 1957), 30, 27. English translation by Ralph Manheim, *An Introduction to Metaphysics* (New Haven: Yale University Press, 1959), 40, 36.

3. Martin Heidegger, *Unterwegs zur Sprache* (Pfullingen: Neske, 1959), 95; English translation by Peter D. Hertz, *On the Way to Language* (New York: Harper & Row, 1971), 9. Hereafter US.

4. Theodore Kisiel, "The Missing Link in the Early Heidegger," ed. J. J. Kockelmans, *Hermeneutic Phenomenology* (Washington, D.C.: University Press of America, 1988), 1–40. The discovery of the manuscript in its entirety of this "Aristoteles-Einleitung" was made by Hans-Ulrich Lessing in the university archive at Göttingen. See Martin Heidegger, "Phänomenologische Interpretationen zu Aristoteles (Anzeige der hermeneutischen Situation)," *Dilthey-Jahrbuch* 6 (1989): 235–74. English translation by Michael Baur, "Phenomenological Interpretations with Respect to Aristotle (Indication of the Hermeneutical Situation)," *Man and World* 25 (1992): 355–93.

5. Martin Heidegger, *Sein und Zeit* (Tübingen: Niemeyer, 1957), 329. Hereafter SZ.

6. This suggestion has been made by David Krell, *Intimations*, 49f.

7. Martin Heidegger, *Logik: Die Frage nach der Wahrheit*, Marburg lecture course of winter semester 1925–26, ed. Walter Biemel, *Gesamtausgabe*, vol. 21 (Frankfurt: Klostermann, 1976), 232–35.

8. This in fact is the conclusion of the course. See Martin Heidegger, *Grundprobleme der Phänomenologie*, Marburg lecture course of summer semester 1927, ed. Friedrich-Wilhelm von Herrmann (Frankfurt: Klostermann, 1975), §22. See the fine English translation by Albert Hofstadter with its indispensable concluding glossary. This should have been the paradigm for all future English translations of Heidegger's *Gesamtausgabe*, but, unfortunately, the paramilitary assaults on scholarship by Heidegger's literary execut(ion)ers changed all that.

9. Theodore Kisiel, "Das Entstehen des Begriffsfeldes 'Faktizität' im Frühwerk Heideggers," *Dilthey-Jahrbuch* 4 (1986/87): 91–120, esp. 91f., 96–102. The data on the symposium of June 1985 is to be found on page 11f. of this issue.

10. This important letter of 20 August 1927 is now published in Dietrich Papenfuss and Otto Pöggeler (eds.) *Zur philosophischen Aktualität Heideggers*, vol. 2: *Im Gespräch der Zeit* (Frankfurt: Klostermann, 1990), 33–38, esp. 37.

11. Martin Heidegger, *Frühe Schriften* (Frankfurt: Klostermann, 1972), 202. Hereafter FS. I have traversed this trajectory from the habilitation ("The Doctrine of Categories and Meaning in Duns Scotus") to *Kriegsnotsemester* 1919 ("The Idea of Philosophy and the Problem of World Views") in more straightforward ways in the following essays: "Das Kriegsnotsemester 1919: Heideggers Durchbruch zur hermeneutischen Phänomenologie," *Philosophisches Jahrbuch* 99 (1992): 105–22; "Kriegsnotsemester 1919: Heidegger's Hermeneutic Breakthrough," paper presented to the Heidegger Conference in Seattle, May 1990, publication pending; and most importantly as chapter 1 in *The Genesis of Heidegger's "Being and Time"* (Berkeley: University of California Press, 1993).

12. Martin Heidegger, *Zur Bestimmung der Philosophie*, *Gesamtausgabe* vol. 56/57 (Early Freiburg Lecture Courses of *Kriegsnotsemester* 1919 and summer semester 1919), ed. Bernd Heimbüchel (Frankfurt: Klostermann, 1987), 62. Hereafter ZBP.

13. Cf. my review of Mark Taylor's *Tears* in *Bulletin de la société américaine de philosophie de langue française* II (1990): 61–66. A later version is reprinted as a "Discussion" in *The Journal of the British Society for Phenomenology* 22, no. 2 (May 1991): 93–96.

CHAPTER 4

Should a Phenomenologist Be Clever?

DOMINIQUE JANICAUD

I realize that the title of my paper may seem puzzling to many of you. If a phenomenologist were not clever, how could he or she even understand the basic principles of Husserl's *epoché* and of the method of eidetic description? Since it is obvious that a phenomenologist should be clever—to a certain extent, at least—why question this requirement? Is it not prejudicial to entertain a suspicion concerning the seriousness of phenomenology? You may feel reassured, however, for I am not ill-intentional. Although I would concede that my title sounds somewhat "analytic," I could defend my choice by pointing out that there is no reason why an ironic inspection of the domain of cleverness should be reserved for analytic philosophers and denied to phenomenologists.

Nonetheless, I do admit to having to offer some preliminary justifications. My aim is not to deal with the psychological and intellectual abilities with which an individual must be endowed in order to become a phenomenologist. Rather, I wish to find a hinge between the question of method (as minimal requirement of scientificity) and the effective and specific practice of phenomenology. If phenomenology strives to become a *strenge Wissenschaft*, that is, a rigorous science, or if it is at least concerned about remaining a rigorous discipline, then it has to be performed with some method, even if only minimally so. If this is the case, then the intelligent use of method would imply less the recourse to personal insights than the application of methodological rules and the enforcement of some sort of "reductionism."

On the other hand, since the time Husserl established phenomenology as an autonomous philosophical movement, it has taken on many forms and has never been reducible to the formal application of rules. Although the methodological concern remained operative even beyond the limits of the Husserlian school (Heidegger, for instance, claimed in *Being and Time* that phenomenology is a *Methodenbegriff*),[1] it is not clear whether it can be given a unified characterization. The phenomenological project as such seems to involve much more than the formulation and application of methodological principles. For surely the concern for the "thing itself" leads to its meaning within the whole of human existence. Along this line, one must remember the beginning of Merleau-Ponty's *Phenomenology of Perception*:

> What is phenomenology? It may seem strange still to have to ask that question, half a century after Husserl's first works. It is nevertheless far from being answered. Phenomenology is the study of essences, and, according to it, all problems amount to defining essences: the essence of perception, the essence of consciousness, for example. But phenomenology is also a philosophy which relocates essences within existence, and does not think that one can understand man and the world otherwise than by starting from their 'facticity'.[2]

Although Merleau-Ponty's statement provides us with a first approach to the phenomenological project, we must go further than it does and be more precise. Let us take note of the twofold character of phenomenology: it studies essences, but also human "facticity." To use more methodological terms, this implies that phenomenology harbors an unavoidable tension between method and project. We shall have to unfold this ambiguity.

My last preliminary remark will be of linguistic import, but it may have some bearing on the ambiguity of phenomenology. What do we mean by "cleverness" or "intelligence"? Do we intend to designate only the success of a certain number of intellectual operations or functions? Surely we also mean that the world has been finely and subtly understood. In English, this last meaning seems to be expressed by the word "understanding" better than by the word "cleverness," which is more denotative of skillfulness. Because the English term "intelligence" only partially overlaps with the senses of the French world *"intelligence"* on which I would like to play, I shall have to use several English expressions to convey these senses. The senses I have in mind are aptly conveyed by the French expression *"en intelligence avec,"* which refers to a close understanding of, an empathy towards, or a collusion with a set of phenomena, a situation, a person, or a group of people. (In a few obvious cases, I shall simply use "understanding" to designate these senses.) The question before us is: Should phenomenology remain alien to this last meaning and to that which it opens up?

Now that I have given some hints regarding my intentions, the main task remains to be carried out. What is required is to unfold the problem of phenomenological method inasmuch as it involves both basic principles and something more, a more comprehensive understanding. As I cannot deal with all the facets of the question, I shall focus first on the minimal methodological requirements without which phenomenology would lose all consistence (in the sense of "cohesiveness"), before turning to the other, more open, albeit quite paradoxical, side of the phenomenological project.

THE NEED FOR A MINIMAL METHOD

The first significant move from an ordinary understanding of phenomena to phenomenology is made by locating, defining, and criticizing the "natural attitude." According to this natural attitude, which Husserl also calls "natural thesis," "the world is always here as reality [*Wirklichkeit*]."[3] This world, which is constantly present [*vorhanden*], can be more or less stable: it can offer both clear certainties and confused images or hallucinations. It also can be studied and known by all of the sciences that Husserl qualifies as being "natural" in that they offer a positive and reliable knowledge of the world as it is.

The radical change of the *epoché* is presented as a "switching off" or bracketing of the natural world.[4] In terms of our understanding of the world, this means putting myself out of play [*ausser Aktion*].[5] I no longer make any use of my spontaneous beliefs. This conversion of my gaze and of my appraisal, this *Umwertung*, lets everything be as it is. The *epoché* does not modify the "facticity" of things (not even of my own being, insofar as I am part of the natural world), but it changes my belief. At any moment and from any standpoint, I can freely "disconnect" my empirical judgments, thereby performing the transcendental *epoché*.

The *epoché*, however, is not an aim per se. Without any methodological fulfillment, it would run the risk of remaining skeptical. As the indispensable way of access to the specific results that Husserl intends to elicit, the *epoché* allows the descriptive attempts and their variations in imagination to reach a pure eidetic level. Henceforth, phenomenological knowledge will give pride of place to *intuition* by making it its "principle of principles": Husserl established "any originally giving intuition as a legitimate source of knowledge."[6]

Recalling these two fundamental phases of the Husserlian method (the reduction and the procedure of eidetic variation in intuition) helps us to formulate these key questions: What is the purport of the phenomenological method in terms of *intelligence* (the French notion) or in terms of understanding, empathy, and collusion? Does this method prevent "reductionism"? There is no doubt that, when it is understood and practiced rigidly, phenomenology as description of eidetic idealities or essences *schematizes* mental life. From the standpoint of positive rationality, however, this schematization is not a bar to its credibility. On the contrary, according to the second rule of Descartes's *Discourse on Method*, one of the basic principles of scientific rationality is to divide each difficulty into as many pieces as are required to resolve it.[7] More generally, there is no scientific procedure that does not break up the bulk of empirical realities in order to test the validity of a hypothesis. Although Husserl reluctantly conceded in the *Crisis* that phenomenology had not yet reached the level of a true science,[8] he never gave up the hope of establishing it as both the ground and the achievement of the whole Western conquest of rational mastery. Husserl, however, stressed the teleology of reason much more than the effective methodological limitations that any scientific enterprise must accept. While criticizing the objectivist and naturalistic deviations of science, he may not have perceived with sufficient acuity the unavoidable "reductionism" that the method of eidetic intuition involves.

Yet we must ask ourselves whether the search for invariant essences, extracted from the flux of becoming, is able to give a comprehensive account of the complexity of our mental life. Indeed, we must question whether the noetic-noematic correlation is even satisfactory and sufficient to account for all of the aspects of intentionality. As may be seen in the interesting volume about Husserl edited by Hubert Dreyfus,[9] the very anticipations of cognitive psychology and of artificial intelligence that one is tempted to find in Husserl's theory of intentionality oblige us to question presuppositions that are shared by all of those fields (and that are perhaps unavoidable) concerning the role of description, the use of patterns, the conception of the noema, and so on. And surely the move of the late Husserl and of recent phenomenologists toward a more holistic and existential approach is a signal that it is necessary to amend the former "reductionism."

On the other hand, if any sort of description can be labeled "phenomenology," then phenomenology may become so flexible, if not vague, that it can no longer be considered a coherent, that is, cohesive discipline. From the Husserlian standpoint, it would amount to going back to natural attitudes, as they are found in empirical life and in fiction, when one describes the environment or conjures up its imaginary variations. To counter this objection, it may be enough to collect a few minimal rules, for example, the restriction to immanent experience and the famous motto "To the things themselves!" But what does "experience" mean? Will everyone agree over that which is immanent to experience? Certainly not. At this point, we face a great difficulty, an example of which will be provided by the work of the French phenomenologist Michel Henry.[10]

Having shown that Husserl's transcendence is still "worldly" (in that it is always defined with regard to the world or to things), Henry argues that one should start from the inner affectivity that he considers the original locus of "phenomenality" as such. Things are not merely coming into presence: they are felt, they are intimate to us. We could not be aware of them, nor even perceive them, without an original self-affection. Starting with this critique of Husserl, Henry is led to vindicate the rights of a phenomenology of immanence, a paradoxical phenomenology that both claims to offer a knowledge of life as such (as absolute self-affection) and recognizes that it is impossible for eidetic intuition to reach that intensely affective life. There is thus a split between the absolute and our intellect, a break that phenomenology tries vainly to overcome, since eidetic intuition prevents it from doing so.

In a small book, the literal translation of whose title is *The Theological Turn of French Phenomenology*,[11] I put forth a methodological critique of the claims and positions of Michel Henry and of some other contemporary French phenomenologists who share many of the same presuppositions. The following brief summary of my critique is intended to show that phenomenology finds itself in a difficult predicament when it severs the connections and abandons the requirements that are involved in eidetic intuition.

My thesis is that Michel Henry's attempt to reach an absolute self-affection, the original and intense revelation (*"Archi-révélation,"* as he says) of life, forces him to execute a complete reversal of the phenomenological project. Instead of describing determinate essences, he proclaims the unutterable tautology of life! Thus he claims that the object of phenomenology becomes life "crushed against itself within the invincible implosion of its pathos."[12] The attributes of this life are very similar to those of the God of Christian theology: absolute self-reference, self-affection, universality, and even eternal life. The only attribute that is lacking is personality, as is the case in the theology of Master Eckhart, to whom Henry explicitly refers. Starting from a convincing critique of the limits of eidetic intuition, such an enterprise fails to overcome Husserl's "reductionism." Rather, it gives way to an anti-phenomenology that, in my view, restores a metaphysics of absolute subjectivity that turns out to be very close to Hegel's thought during his Frankfurt period, that is, before the building of the complete system of speculative dialectics.

This example illustrates the methodological predicament that undermines the unfolding of contemporary phenomenology when it gives up the requirements (and the unavoidable "reductionism") of the basic Husserlian claims. It cannot be denied that, even in Husserl's work, phenomenology has never overcome the tension between its project and its method. In the essay "Phenomenology as Rigorous Science," Husserl set out the problem, but did not resolve it. The more phenomenology sets binding rules, the more it runs the risk of becoming formal, that is, the more it incurs the risk of turning into a mere methodology of eidetic description. In that case, it would be reductive in the same limited and justified sense as is any inquiry of positive science. By the same token, however, it would also fail to open itself to the depth of the transcendental dimension and to the enigma of "appearing" as such.

In fact, Husserl never gave up the claim that phenomenology should remain philosophical in the strongest sense of the word, facing phenomena and phenomenality with the utmost radicalness, always questioning and never accepting to reduce the reduction, that is, the *epoché*, to a mere methodological tool among others. This makes the relation between phenomenology and science appear to be very paradoxical, if not contradictory—at least as long as one conceives of phenomenological rigor on the model of scientific rigor in general. Yet it makes greater sense to understand the Husserlian demand for rigor in phenomenology as a search for a *sui generis* rigor. From this perspective, if phenomenology secures a rigor of its own, then even on its first, mostly formal level it should never be reductive in the same sense as behaviorism, sociobiology, and cognitivism are reductive, that is, in a straightforward positivistic fashion. Its procedure should continue to be subordinated to its philosophical aims and ends. That is why phenomenological understanding, even within the limits of its minimal methodological procedures, needs something other than methodological principles, something that might even upset any sort of rule, which I shall provisionally call "openness."

THE OPENNESS OF PHENOMENOLOGICAL UNDERSTANDING

One might simply characterize this need for openness by appealing again to the famous motto *"zu den Sachen selbst,"* which, as was stated earlier, is less a methodological rule than a manner of password or emblematic call. It has to be kept in mind that this slogan was a reaction against the neo-Kantian conception of philosophy that restricted the scope of knowledge to the examination of its conditions of possibility. Since the domain of the *Ding an sich* had been ruled out as inaccessible, philosophy was thought to lack an effective content and a living relationship to reality. The only remaining tie to the concrete world was taken to reside in the ethical law. Husserl's cleverness consisted in finding a theoretical means to recover "real things" without lapsing back into metaphysics. This all too rapid summary may give rise to a great misunderstanding unless we keep in mind two points. First, that the phenomenological reduction bars any relapse into realism or empiricism. Second, that, thanks to the reduction, things are again given according to their modes of appearing, the latter ranging from the most "subjective" layers of perception and imagination to the most "objective" strata of knowledge.

In the first of the lectures delivered at the university of Göttingen in 1907, Husserl elucidated very clearly the novelty of the phenomenological project as the most radical response to the following two requirements: critique of natural knowledge and openness to phenomena.[13] This reference to the constitution of phenomenology as an autonomous orientation and discipline again shows that phenomenological understanding is not a vague openness, but rather that it is determined by a context that is critical of the natural attitude as well as, on a second level, of Kant's criticism of metaphysical knowledge. Paul Ricoeur has given an apt formulation of the specificity of phenomenology: "it deals—as an autonomous problem—with the way in which things appear."[14] The limitation of phenomenology's concern to "the way in which things appear" does not preclude the possibility that there may be different *styles* within phenomenology, different ways of reading the text of phenomenality. Ricoeur himself recognizes two phenomenological styles that were in existence even before Husserl's foundation of phenomenology as such: Kant's "critical phenomenology" (we should not forget that in the letter to Marcus Herz, Kant announces that metaphysics will be preceded by a phenomenology);[15] and Hegel's attempt to build an ontological and spiritual phenomenology. And, as Ricoeur says, other phenomenological styles are possible, provided that the phenomenological openness remains aware that a critical treatment of the question of "appearing" per se is needed.[16]

Certainly phenomenology is both older and younger than Husserl's works. We already find an invitation to a phenomenological philosophy and to a phenomenological openness in a beautiful and mysterious text that goes by the title "The Oldest Systematic Program of German Idealism": "People bereft of aesthetic sense are our literalist philosophers. The philosophy of spirit is an aesthetic philosophy."[17] If we pick these two sentences freely out of their historical context, it seems to me that they can offer us an inspiring motto for the openness that a phenomenological philosophy continues to require. The aesthetic sense in question is to be understood not only as the sense of beauty, and not only as the a priori formal understanding of space and time, but also as the sensitiveness to phenomenality, to the coming into sensible presence of things and beings, or to appearing as such.

In this appeal to an aesthetic sense, we should therefore listen to much more than to the traditional distinction between letter and spirit. The *aisthēsis*, as the finite coming into presence of our perceptions and intellections, is the very field of phenomenology. As a call to let the eidetic intuitions be relocated in their physical preconditions and in their embodiment, the aesthetic sense of phenomenology should first of all prevent any regress to intellectualism. It should also allow phenomenology "to develop within a double precariousness": precariousness in the face of the phenomena as they appear (they might be mere appearances) and precariousness in the face of appearing as such (the source or the origin of the upsurge of phenomena).[18]

Nobody succeeded better than Merleau-Ponty in conjuring up and in analyzing the ambiguous wealth of this precarious openness without severing the ties or the threads of understanding, empathy, and collusion. In November 1960, Merleau-Ponty wrote the following working note, which is found at the end of *The Visible and the Invisible*: "It is a question of creating a new type of intelligibility (intelligibility through the world and Being as they are—'vertical' and not *horizontal*)."[19] I think that this quotation aptly points to the very matter I have been aiming at since the outset of his paper and expresses it better than I could have conveyed it without its help: the new intelligibility that is needed is not the intelligibility of the pure spectator, the Cartesian subject who looks for the complete transparence of its horizon of objectivity. It is the understanding of the flesh of the world, the understanding of the chiasm between world and self—between outside and inside.

One might be tempted to reduce this to a mere reversal of intellectuality into the opacity of the body. Merleau-Ponty's approach, however, is more subtle. The consciousness of the impossibility of a "total and active grasp" or of an "intellectual possession"[20] does not lead him to give up the attempt to understand the world. On the contrary, there is no sense of the flesh of the world without an understanding of the reversibility or of the chiasm: "the idea of *chiasm*, that is: every relation with being is *simultaneously* a taking and a being taken, the hold is held, it is *inscribed* and inscribed in the same being that it takes hold of."[21]

The new intelligibility is "vertical" in that it is not content with producing and laying out an objectivity that would spread out in front of us. Rather it shows the upsurge of the world, that is to say, the upsurge of a *flesh* that is the simultaneity of three phenomena: world, body, and self. Another passage by Merleau-Ponty sheds light on the point I have just made: "The flesh of the world is not *explained* [my emphasis] by the flesh of the body, nor the flesh of the body by the negativity or self that inhabits it—the three phenomena are *simultaneous*."[22] The new phenomenological intelligibility unfolds this intertwining of the visible and the invisible that is elicited and supported by our body. It is thus able to display the aesthetic sense that was invoked a moment ago. Phenomenology is no longer either formal or a *Buchstabe* (a mere apprenticeship of the letter). It is both spiritual and bodily: it lets things happen as the "stars of our life."[23]

Is this too beautiful a program? At the very least, it allows us to overcome the superficial and sterile opposition between intellectualism and anti-intellectualism and the rigid dichotomy that threatens the unity of phenomenology, namely, that between the Husserlian concern for method and a wild "existential" phenomenology. It requires the overcoming of the widespread instrumental conception of understanding, a conception that is to be found in Bergson's works and against which Heidegger reacted when he spoke of "the spirit falsified into cleverness [*Intelligenz*]," that is, of the spirit treated as an instrument.[24] The new intelligibility in the sense hinted at by Merleau-Ponty is not a falsified spirit; it is precisely the opposite. It removes the metaphysical rigidity of the spirit as principle in order to render it flexible and to open it to the immanence of our being-in-the-world.

To counterbalance the possibly excessive ambitions of this paper, I propose some limited and provisional concluding remarks. Nietzsche wrote that any victory may quickly turn into a defeat: thus often the triumphs of our cleverness are such that they are easily rebuked by elementary or "idiotic" realities. Consequently, the answer to the question raised in this paper's provocative title cannot be simple. It is all too obvious that a phenomenologist should be clever; but what truly matters is to determine *how* he or she should be so. This cannot be determined on too general a level.

We saw that the new intelligibility that is needed does not consist either in using a few formal rules or in unfolding a vague openness. Rather it consists in finding a specific and unceasingly renewed access to the moving limits of phenomena. In fact, we, as phenomenologists, have to accept and to appropriate a double limitation. The first is the fundamental, critical and postcritical, limitation imposed by a philosophy of finitude that renounces metaphysics (as *metaphysica specialis*) and undertakes to explore experience fully in its phenomenal boundaries. The second limitation is imposed by the minimal methodological constraint that phenomenology cannot grasp the phenomena in all their aspects and shades, but must perform the transcendental reduction in order to view their constant and essential features. If one forgets this twofold limitation, which seems constitutive of phenomenology, then one incurs the risk of relapsing into metaphysics, theology, or some rhetorical pathos. Too clever would be the philosopher who would always be looking for the truth of phenomena *behind* them, as if phenomenology were only a means to attain a higher dimension. In my view, the "good" phenomenologist humbly accepts not to be too clever, at least not more subtle or more profound than phenomenal realities. In keeping with Nietzsche's advice, he or she will be superficial owing to his or her profundity.

One could dream of a more scientific, rigorous, and formal phenomenology, or, on the other hand, of a more suggestive, feminine, and provocative one. By offering the guiding thread of understanding, however, I have taken into account phenomenology as it has been at its best and as it may still flourish: unsatisfactory, but disclosing insights; minimally "reductionist," but helpful against narrower reductive strategies; eidetic and trans-eidetic; too clever to be scientific, not clever enough to be art.

NOTES

1. See Martin Heidegger, *Sein und Zeit*, 11th ed. (Tubingen: Niemeyer, 1967), 27.
2. Maurice Merleau-Ponty, *Phénoménologie de la perception* (Paris: Gallimard, 1945), 1.
3. Edmund Husserl, *Ideen I* (Halle: Niemeyer, 1928), §30.
4. "*Ausschaltung*," "*Einklammerung*" (ibid., §31).
5. Ibid., §54.
6. Ibid., §24.
7. "Le second de diviser chacune des difficultés que j'examine-rais, en autant de parcelles qu'il se pourrait et qu'il serait requis pour les mieux résourdre" (Descartes, *Discours de la méthode* [Paris: Vrin, 1947], 18).

8. Edmund Husserl, *Die Krisis der europäischen Wissenschaften und die transzendentale Phänomenologie* (The Hague: Martinus Nijhoff, 1954), §1.

9. Hubert Dreyfus (ed.), *Husserl, Intentionality, and Cognitive Science* (Cambridge, Mass.: MIT Press, 1982).

10. On the principles of phenomenology, see Michel Henry, "Quatre principes de la phénoménologie," *Revue de métaphysique et de morale*, 1 (1991): 3–26.

11. Dominique Janicaud, *Le tournant théologique de la phénoménologie française* (Combas: Les éditions de l'Eclat, 1991).

12. "C'est écrasée contre soi dans l'implosion invincible de son pathos que la vie est l'Archi-révélation." Michel Henry, *Phénoménologie matérielle* (Paris: Presses Universités de France, 1990), 132.

13. Edmund Husserl, *Die Idee der Phänomenologie*, Husserliana II (The Hague: Martinus Nijhoff, 1958). See, in particular, the first and the third lectures.

14. "On traite comme un problème autonome la manière d'apparaître des choses." Paul Ricoeur, *A l'école de la phénoménologie* (Paris: Vrin, 1987), 141.

15. As Ricoeur mentions it (ibid, 141). See Kant, An Marcus Herz, 21 February 1772 (*Akademie-Ausgabe*, X, 123).

16. See Ricoeur, *A l'école de la phénoménologie*, 142–44, 158–59.

17. See the critical edition published by Christoph Jamme and Helmut Schneider, *Mythologie der Vernunft* (Frankfurt: Suhrkamp, 1984), 12. ("*Die Menschen ohne ästhetischen Sinn sind unsere Buchstaben Philosophen. Die Philosophie des Geistes ist eine ästhetische Philosophie*").

18. Ricoeur, *A l'école de la phénoménologie*, 144.

19. Maurice Merleau-Ponty, *The Visible and the Invisible*, trans. Alphonso Lingis (Evanston: Northwestern University Press, 1968), 268.

20. Ibid., 266.

21. Ibid.

22. Ibid., 250.

23. Ibid., 220.

24. Martin Heidegger, *Introduction to Metaphysics*, trans. Ralph Manheim (New Haven: Yale University Press, 1959), 38; *Einführung in die Metaphysik* (Tübingen: Niemeyer, 1953), 35 ("Der so zur Intelligenz ungefälschte Geist . . .").

PART II

The Boundaries of the Individual and the State

CHAPTER 5

Homeworld/Alienworld

Toward a Generative Phenomenology of Intersubjectivity

ANTHONY J. STEINBOCK

In this work,[1] I want to formulate the possibility of a transcendental philosophy of the social world that is nonfoundational. I wish to do this by advancing a new dimension of phenomenology, a "generative" phenomenology. A generative phenomenology will be evoked primarily through the intersubjective and geo-historical Husserlian concepts of homeworld [*Heimwelt*] and alienworld [*Fremdwelt*] .

The very nature of this project appears untenable. How can a *transcendental* philosophy of the social world be *nonfoundational?* Is not transcendental philosophy as the doctrine of the constitution of the world by subjectivity an ahistorical attempt to seek the foundation for society in the absolute individuality of the ego?

In what follows, I first will outline the phenomenological concept of foundation as well as specify its dangers for a philosophy of intersubjectivity. In the second section, I will sketch the methodological and thematic possibilities that are open to transcendental phenomenology. These diverse methodological and thematic positions within phenomenology are significant because they circumscribe a field of investigation that remains transcendental but nonfoundational, historical, and intersubjective. In the final section I will highlight various themes peculiar to a generative phenomenology.

I wish to address this project within the context of Husserlian phenomenology for two reasons. First, it has long been thought that Husserl, following Descartes, remains philosophically indebted to the concept of a transcendental ego, and further, that intersubjectivity is one of Husserl's major blind-spots. This is one reason that Husserlian transcendental phenomenology has been—directly or indirectly—the main catalyst of the contemporary challenge to transcendental *qua* foundational thought.[2]

Second, it is Husserl himself who suggests the systemic, epistemological, historical, and intersubjective analyses that open the possibility for a transcendental theory of the social world that is nonfoundational. He does this (1) through his descriptions of the novel geo-historical intersubjective features of homeworld and alienworld that depart radically from a foundational account of intersubjectivity; (2) by elaborating the concept of constitution as a "liminal" process of historical appropriation of sense and reconstitution of normative lifeworlds; (3) by exploring the constitutive role of communication and narrative that usurps the foundational role of intropathy; (4) by reconsidering how birth and death are essential features in world constitution; (5) by suggesting the co-relativity of homeworld and alienworld as well as the axiological asymmetry of this structure; and, finally, (6) by investigating the ethical participation of phenomenology itself as historical "critique" in the development of the generative framework. As a result, phenomenology becomes a normative undertaking.

FOUNDATIONAL PHENOMENOLOGY AND THE SOCIAL WORLD

The term "foundation" [*Fundierung*] was first introduced by Husserl in the third Logical Investigation as a *logical* concept. Foundation is a relational concept characterizing the essential laws that obtain between parts and parts, and between parts and wholes. For example, if part P cannot exist without supplementation [*Ergänzung*] by or association with Q in an encompassing unity, then P is said to require foundation by Q. Relationships of foundation can be either reciprocal or one-sided. Reciprocal relations are those in which, for example, two parts mutually found one another such that neither could exist without the other. This is the case, for instance, where color and extension are concerned.[3] This mutual dependency, linked with the inability to present the moments separately, is not a subjective feature due to the limits of mental representation, Husserl cautions, but an "objective" or "ideal" one, which is to say, "it could not be otherwise" (LU II: 238).[4] In the case of one-sided relations of foundation a part can be *independent*, that is, separately presentable.[5]

The search for a one-sided relation of foundation in terms of an all-encompassing foundation that has no further presuppositions was not undertaken in the *Logische Untersuchungen* (1900–1901). One would be hard pressed to detect such an explicit concern articulated prior to 1912, that is, prior to *Ideen I*. In this work, however, the notion of foundation is linked to the notion of "evidence" in such a way that foundation becomes essentially equivalent to "grounding" [*Begründung*]. Evidence is the fulfilling "self-presence" of something as it is itself; it remains a lasting acquisition that Husserl calls cognition or knowledge [*Erkenntnis*].

At the same time that Husserl ties the notion of foundation to evidence, he puts forward a Cartesian idea of philosophy. Briefly stated, this Cartesian idea is based on the "maxim of indubitability."[6] The result of this peculiar confluence, which culminates in the "Cartesian way," is that the ego emerges as an evident, absolute, *and independent* sphere of being and hence as foundational for (that is, grounding for) a relative, dubitable, and dependent sphere of being: the world.[7]

As is well-known, the terminology used to express a relation of foundation, being "foundational for" and being "founded upon," avails itself to metaphors of layering or stratification, structural metaphors that Husserl employed liberally. These metaphors can appear quite innocent when clarifying typically different acts. For example, in the context of Habermas's distinction between illocutionary and perlocutionary speech-acts, one can say that perlocutionary acts are founded upon illocutionary acts. An act is perlocutionary when it takes the illocutionary content as a means to a strategic end. If the strategic element is absent, the act nevertheless remains a complete act, precisely as communicative action oriented toward reaching understanding.[8] According to Husserl, the upper levels of the foundational whole, say, of a perlocutionary act, can "fall away" [*fortfallen*] without diminishing the completeness or the independence of the underlying intentional experience, what Husserl designates as the "remainder." An illocutionary act, then, could retain its intentional integrity should the perlocutionary component be removed (Hua III: 237).[9]

The tendency to understand relations of foundation becomes pernicious, however, when it is extended to the relation of consciousness to world and of ego to alter ego. This is uniquely a "Cartesian" move. This Cartesian move not only gives credence to the contention of §33 in *Ideen I* that the "phenomenological residuum" after the *epoché* is an *absolute sphere of being*, but justifies the claim espoused in §49 that absolute consciousness is the residuum of world-annihilation. Because the being-sense of the world is *founded on* subjectivity in the foundational unity *cogitatio-cogitatum*, noesis-noema, subjectivity-world, the world can fall away without diminishing the integrity of the subject! Put differently, the residuum, the being of consciousness, while "indeed necessarily modified" as Husserl contends, nonetheless retains its independent existence as founding or grounding, as absolute being or concrete consciousness.

Finally, the contention that one can remove one-sidedly the founded layering where *subject and world* are concerned has dire repercussions for a theory of the social world. In *Ideen II*, Husserl maintains that within the communicative environing-world [*Umwelt*], every person has an "egoistical environing-world." There is, accordingly, a "one-sided removability" [*einseitige Ablösbarkeit*] of an environing-world in relation to another environing-world that makes the egoistical world out to be "an essential core of the communicative environing-world" (Hua IV: 193). By articulating social phenomena in terms of foundation, one is led to assert the primacy of the ego upon which the social whole is founded.

This notion of foundation is characterized as a one-sided relation of foundation that is developed in terms of the idea of evidence within a Cartesian framework. In the fifth Cartesian Meditation, Husserl begins by abstracting from everything alien with the result that he only really wins back the logical "other," a "second I," an "alter ego"; because of his abstractive starting point, he can never really account for the *alien* or the dimension of a historical, communicative, cultural *Fremdheit*. Furthermore, the notion of constitution, while taken to the level of body in terms of "passive synthesis," is not carried out beyond my body and another's body. It remains within an I-thou or at best an I-you relation where language and communication are not constitutive features in his theory of intropathy. Finally, the Cartesian analysis is a static analysis, an account in which the problem of facticity, and eventually history, is absent.

Having noted the difficulties with Husserl's Cartesian account of intersubjectivity that is tied to the notion of foundation, it should be stated that it remains another question whether or not the phenomenological method is intrinsically dependent upon this particular idea of foundation or this idea of philosophy. It also remains a question whether and to what extent a philosophy of foundation is essentially and inherently *transcendental*.

In the following section, I wish to suggest the possibilities that are open to transcendental philosophy and thereby to delimit roughly the method and phenomena appropriate to a nonfoundational transcendental phenomenology of the social world. (See tables 5.1 and 5.2.)

Table 5.1. Methodological Scope

Transcendental procedure / Phenomenological method	Cartesian	Phenomenological psychology	Critical
Static	Progressive-intuitive	Progressive-intuitive/ Psychological-regressive	Regressive ontological
Genetic	—	Psychological-regressive-reconstructive/ Progressive-intuitive	Regressive-reconstructive
Generative	—	—	Regressive intersubjective-geo-historical

Table 5.2. Thematic Scope

Transcendental procedure / Phenomenological method	Cartesian	Phenomenological psychology	Critical
Static	Atemporal structures of consciousness	Conscious intentional life	Lifeworld structures
Genetic	—	Temporality monadic ego/ Facticity	Territory: World as horizon/ Earth as ground
Generative	—	—	Generativity: Homeworld/ Alienworld

TOWARD A NONFOUNDATIONAL TRANSCENDENTAL PHENOMENOLOGY

The material I use to outline these diverse dimensions of transcendental phenomenology come from Husserl's published and unpublished writings that range from the so-called "transcendental turn" about 1905–7 to reflections occupying Husserl near the end of his life. Let me say a word concerning the development of Husserl's thought in relation to these methods and phenomena.

The dimensions of transcendental phenomenology adumbrated above are not unambiguous or unproblematic. True, there are privileged moments when Husserl does explicitly distinguish between a static and a genetic method or when he criticizes his "Cartesian way" in light of new methodological alternatives. My point is that these alternatives do not represent discretely demarcated developmental stages in Husserl's thought. This makes a simplistic distinction between an "early" and a "late" Husserl problematic. We do not find fixed, clear-cut stages, but *strains* of thought or methodological motivations running throughout his work that are often interwoven with other strains or motivations. When developed systematically and consistently, however, these strains have quite distinct and irreducible implications. What I address here are not so much the "stages" of Husserl's thought as systematic lines of methodological issues.

The second point I would like to make is that *in practice* Husserl does not first conceptualize a method and then execute it. Rather, the conceptualization of method is accomplished through its execution: the particular methods develop as he attempts "to describe" a vast array of phenomena. Thus, Husserl works out the meaning of the methods through phenomenological investigations themselves. A generative phenomenology by its very nature, however, will have to transcend even the historical figure "Husserl."

Let me begin explicating tables 5.1 and 5.2 by focusing on three types of phenomenological method: static, genetic, and, as I shall propose, "generative." Static method has two functions. On the one hand, static method can function as a *constitutive* inquiry into the way in which phenomena are given. On the other hand, static method can be carried out in the natural attitude as an eidetic inquiry, that is, as an ontology.[10] In this case, static method would analyze "structures," for example, possible objects, types, regions of being, and so on. Common examples of phenomenological structures include the noesis or the noema, intentionality, modes of fulfillment and disappointment, the relations of foundation among acts, or even the pre-given foundational layers of the lifeworld. In a static analysis, whether constitutive or ontological, the role of temporality is not considered.

Compatible with a static constitutive approach to phenomenology is what Husserl regards as the "Cartesian way."[11] It takes the maxim of indubitability as its clue to the transcendental dimension by exercising a "progressive" or an intuitive-reflective procedure in order to gain the apodicticity of the ego as its secure point of departure.

Genetic phenomenology examines various levels of temporal conscious life under the rubric of primordial constitution [*Urkonstitution*]. Moreover, in a genetic analysis the living present [*lebendige Gegenwart*] replaces the notion of a punctual present, and the notion of "horizon" is analyzed modally as a nexus of indicating implications. The purview of genetic method includes the genetic laws of apperception and motivation, passive synthesis and active genesis, and the role of sleep and forgetfulness in the constitutional account of the world. It also treats instinct-intentionality, the unconscious life, the role of habituation, and normality and abnormality.[12] Ultimately the genetic method describes the development of the *factical* concrete ego or "monad" as constitutively normal or abnormal.

When the lifeworld becomes an explicit problem in genetic analysis, it is regarded not in terms of its modes of givenness, but in its modes of *pregivenness*. Specifically, the lifeworld understood transcendentally is understood as "world-horizon" [*Welthorizont*] and as "earth-ground" [*Erdboden*]. These two modalities make up the concept of the lifeworld as "territory."[13]

Compatible with a genetic methodology is what Husserl terms the "second way" or the way through phenomenological psychology. The second way is distinguished from the Cartesian way by taking "the world" as a possible starting point for phenomenological analysis and by abstracting from the sphere of objectivity in order to gain the phenomenological region "pure psyche" and pure psychic *intentional* life (see Hua VIII: 41, 275, 283). Phenomenological psychology begins by following out *mundane* "implications" of intentional life or "horizons," and, in particular, the "other" or the "second" subjectivity. The second way, however, is fundamentally ambiguous because Husserl subordinates the problem of world to the Cartesian framework. The result of this attempt is the well-known phenomenological impasse, the *Cartesianische Meditationen*; where the problem of intersubjectivity is concerned, this attempt culminates in the fifth Cartesian Meditation.

Before moving on to a generative methodology, let me mention a third procedure of transcendental phenomenology. In contrast to a reflective-progressive procedure, this way is "critical" and "regressive." The possibility of a regressive analysis was disclosed for Husserl by articulating the differences between ontological and constitutive methods. More specifically, a regressive procedure was articulated when he began to examine the difference between static and genetic methods (see, for example, Hua XI: 345, XV: 614). This procedure was carried out in Husserl's "Kant-Rede" or the "Kant-Speech" and promulgated primarily in the *Krisis*.[14] It is called "regressive" because, beginning from natural experience, it undertakes a *critique* of presuppositions and *questions back* from the pregivenness of the world *qua* the "world of life." A generative methodology can only be pursued as a critical-regressive procedure of transcendental phenomenology.

Distinct from both static and genetic methods is the possibility of a generative style of phenomenology. Generative phenomenology is concerned with generativity [*Generativität*] in a twofold sense: as generation or becoming, and as a mode of constitution that takes place over the generations. This style of inquiry is directed toward cultural, historical, normative, and intersubjective phenomena. Although a genetic account does take into consideration the past and the future in the constitutive formation of subjectivity, and although it does allow for the problem of "the other," a genetic theory of constitution is limited to individual constitution or, at most, to an intersubjective nexus of contemporaries. That is, pre-egoic analyses do not necessarily challenge egoic constitution (hence the possibility of a genetic phenomenological psychology). Let us recall, for example, that the fifth Cartesian Meditation, which asserts the priority of the subject as the starting point and foundation for world and intersubjective constitution, is premised on the genetic analyses of passive synthesis. Structurally speaking, genetic phenomenology presupposes generative phenomenology.

Generative method, on the other hand, integrates alienness from the start into the problem of constitution, as constituting. It does this by accounting for the communal reconstitution of normatively significant geohistorical territories. These generative concepts are termed homeworld and alienworld.[15]

HOMEWORLD/ALIENWORLD

Generative analysis marks a shift in Husserl's phenomenology of intersubjectivity insofar as it opens the possibility of a transcendental phenomenology of the social world that is nonfoundational. Thus it breaks with the egological account espoused in the fifth Cartesian Meditation. Particularly prominent and decisive in this regard are the notions of "homeworld" and "alienworld" that, to the best of my knowledge, first appeared about 1920 and were then taken up more rigorously in terms of generativity about 1930.[16]

Although various works from Patocka in 1936 to Bernet in 1989 introduce the concepts of homeworld and alienworld, I have not found any works that treat this conceptual pair as the topic of a sustained, systematic analysis of intersubjectivity; that is, they do not take them as the matter of a unique transcendental phenomenological method, nor do they place them in the context of a new generative constitutional account. Finally, they do not explicate the problem of normality and abnormality as constitutive features of the problematic of homeworld and alienworld.[17]

Klaus Held has offered the most thorough and systematic treatment of the concepts "homeworld" and "alienworld" to date, taking advantage of material published, but for the most part neglected, in Husserl's *Nachlaß* (Hua XV). But even Held's article, which is otherwise a concise summary of sometimes cryptic and disparate material, misses its sense and its radical implications by interpreting the structure of homeworld and alienworld as an enriched reiteration of an egological analysis, a Cartesian foundational approach mirrored, as it were, on a higher level.[18]

Although a transcendental generative analysis of intersubjectivity via homeworld/alienworld is broached in the context of Husserl's emphasis on the lifeworld, what I am designating as a generative phenomenology does not merely have as its theme the celebrated concept of the lifeworld. The problematic of homeworld and alienworld is *qualitatively distinct* from the lifeworld and requires generative analyses. The homeworld, Husserl clarifies, is the *normal* lifeworld, and the alienworld is the *abnormal* lifeworld with its own style (Hua XV: 210). The process integral to understanding the constitution of homeworld/alienworld is the process of normalization (see Hua XV: 148ff. and text 14).[19]

Normalization is not action in accordance with norms, given in advance, but the very genesis of normality and abnormality. It is a process of selection and exclusion [*eingrenzen und ausgrenzen*] as Waldenfels would say,[20] a process that gives rise to "concordant," "optimal," "typical," and "familiar" modes of givenness and pregivenness. Intersubjectively and historically, normalization is the process of simultaneous appropriation and disappropriation of sense that "stems" from a tradition.[21] Accordingly, normalization is the generation of various normal orders for a community in the unity of a tradition (see Hua XV: 226ff.; Beilage XIII).

Moreover, constitution as the reconstitution of sense goes beyond individual subjects and the synchronic existence of individuals. This entails integrating the important roles of birth and death, language and communication, myth, and ritual for the reappropriation of the homeworld (see Hua XV). More radically, generative phenomenology investigates the normative roles of children, animals, and even geology in the formation of common worlds.

Homeworld and alienworld are co-constituted as co-relative through two types of experiencing that I term "liminal." These types of experiencing are liminal not only because they posit "limits" [*Grenzen*], but because they delimit home from alien co-generatively in and through their co-constitution. One mode of this liminal encounter is appropriation. Through "appropriative" experience the alien is co-constituted *as* alien while the home is reconstituted as home. Through another liminal movement, "transgressive" experience, the home is co-constituted as home through the constitution of the alien.

This dual liminal constitutive movement means that homeworld and alienworld are *co-generative* concepts. This is one of the basic reasons why the structure homeworld/alienworld is not assimilable into a foundational theory of social ontology and why it cannot be pigeonholed into a Cartesian account such as the fifth Meditation. First, the "home" is already an intersubjective sphere from the very start. Second, whereas the other was said to be founded in the original sphere or the ego, the alienworld is not founded on the homeworld. The home is not an original sphere; the home is only home because it is simultaneously delimited from the alien. In the Cartesian account, Husserl maintained that in the case of world-annihilation the being of consciousness could remain as a phenomenological residuum. In a generative account, the destruction of the alienworld would entail a simultaneous destruction of the homeworld since the negation of either home or alien would be the negation of the entire "generative framework." I call this irreducible, co-relative, and co-generative structure, which is expressed as homeworld/alienworld, a liminal structure.

Although Husserl does analyze the process of normalization with respect to particular lived bodily being (Hua XV: 154; and see Hua XI), the process of normalization is ultimately an intersubjective process that cannot take its *departure* from an analysis of a "subject." This is the case for two reasons. First, Husserl contends that the so-called "first" sphere of normality is the intersubjective homeworld:[22] an individual is normal only in and by virtue of the normal historical community, the homeworld, that is, the "subject" is always the subject *of* a normal cultural world.[23]

Second, not only is the subject necessarily constitut*ed* in a homeworld, but, strictly speaking, the very notion of "subject" must be considered abstract. For Husserl, the subject receives a historical and intersubjective qualification as *"Heimgenosse"* or home-comrade (Hua XV: 221–23, 233–35). In this way, Husserl hints at a constitutive account *of* the subject *as Heimgenosse* within an interpersonal context. Accordingly, what was known previously as the primordial subject is now expressly understood as being co-constituted in an intersubjective and generatively constituted world.[24]

To be sure, Husserl never abandoned the *logical* concept of *Fundierung* as such. Yet it is equally important to note that the homeworld is never portrayed as a "foundation."[25] Further, it can never be a foundation or a residuum because as homeworld, it is co-generative with an alienworld (see Hua XV text 35). Nevertheless, the homeworld as the familiar world, the world of appropriated sense, is a *privileged* place. Normality is not the conformity to what is average, but the concordant [*einstimmig*], typical, familiar, experiential process that functions as "optimal" or "best" for aesthetic, kinaesthetic, vital, and veridical contexts. The homeworld is not just one world among others, and it is not exchangeable or reversible with another. It is not a We-world, but *our* world, a possessive world in the sense that we belong to it; it is a world whose sense is acquired by the process of appropriation and disappropriation (Hua XV: 163, 214–16, 437).

Thus, for us, an alien language is not a so-called "second language" that one-sidedly depends upon a "first" language; it is a "foreign language" that only makes sense as such in relation to our "home" language. Indeed, Husserl insists that the alienworld has its own style, its own way of accepting the world, its own normality, as it were. But this is already an abstract way of speaking, for this alleged "other normality" is experienced from the perspective of *our* normality not only as discordant [*unstimmig*], as rupturing our concordant experiences (Hua XV: 216), but as normatively unfamiliar, nonoptimal, not relevant for us in the same way a home is. In this sense it is constitutively "abnormal." We cannot quite integrate it or appropriate it as speaking to or forming our common world. The alien, the abnormal, arise as such only *in relation to* our traditions, language, rituals, sciences, and presuppositions that make those sciences and cultural values meaningful (Hua XV text 27). It is the *co-relation* and co-generation of the home and of the alien that is disclosive of sense.

To be sure, Husserl, as a good phenomenologist, is interested in *modes* of accessibility, that is, modes of givenness or pregivenness, and not merely in the fact *that* something is given. And this interest carries over to his theory of intersubjectivity. It is for this reason that Husserl attempts to identify the mode of accessibility of the alienworld for the homeworld. It is also the reason why he maintains that the alienworld is not accessible to us in the same way that the homeworld is. If it were accessible in the same way, the alien would be reducible to the home. The alienworld is accessible to the homeworld in a qualified way, precisely as *"inaccessible. in the mode of incomprehensibility."*[26] In other words, its mode of accessibility is inaccessibility. This inaccessibility is due to the generative depth of both the alien and the home.

The homeworld is not an immediately given starting point that has the status attributed to an independent ego. In fact, the starting point of a constitutional analysis of intersubjectivity is the structure homeworld/alienworld from the perspective of the homeworld. It is a peculiar starting point indeed, since it is a point of departure that is already in process, already with an orientation sketched out by the homeworld's relation to an alienworld. If we take Husserl's descriptions of homeworld/alienworld seriously, then there is no prospect of a third party capable of spanning this dyad. For this dyad becomes the historical, a priori structure of intersubjective experience. There is no familiarity that overarches familiarity and nonfamiliarity. And despite Husserl's claim to the contrary—reading Husserl against Husserl— there can be no constitutive account of "the one world" subtending or encompassing homeworld/alienworld. Home and alien arise through a co-generative delimitation.

By the same token, a *pensée en survol* cannot abate the privilege of the homeworld, because this privilege is a historical privilege developing in communal contexts, secured through the lived body, and anchored by discursive practices and spatio-temporal co-habitation (Hua XV: 161). This historical privilege attests to a fundamental *asymmetry* such that the homeworld is noninterchangeable with an alienworld. Such an asymmetry, which is due to a privilege that is ultimately unbreachable, I shall call an "axiological" asymmetry.

In the final analysis, this fundamental axiological asymmetry would have to be felt in transcendental generative phenomenology itself by acknowledging its own presuppositions and historical situatedness.[27] In a generative phenomenology, *"the phenomenologist and phenomenology themselves stand in this historicity"*![28] Phenomenology becomes the task not only of "describing" essences, especially those pertaining to the intersubjective sphere, but of participating in the becoming of the essence of intersubjectivity from the perspective of the home. That is, phenomenology becomes a normative project as well. Ultimately, co-generation and axiological asymmetry require of phenomenology and of the phenomenologist a dual mode of responsibility: that they be ethically "critical" of the home and ethically "responsive" toward the alien.

CONCLUSION

The radical nature of a generative phenomenology of geo-historical intersubjectivity remains to be seen. Nevertheless, both methodologically and thematically, it opens the possibility, suggests the uniqueness, and advances the direction of a nonfoundational, transcendental phenomenology of the social world. It does this by beginning from the pregivenness of geo-historical worlds that are normatively significant rather than from the apodicticity of the ego or absolute givenness. Its point of departure is not the I, the "original" sphere, or even the We (for in the latter instance, intersubjectivity would indeed be just a plural parallel to an egology). Rather, it takes the liminally co-generative structure, homeworld/alienworld, as the new beginning for such an analysis. It does not formulate the problem of intersubjectivity in terms of a one-sided relation of foundation, as, for example, the fifth Cartesian Meditation does in the form of ego and alter ego, implicitly skirting the problem of the alien. Instead, due to the unique structure expressed in the co-relativity and axiological asymmetry of homeworld and alienworld, it challenges the possibility of an abstract reversibility of perspectives (also required in the fifth Meditation for the constitution of an intersubjective context). Further, calling into question the status of intropathy as a synonym for *Fremderfahrung*, it integrates the role of communication and narrative in a constitutive analysis of the social world. Finally, the notion of constitution is taken beyond the dimension of a synchronic sense-bestowing consciousness. It not only integrates the alien from the very start in the process of constitution, but also inquires into this process as the generational reproduction of the social world and the generative framework.

NOTES

1. I would like to thank the Husserl Archives in Leuven for their kind permission to consult and to cite the manuscripts of Husserl.

2. See, for example, Theodor W. Adorno, *Zur Metakritik der Erkenntnistheorie* (Frankfurt am Main: Suhrkamp, 1971); Michel Foucault,

L'archéologie du savior (Paris: Gallimard, 1969); Jürgen Habermas, *Theorie des kommunikativen Handelns, Band I: Handlungsrationalität und gesellschaftliche Rationalisierung* (Frankfurt am Main: Suhrkamp, 1987); hereafter *Kommunikativen Handelns I*; Jürgen Habermas, *Theorie des kommunikativen Handelns, Band II: Zur Kritik der funktionalistischen Vernunft* (Frankfurt am Main: Suhrkamp, 1987); and Michael Theunissen, *Der Andere: Studien zur Sozialontologie der Gegenwart* (Berlin: de Gruyter, 1977).

3. The *Logische Untersuchungen: Band II/1* (Tübingen: Niemeyer, 1968), §16; hereafter cited as LU. All translations of Husserl's texts are mine.

4. See E. Levinas, *Theorie de l'intuition dans la phénoménologie de Husserl* (Paris: J. Vrin, 1989), 161.

5. A nonindependent part is called a "moment"; a part that is independent relative to the whole is called a "piece" (LU II.1: §17). Moments and pieces hang together contextually according to the relation of foundation in encompassing wholes, which themselves can require founding (LU II.1: §14, prop. 1).

6. This maxim is opposed to the earlier "principle of presuppositionlessness" espoused in the *Logische Untersuchungen*. See LU II "Einleitung," §7. And compare *Erste Philosophie (1923/24): Zweiter Teil: Theorie der phänomenologische Reduktion*, ed. R. Boehm (The Hague: Martinus Nijhoff, 1959), 35. Hereafter, Hua VIII. ("Hua" will indicate *"Husserliana"* followed by the volume number.)

7. *Ideen zu einer reinen Phänomenologie und phänomenologischen Philosophie. Erstes Buch: Allgemeine Einführung in die reine Phänomenologie*, ed. W. Biemel (The Hague: Martinus Nijhoff, 1950), §§44, 46, 49; hereafter Hua III.

8. Habermas, *Kommunikativen Handelns: Band I*, 443–44; and see 388, 394. Similarly, Husserl contends that an intentional experience that "values"—though founded upon perceiving and judging—is identified according to its "highest" component as a valuing experience.

9. Accordingly, for Husserl perceiving can remain intact if judging or valuing is "stripped off." Nevertheless, Husserl adds, there is a certain phenomenological "modification" of the bottommost layer, the remainder, in the process of this falling away, although he does not specify the phenomenological character of this modification.

10. See Hua III: 358ff., 371ff.

11. See *Die Krisis der europäischen Wissenschaften und die transzendentale Phänomenologie. Eine Einleitung in die phänomenologische Philosophie*, ed. W. Biemel (The Hague: Martinus Nijhoff, 1954), §43; hereafter, Hua VI. And see Hua VIII: 44ff.

12. Aside from the writings published in *Zur Phänomenologie der Intersubjektivität*, volumes XIII, XIV, and XV, ed. Iso Kern (The Hague: Martinus Nijhoff, 1973), see Hua XI, *Analysen zur passiven Synthesis*, ed. M. Fleischer (The Hague: Martinus Nijhoff, 1966), and the D 13 Manuscripts.

13. See Hua VI: §37; Edmund Husserl, "Grundlegende Untersuchungen zum phänomenologischen Ursprung der Räumlichkeit der Natur," in *Philosophical Essays in Memory of Edmund Husserl* (Cambridge, Mass.: Harvard University Press, 1940), 307; and Hua XV: 206.

14. *Erste Philosophie (1923/24). Erster Teil: Kritische Indeengeschichte*, ed. R. Boehm (The Hague: Martinus Nijhoff, 1956), 230–87. And see Hua VI: 114ff., and Beilage XVI.

15. For reasons I cannot specify here in detail, a generative phenomenology does not exist in a Cartesian or psychological form.

16. See Ms. A V 10 I, entitled: "Umwelt, Heimwelt." And see Hua XV: 67. The concepts homeworld and alienworld have occasionally surfaced in secondary literature on Husserl's phenomenology. The first to have mentioned this theme, I believe, is Jan Patocka in 1936. (See the French translation of the original Czech, *Le monde naturel comme problème philosophique*, trans. Jaromir Danek and Henri Declève [The Hague: Martinus Nijhoff, 1976].) In 1940 Landgrebe also mentioned these notions. ("Welt als phänomenologisches Problem," which first appeared in English translation, "World as Phenomenological Problem" in *Philosophy and Phenomenological Research* I.1 [1940]. The German text first appeared in *Phänomenologie und Metaphysik* [Hamburg, 1949].) In 1956, the notion of homeworld is briefly addressed by Diemer (Alwin Diemer, *Edmund Husserl: Versuch einer systematischen Darstellung seiner Phänomenoloqie* [Meisenheim am Glan: Hain, 1956], 2. verbesserte Auflage, 1965, 243ff.; hereafter cited as *Edmund Husserl*). Toulemont, following Landgrebe, treats the pair *"monde familier"* and *"monde étranger"* in 1962 (René Toulemont, *L'essence de la société selon Husserl* [Paris: Presses Universités de France, 1962], 184ff.). Waldenfels in 1971 again brings the notion of homeworld into relief (Bernhard Waldenfels, *Das Zwischen Reich des Dialogs* [The Hague: Martinus Nijhoff, 1971]). Homeworld and alienworld are also treated in his "Heimat in der Fremde," in *In den Netzen der Lebenswelt* (Frankfurt am Main: Suhrkamp, 1985), 194ff. More recently, Bernet treats homeworld in a

piece devoted to the themes of world and subject (Rudolf Bernet, "Le monde et le sujet," in *Philosophie* 21 [Winter 1989]:57–76).

17. The connection of the homeworld to normality is suggested by Diemer, *Edmund Husserl*, but is not explicated. On the other hand, the important role of normality is brought out more explicitly by Waldenfels, but is not tied to the problem of homeworld and alienworld. See his *Ordnung im Zwielicht* (Frankfurt am Main: Suhrkamp, 1987), especially section B.

18. Klaus Held, "Heimwelt, Fremdwelt, die eine Welt," presented at "Husserl-Ausgabe und Husserl Forschung," Leuven, 21–24 September 1988. This article is published in German in *Phänomenologische Forschungen*, Band 24/25 (Freiburg: Alber, 1991), 305–37. The notion of homeworld is also mentioned in his "Husserl's These von der Europäisierung der Menschheit," in *Phänomenologie im Widerstreit*, ed. Christoph Jamme and Otto Pöggeler (Frankfurt am Main: Suhrkamp, 1989), 13–39. See also Elmar Holenstein's response to Held in this collection of essays, "Europa und die Menschheit. Zu Husserls kulturphilosophischen Meditationen," 40–64.

19. The notions of normality and abnormality permeate the writings of Husserl, ranging from work prior to the *Logische Untersuchungen* to his last reflections. Yet it is virtually unrepresented in the literature on Husserl. This is all the more surprising since the process of normalization is essential for him, not only for the formation of a lived body, but also for the genesis of formal logic and the formation of a common world.

Those who have made contributions to the subject of normality and abnormality include Maurice Natanson, "Philosophische Grundfragen der Psychiatrie" in *Psychiatrie der Gegenwart*, ed. Grühle (Berlin: Springer 1963); Richard Grathoff, "Über Typik und Normalität im alltäglichen Milieu" and Gerd Brand "Die Normalität des und der Anderen und die Anomalität einer Erfahrungsgemeinschaft bei Edmund Husserl" in *Alfred Schütz und die Idee des Alltags in den Sozialwissenschaften*, ed. Walter M. Sprondel and Richard Grathoff (Stuttgart: Enke, 1979). And see R. J. Folter in his dissertation "*Normaal en abnormaal: Enkele beschouwingen over het probleem van de normaliteit in het denken van Husserl. Schütz en Foucault.*" These studies, however, fall short of a systematic examination of the connection between normality and abnormality and the formation of homeworld/alienworld.

20. See Bernhard Waldenfels, "Auf der Schwelle zwischen Drinnen und Draussen," in his *Der Stachel des Fremden* (Frankfurt am Main: Suhrkamp, 1990), 28–40.

21. Hua XV: 463: "Rückgewendet sehe ich alsbald, daß, was vordem für mich als Welt in Geltung war, seinerseits immer schon Bestände hat, die aus solcher Tradition stammen." And see Hua XV: 165.

22. Ms. B III 3, 41b: "Das erste Normale ist also [das] der einstimmigen Heimwelt und das der ihr zugehörigen Subjekte, die in Beziehung auf sie stimmen."

23. Hua XV: 142: "Der Normale ist normal in und vermöge der normalen Gemeinschaft." And Hua XV: 155: "Die erste und universale Normalität ist die, daß die transzendental Intersubjektivität überhaupt eine Welt konstituiert als normale *Erfahrung*welt der normalen Menschheit." See Hua XV: 138ff., 180, and 233.

24. Ms. C 17 II, 9: "Jedes Primordiale ist Reduktionsprodukt von einem intersubjektiv und generativ konstituierten Sinn, der Seinssinn ist aus der intersubjektiv zusammenstimmenden Erfahrung eines jeden, einer Erfahrung, die schon auf die Intersubjektivität Sinnbeziehung hat." And Ms. C 17 II, 7: "Die Transcendenz in der die Welt konstituiert ist, besteht darin, daß sie mittels der Anderen und der generativ konstituierenden Mitsubjekte konstituiert."

25. Husserl does speak at least once of a founding relation between normal nature and normal world (Hua XV: 156).

26. Hua XV: 631: "Im mittelbaren Horizont sind die fremdartigen Menschheiten und Kulturen; die gehören dazu als fremde und fremdartige, aber Fremdheit besagt Zugänglichkeit in der eigentlichen Unzugänglichkeit, im Modus der Unverständlichkeit." (The emphasis in the English is mine.)

27. This project began with a *Phänomenologie der Phänomenologie* initiated in 1930 (Ms. B II 6) and became one of the main themes of the "Sechste cartesianische Meditation." See Eugen Fink, *Husserliana Dokumente Band II/1*, ed. Hans Ebeling, Jann Holl, and Guy van Kerckhoven (Boston: Kluwer, 1988).

28. Hua XV: 393: "Aber der Phänomenologe und die Phänomenologie stehen selbst in dieser Geschichtlichkeit."

CHAPTER 6

Constituting the Transcendent Community

Some Phenomenological Implications
of Husserl's Social Ontology

H. PETER STEEVES

[T]here arches over the single individuals in their genuine self-love and love of neighbor the idea of a social individuality as an individuality of a higher order; or better, the human community has over itself in a similar manner to the single I an individual idea: The individual idea of the true human community and a true human life in community.

—Edmund Husserl

This statement by Husserl seems to bear on deeply ethical notions, yet it finds the root of its meaning in basic ontological studies. As we investigate the constitution of the Ego, we come to realize that the Other is constituted simultaneously. Thus a fundamental concept of community is a basic ontological commitment. Building on this notion, we can uncover several layers or levels of community, finally realizing that they lead to a concept of a "universal community," a "true human community," with necessary ethical and religious implications.

Such is the task before us. Starting with Husserl's conception of empathic perception as outlined in the fifth Cartesian Meditation, we will move to establish the constitution of the various levels of community that such a phenomenology of social ontology implies. Key to the argument overall will be Husserl's notion of apperception; thus we will address the specific application of "pairing" and then indicate how such a notion leads to the transcendent, universal community where the connection between the constitution of the Ego and the living of a "true human life" will be made clear.

EMPATHIC PERCEPTION AND THE CONSTITUTION OF THE EGO AND THE OTHER IN *CARTESIAN MEDITATIONS*

Husserl begins the fifth Meditation with an apparent dilemma: "When I, the meditating I, reduce myself to my absolute transcendental ego by phenomenological epoché do I not become *solus ipse*"?[1] That is, he asks, how is it that I can come to believe in other egos if I must bracket all statements of fact concerning the external world? Such is the motivating question behind both the notion of empathic perception and the discovery that a reduction to the level of a windowless monad is impossible. James Hart, however, is correct in explaining that the attempt to perform such a reduction need not be considered a failure, since

> it is continuous with the results of the project of bracketing all forms of belief (*doxa*) in regard to being: At the most basic level of the primal passive streaming this is not possible. Thereby the true value and the great discovery of the primordial reduction comes to light. Only in attempting the radical reduction do we obtain the evidence that an absolute disengagement from an elemental world-substrate (identity synthesis) and from the co-presence of the Other is not possible.[2]

Thus the Ego and the Other are constituted together, and a basic level of community forms the foundation of our ontology. Before considering such issues in detail, however, let us first show how Husserl successfully demonstrates this point in the fifth Meditation by outlining step by step the argument for empathic perception.

Husserl begins with a *reductio* argument in which he first assumes that it is possible to reduce all experience to a "sphere of ownness" in which everything that is not basic to us is screened off. Husserl then suggests that we make an attempt to reduce all relational predicates from our experience until we are left with only those monadic qualities that are inherent to our nature and that are not dependent on any outside being or state of affairs. Toward this end, we block off all "alien" and "other-spiritual" things, abstracting the characteristic of belonging to the surrounding world, that is, the "world for everyone" in which we are "capable of mattering or not mattering" (CM 95). Once this is accomplished, we look to see what is left. Husserl remarks that there is a certain stratum of Nature still in this "peculiar epoché," although it is not the Nature of natural science since it has lost its sense of being experienced by everyone (CM 96). In addition, there are some predicates left to us in this "kind of world"—specifically those "value" predicates and predicates of "work" directly associated with the Ego (CM 98). It is at this point, however, that we come to realize something truly amazing. We have reduced experience to things only in our sphere of ownness, yet we find that the "psychic life of my Ego . . ., including my actual and possible experience *of* what is other, is wholly unaffected by screening off what is other. . . . [Which is to say that] I, the reduced 'human Ego' . . . am constituted . . . as a member of the 'world' with a multiplicity of 'objects outside me,'" including the possibility of other Egos (CM 98).

The question, then, is how it is that we actually come to constitute empathically an alter ego? In other words, how do we conjure another original sphere, one that is not our own? Clearly, our original sphere was not what we had expected. We were unable to reduce experience completely so as not to have a notion of Others. This still leaves us, however, with the problem of accounting for the process by which we can securely have access to the Other's essence (CM 109). For this, Husserl invokes the notion of appresentation.

Appresentation is a making "co-present"—a "making present to consciousness a 'there too', which nevertheless is not itself there" (CM 109). This process occurs, for example, in everyday experience when we perceive objects as wholes. When I see a house, I do not have the experience of seeing "the front of a house," although the front of the house is all that is actually in my field of vision. Instead, there is an apperception of the back of the house—a making present to my consciousness a "there too" in that, although all I physically see is the front of a house, the back is "there too" for me; I thus can say, "I see the house."

A question arises at this point as to the nature of apperception. Is it a matter of induction or inference? Husserl's answer is an emphatic "No." "Apperception," he writes, "is not inference, not a thinking act. *Every* apperception . . . points back to a *'primal instituting*,' in which an object with a similar sense became constituted for the first time. . . . [There is thus] an *analogizing transfer* of an originally instituted objective sense to a new case" (CM 111). Consequently, apperception can be seen to work on a deeper level than everyday normal perception. Husserl illustrates the point further with an example of a child first encountering a pair of scissors. At first, the child apprehends them as a mere object; after finally grasping them in their "final sense," however, she will then always see scissors *as* scissors at first glance (CM 111). A judgment will not take place once the transfer of sense occurs.

A fascinating aspect of this notion of the role of apperception and judgment is made clear when it is applied to our inquiry into the constitution of the Other. In this case, the only primal instituting we have to go on is our Ego, thus it would seem that the Ego must act—at least in some foundational way—as a primordial agential model for our grounding of the idea of an Other. This is one sense in which it is clear how Husserl can claim that the notion of the Other is inherent in the notion of the Self.

Husserl calls the exact mechanism for this appresentation of the Other "pairing." Pairing is a "*universal* phenomenon of the transcendental sphere . . . a *primal form of that passive synthesis* which we designate as 'association'" (CM 112). Furthermore, "[i]n a *pairing association* . . . two data are given intuitionally . . . as data appearing with mutual distinctness . . . [and] *found phenomenologically a unity of similarity* and thus are always constituted precisely as a pair" (CM 112). Thus, the Other—during this pairing—takes from my Ego the sense of animated body; my Ego is always available for this move since I "am always prominent in my primordial field of perception, regardless of whether I pay attention to myself" (CM 113).

The result of this is that a second animated body is now within my personal experience. There is, however, still a question as to how we endow this second organism with existent status and a "sphere of ownness" all of its own. As Husserl puts it: "What makes this organism another's, rather than a second organism of my own?" (CM 113). The answer has to rest in an appeal to further evidence, but we are limited as to what we can allow as evidence since we are still operating in a reduced world. Clearly, the notion of a presentation that fulfills our horizonal anticipation of the Other is excluded as is any similar notion involving a sort of "*hyle*" and "filling" that depends on evidence found outside our reduced world. Of such evidence Husserl remarks that we must "exclude it *a priori*" as it would lead over to another original sphere and, in a sense, assume what we are trying to prove (CM 109).

The evidence that we can allow is not evidence that "gives something originally," but rather evidence that consistently verifies something indicated: "[t]he character of the existent 'other' has its basis in this kind of verifiable accessibility of what is not originally accessible . . . [in that the] experienced animated organism of another continues to prove itself as actually an animate organism, solely in its changing but incessantly *harmonious* '*behavior*'" (CM 114). Of course, such experiences would not be possible if there were not an original "set" to allow for an analog. It is in this way that we understand Husserl's claim that the Other is a "phenomenological modification of myself" (CM 114).

Finally, the Ego is used as the primordial model for the Other in one other sense, namely, in the way in which I further define the Other's existence by seeing him as a possible, but never actual, version of me as I am located in space. The argument is that I am always Here while the Other is always There. I define There as what I could call Here if I were the Other. Since I can "convert any There into a Here," it follows that my perspective is arbitrary (CM 116). This makes room for Others in a sort of "logical space." I realize that "I apperceive . . . [the Other] as having spatial modes of appearance like those I should have if I should go over there and be where he is" (CM 117).

Such is Husserl's argument for empathic perception. Yet clearly, it is not the case that the relationship of defining and constituting is solely one-sided. Inasmuch as I define and act as a model for the Other, so too am I defined and constituted by him. This is the nature of apperceptive pairing and the key to understanding Husserl's argument. We turn now to investigate the notion in more detail.

THE RECIPROCAL RELATION OF PAIRING

Michael Theunissen suggests that "[i]n its universal transcendental signification, pairing is an originary form of the passive synthesis of association . . . [yet it does not] includ[e] analogizing apperception of the alien body within it.[3] Consequently, analogizing apperception is a unilateral function and the only possible link between my functioning body and the body of the Other. This is to say that pairing requires two data to "stand out in consciousness as similar: the purely passively registered similarity of the data motivates their association as a pair."[4] Although there is a presentness of my functioning body, there cannot be a presentness of the Other in the same manner, for to posit such would be to "run counter to [our] precept to disregard all the constitutive operations of the Other."[5] Without two matching data, pairing cannot take place. Alternatively, a one-sided transfer of meaning would occur: the Other taking up the sense "functioning body" from me. But this is clearly not what Husserl thinks that he has accomplished or what he deems necessary.

Theunissen attempts to fortify Husserl's account of empathic perception by maintaining that there are actually two forms of pairing: the pairing that precedes the understanding of the alien body and the pairing that follows the understanding of the alien body. The distinction is based on the objects that are being paired. In the first instance, personal-human objective I's are paired. In the second instance, physical bodies [*Körper*] are paired.

Pairing that precedes the understanding of the alien body is understood not by a passive synthesis of association between organic bodies [*Leiber*], but rather by a passive synthesis of association between physical bodies [*Körper*]. It is not the ego in any of its formulations (that is, the absolutely unique ego, the primordial ego, or the personal-human objective I, to use Theunissen's terminology) that is paired. Rather, the organic bodies are related through an analogizing apperception that *assumes* a *Körper* pairing. According to Theunissen, such a notion is supported in Husserl's discussion of the constitution of other bodies in §54 of the *Cartesian Meditations*. Here Husserl explains:

> The body that is a member of my primordial world (the body subsequently of the other ego) is for me a body in the mode There. Its manner of appearance does not become paired in a direct association with the manner of appearance actually belonging at the time to my animate organism (in the mode Here); rather it awakens reproductively *another*, an immediately similar appearance included in the system constitutive of my animate organism as a body in space. . . . *Thus the assimilative apperception becomes possible* and established, by which the external body over there receives analogically from mine the sense, animate organism, and consequently the sense, organism belonging to another "world," analogous to my primordial world. (CM 117–18)

Reading "animate organism" as "organic body" (or *Leib*), it is clear that the relating of my organic body to the organic body of the Other is an analogizing apperception that is not a pairing, but rather one that assumes a physical body pairing. Yet, given this, how is it that the pairing of physical bodies can actually be said to be a reciprocal relation? If *Körper* are truly paired, then it is not only the case that the Other's physical body is defined (foundationally constituted, as it were) by my personal physical body, it is also the case that my personal physical body is so defined by the alien *Körper*. Thus, as objects in the world, physical bodies are interdefined, and with each encounter of the Other, "I take part in the alien primordinal positing of my organic body as a pure physical body."[6] My physical body is taken *as* a physical body for the Other, and "[o]nly now can one truly say that my body is a thing like any other thing. It is for the Other an 'environmental object,' in no way different from the chair and the table, next to which it makes its appearance in the alien surrounding world."[7] The pairing relation is fulfilled as the *Körper* achieve their sense and arise with meaning together.

One might question Theunissen here by turning his own line of reasoning against him. If pairing requires a basic correspondence between the objects to be paired, it might be asked, does not a pairing of *Körper* assume a proto-pairing that established the physical bodies as similar objects capable of undergoing the pairing? That is, how can we know that two objects are capable of being paired as physical bodies? What prevents the necessity for a preestablished similarity from becoming an infinite regress?

We can attempt to defend Theunissen here by appealing to the notion of pairing as a primal form of association. Recall that Husserl has suggested that primitive objects are given intuitionally as data appearing with mutual distinctness yet founding phenomenologically a unity of similarity. There is enough similarity between these primitive objects for the pairing to "stick," that is, when the passive synthesis "engages" and the attempt is made to pair my physical body and the physical body of the Other, the pairing succeeds.[8] Consequently, there is the mutual transfer of sense that is typical of the pairing process.

It must also be pointed out at this juncture that such a move saves Husserl from solipsism. This is one of the fringe benefits of the notion of pairing. Although it is clear that the external object receiving the sense I already have for my personal physical body prospers from such a transfer of sense (in fact, such is the necessary founding step for constituting Others in the full sense of "alien Egos"), one can ask what is it that the object being constituted as "my *Körper*" receives from the mutual transfer of sense.

My physical body is constituted as an external object. This, then, keeps the theory from falling into solipsism. The argument is intuitive: I can experience my face when I shave, my hands when I play guitar, my feet when I play tennis, and so forth. But I cannot experience my body at this level *as a whole*—especially as an external whole. Such is one of the senses that my physical body receives from the pairing with the other physical body—a body that *is* experienced as a whole. Consequently, I transcend the purely solipsistic attitude. Without the Other, I would never have a sense of myself as a whole; I need the Other in order to understand the *full* sense of myself. It is at this point that we begin to see the true significance of the reciprocity of the pairing relation.

Having thus established a form of pairing that precedes the understanding of the alien body, we move to consider the post-pairing that follows the understanding of the alien body. To begin such an analysis, Theunissen considers Husserl's statement that the ego and alter ego are always and necessarily given in an original pairing. To what sort of thing could "ego" be referring in this instance?

There are three possibilities: the absolutely unique ego, the primordinal ego, or the personal-human-objective I. Theunissen rejects the first two interpretations as analytic impossibilities. "To be sure," he explains,

> the alter ego is always and necessarily given on the basis of my absolutely unique ego and my primordinal ego. But my absolutely unique ego would not be absolutely unique if it were only given in an original pairing with the alter ego. And, in the same way, my primordinal ego would not be primordinal if it needed the alter ego as a condition for its own givenness.[9]

Thus the ego to which Husserl is referring must be the personal-human-objective I. This is to say that the analogizing apperception of the Other's body precedes the pairing of egos as personal I's. In this way, the egos arise, as it were, as personally owned. This is truly a reciprocal pairing relationship as is evidenced by Husserl's further discussion of this level of constitution of the Other. Although the Other is, in a sense, "phenomenologically a 'modification' of myself," he writes, "[I get] this character of being 'my' self by virtue of the contrastive pairing that necessarily takes place"(CM 114). The alien body and my body are now paired and ownership is established: myself as *my* self and the other as the *Other's* self.

There are, then, two forms of pairing—one preceding and one following the understanding of the alien body. Through this relation of reciprocity, the Ego and the Other arise together as animate, lived, bodily, organic, personal, and owned selves. Thus we come to understand what it means for the relation of pairing to be truly reciprocal: without the Other, there is no I. That is to say that "I am aware of myself in a personal and self-referential way through being first of all the beneficiary of a gracious act of attention by Others. In a genetic-constitutional sense I am, first of all, the Other to Others."[10]

THE FURTHER CONSTITUTION OF COMMUNITY

We now turn to investigate the various forms and levels of community constituted either in conjunction with or as a result of the constitution of the Other. If it is true that the Other and the Ego arise together, and if, therefore, I always constitute myself as a member of a community and not as an isolated monad in the strict sense, then it is clearly a valid and worthwhile endeavor to attempt to uncover the character of the community in which I participate.

At its most basic level, we understand community to represent the notion of intersubjective Nature. This takes place through an identity of appearance systems that leads to "perceiving that the other Ego and I are looking at the same world . . . though this perceiving goes on exclusively within the sphere of my ownness" (CM 124). The argument begins by understanding that my Here point is a There point for the Other; and although the Other appears to me There, he takes his point as a Here. This notion of shifting spatial perspective can be enlarged to cover the whole of Nature as well:

> "[M]y" whole Nature is the same as the Other's. In *my* primordial sphere it is constituted as an identical unity of my manifold modes of givenness—an identical unity in changing orientations around *my* animate organism (the zero body, the body in the absolute Here), an identical unity of even richer multiplicities that, as changing modes of appearance pertaining to different "senses," or else as changeable "perspectives," belong to each particular orientation as here or there and also, in a quite particular manner, belong to my animate organism which is inseparable from the absolute Here. . . . *In the appresented other ego* the synthetic systems are *the same* . . . except that the *actual* perceptions and the modes of givenness actualized therein, and also in part the objects actually perceived, are *not the same*; rather the objects perceived are precisely those perceivable *from there*, and *as* they are perceivable from there. (CM 123)

We might clarify Husserl's point with the following illustration. If all of reality can be imagined as being filled by a three-dimensional Cartesian graph system, then we take our Here point as the origin. But we take the Other's There point as an actual Here point for him and as a possible Here point for us as well: our origin can shift and thus change any potential There into a Here. This underlying matrix of possible points of perspective is the first notion of an intersubjective Nature and, thus, of a community. We have not only the notion of the Other and the Ego given to us, but also the notion of the *matrix* as well. The matrix is common to my Ego and to the Other. If, for the sake of argument, we say that my Here—my point of perspective—is the origin point A $(0,0,0)$ and the Other's Here—the Other's point of perspective that I call a There point—is located at point B $(1,2,3)$ as viewed from my perspective, then we can imagine turning the There point B into a Here point (figure 6.1).

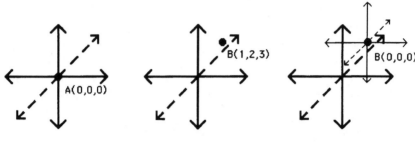

Figure. 6.1

This can occur because the actual points A and B, no matter what coordinates are assigned to them as our origin shifts, are common to the Ego and to the Other. Whether point A is seen as (0,0,0) or (1,2,3), it is still point A for both of us. Thus the Other and I can be said to share an objective Nature— since this illustration not only applies to spatial perceptions, but to other sensual perceptions of the world as well. This is the first level of community: a common nexus of possible perspective reference points.

This argument is directly relevant to the "bootstrap problem" we encountered in the section above when we suggested that the Ego and the Other emerge together and as interdependent. To use our current metaphor, we maintain that with the formation of the notion of Here comes not only the notion of There, but the whole underlying grid or matrix as a schema into which all of the Here and There points fit as well. Indeed, the very notion of Here assumes this grid and thus a foundational sense of community.

The second level of community involves three steps and follows fairly straightforwardly from the first level. As Husserl points out, "[a]fter the first level of communalization and (this being almost equivalent) the first constitution of an Objective world, starting from the primordial world, have been sufficiently clarified, the *higher levels* offer relatively minor difficulties" (CM 129).

We begin by noting that the Other's intentional life is parallel to my own. He has a horizon with retentions and protentions and a full field of sensory experience with a glancing ray of attention that he can focus here and there. Second, we recognize that there is a plurality of Others and that I can imagine myself not only as the Other's Other, but as the Other's Other's Other.

This cries out for further clarification. Realizing that there are multiple Others and that they all have an intentional life that is structured similarly to my own, I can imagine how I am not only the Other's (let us call him "Edmund") Other, but also that another Other (let us call him "Martin") might see me as Edmund's Other as well. That is, I realize that Martin takes Edmund as an Other, and Martin realizes that Edmund takes me as an Other, thus I am an Other "twice-removed": an Other for Martin's Other. Slowly, a network of Other-taking develops. When I begin to take this networking *as* a community and no longer need to make the judgment (that is, to work through the argument presented in this paragraph), I have realized a higher, intermediate sense of communalization. Even when I do not perceive the various members of the "network," I have the community. I am constituted within "*a community of men* . . . [and] even as solitary [I have] the sense: member of a community—there is implicit a *mutual being for one another*, which / entails an *Objectivating equalization* of my existence with that of all others—consequently: I or anyone else, as a man among other men" (CM 129).

Finally we come to the highest level of community, the one at which one takes the community *as* one's own, distinct community. The concept at work here is one of orientation: let us call a community that is taken as one's community a "culture." Husserl explains that

> [e]veryone, as a matter of a priori necessity, lives in the same Nature, a Nature moreover that, with the necessary communalization of his life and the lives of others, he has fashioned into a *cultural world* in his individual and communalized living and doing—a world having human significances. (CM 133)[11]

This leads to interesting complications. As each individual comes to recognize his community *as* his community, he realizes that within the plurality of Others, his cultural perspective is but one of the possible perspectives in the world. Furthermore, Husserl maintains that this highest level of community is fashioned historically and that there is thus a multiplicity of cultural worlds. There are two important points to be made here. First, there is a sense in which a culture is a very personal and restricted thing. That is to say, an individual's culture is *his* culture both in the sense that it helps to define him and that it is unavailable to outsiders. Members of a specific culture must acquire an understanding of their culture and of the historical process through which it has been constructed in order to have an understanding of their present. In this sense, culture is *Self*-defining. Yet it would seem that another important aspect of culture is the way in which one is restricted from acquiring an understanding of alien cultures. Husserl explains that an understanding of culture "is essentially possible to all members of that community, with a certain originality possible, to them alone / and barred to anyone from another community who enters into relation with theirs" (CM 133).

At first it might seem that Husserl has set the groundwork for a type of postmodern relativism in which the agenda is truly a negative project in opposition to the goal of the social ontological studies that have been undertaken here. This, however, brings us to the second important point to be made. Although culture may be historically fashioned by a specific community and although it might seem that members of alien cultures are "barred" from intercultural understandings, culture is not completely inaccessible to nonparticipants. In the same way that the alien body can come to be understood on all of its various levels, so too can we achieve an understanding of a member of an alien culture as a member of that particular culture. Husserl characterizes this experience as a "sympathetic understanding" that takes place on various levels. "At first," he writes, "such an individual necessarily understands men of the alien world as generically men, and men of a 'certain' cultural world. Starting from there, he must first produce for himself, step by step, the possibilities of further understanding" (CM 133). The phenomenological project becomes, as it were, a bridge between cultures that allows an understanding that is not contingent in any important way on one's own immersion in one's culture or historically formulated narrative.

Thus we have achieved a constitution of both the Other and the Ego as members of a community on a variety of different levels and have shown— by means of a brief sketch—the general focus of Husserl's notion of social ontology and the power of the pairing relationship that allows the Ego and the Other to arise together in all of their varied senses. But the last point that we have attempted to investigate, that is, the question of the collapse of our phenomenological, ontological theory into relativism, must not be passed over too quickly; for herein lies both the greatest threat to this project as well as the motivation behind the discovery to which we have been leading and to which we now turn.

THE TRANSCENDENT COMMUNITY AND
THE PROBLEM OF RELATIVISM

The move to constitute the final level of community, that is, the transcendent community, although it appears to be a more radical step than is generally taken by those in the tradition of Husserlian social ontology, is actually a natural extension of the same processes in which we have been engaged throughout. The move is simple, but the implications are complex.

We first begin by attempting a reduction of a higher level similar to the reduction attempted in §42 of the *Meditations*. Husserl, engaged in a reduction of the Ego, is concerned about falling into solipsism. Thus he poses the question: "When I . . . reduce myself . . . by phenomenological epoché do I not become *solus ipse*" (CM 89)? We know that the answer is "no," for there is a fundamental concept of community and relation to the Other that we are committed to at this level. Such a notion is indeed necessary for the very concept of my Ego. Similarly, having established the concept of our community (that is, culture) as a basic ontological commitment, we are now concerned about falling into relativism. Thus we pose the question: "When, after the reduction and the ontological investigations that we have undertaken above, we are left with a notion of our being in our community, do we not, in fact, become isolated and trapped in this community, unable to move outside our own 'system'?"[12] If we cannot answer "no" to this question as well, then we are left with a similar, yet more devastating, problem than that with which the solipsist is faced. The solipsist is forced to admit that all he has is himself—his consciousness, his perceptions, his Being, and so on. There is no point of contact with an external world; indeed, any talk of an external world is meaningless. The relativist is in a similar situation. He is forced to admit that all he has is his own culture (system)—his interpretation, his language, and his perspective. There is no point of contact with a community, system, or perspective beyond and above his own; indeed, any talk of such things is meaningless.

Consequently, if something like Truth is defined as being nonperspectival, then we are doomed never to know it. If the transcendent community is a community in which we all participate, live, and find meaning, then this, too, is something we may never know, since all that we have is our own isolated community with its particular significances and meanings that are there just for us. We thus have a perspective from which we can never escape and a community that carves the world into meaningful bits before we even get our hands on it. To try to escape from either is like running from one's own shadow.

But are we committed to relativism as a result? We wish to answer "no" to this question just as Husserl declined solipsism. How this is possible will become evident when we attempt to reduce our experience to what is purely of our own culture. Undertaking this project, we begin to screen off everything that is "culturally other." We take away the notion of absolute significance and understand things as only having significance according to our cultural standards. We discard the notion that a thing exists in any one absolute sense and instead accept that it is always viewed from our own particular perspective; thus it is continually subject to interpretation. We continue to reduce the world to a "sphere of own-culturalness" and it is at this point that something remarkable strikes us. Using an adaptation of Husserl's words (from his refutation of solipsism in §44), we discover that

> [t]he psychic life of my [culturally-immersed] Ego . . . including my whole world-experiencing life and therefore including my actual and possible experience *of* what is [culturally] other, is wholly unaffected by screening off what is [culturally] other. . . . I, the reduced[, communal, culturally-immersed Ego] . . . am constituted, accordingly, as a member of the [transcendent] "world" with a multiplicity of "objects [with various significances] outside [my culture]." (CM 98–99)

This is to say that just as we are committed to the notion of community, since the Ego is foundationally constituted as a member of a community of Others, so too we are committed to a notion of a transcendent community, since our community is foundationally constituted as one community among others. The solipsistic reduction did not hold insofar as the Other was a basic notion necessary for the understanding of the Ego. Thus the relativistic reduction also does not hold insofar as the transcendent community in which we all participate is a basic notion necessary for the understanding of our own culture. To comprehend our community *as* our community, that is, our culture, does not make sense unless we have established the notion of the group.

At this point, although we might agree that the notion of a community of communities is necessary for an understanding of our own community, it is still not clear why we use the term "transcendent" and what we hope to accomplish by using it.[13] One response would be to say that when we take the multiplicity of communities *as* a community, we label this one big meta-community as "transcendent"; in other words, it is purely a linguistic device. But this does not capture everything we mean when we use the term "transcendent." The transcendent community is one that encompasses all perspectives, interpretations, cultural significances, and so on. It is not just the conglomeration of all actual communities and their individual perspectives; neither is it the conglomeration of all actual and possible communities. Rather, the transcendent community is greater than the sum of its parts. To understand this more fully we now turn to the second half of the argument: the relation of apperception to the transcendent community.

Maintaining our parallel to Husserl's original arguments, we invoke the basic phenomenological process of apperception and suggest that such a process is passively functioning in our understanding of community and culture as well. Recall that I never have "the-side-of-the-house-appearing-to-me-now" as the content of my consciousness when I look at a house, rather I have the *whole* house. It would be foolish to fail to recognize that my perception is perspectival. As I move around the house, I am aware of a multiplicity of perspectives, but never do I escape each individual perspective. No matter how I view the house, it is always from my particular perspective at the time. Nevertheless, the object of my consciousness is the whole house, for the sides that are not appearing to me now are constantly being apperceived. The perspective is perceived but the whole is given.

Similarly, it would seem that we have but one cultural perspective on an object. Surely there are a variety of interpretations within a culture, but there is a certain inescapable communal immersion that accompanies each interpretation. That is, there is a sense in which the house might appear as a "two-story provincial" or a "timber-framed" or even a "nice fixer-upper for a growing family"—differing interpretations, but each somehow dependent on the elements included in one's particular cultural system. For example, an appreciation of the aesthetics of timber-framing, or of the historical significance of a certain style, what structures we are willing to declare to be houses, even the language that we use when discussing a house, each of these is dependent on our own immersion in a certain narrative or cultural system. What we want to suggest now, however, is that other interpretations of the object—interpretations ranging beyond those available in our own culture—are "apperceived" in a passive way so that the given object is never "the-house-as-it-appears-to-me-within-my-cultural-understanding," but rather the transcendent house, that is, the house as a whole—the house in its entirety, as it might be seen and understood from a transcendent, all-encompassing perspective. Clearly, all we ever seem to possess at any given time is our own perspective that is dependent on our community, just as all we seem to possess in terms of perception is one specific visual angle. But, in both cases, the whole is actually given. In this way it can be said that we participate in the transcendent community. If we realize that our communal perspective is but one possible, relative perspective and that it is a member of a group of such perspectives, we can come to take the group *as* the transcendent community. Even if we fail to make this judgment, however, it is still clear that we are participating in the transcendent community—it is phenomenologically inescapable.

Our understanding of our participation, however, can vary. The longer that I walk around the house and the more vantage points that I occupy in order to perceive it, the better my understanding of the house will be. Looking at it first from this angle and then from that angle enriches my understanding of the whole.[14] Although each new angle is still *my* angle, each one adds to the overall experience of the house. Similarly, as I take up other possible cultural perspectives on the house, for example, how an Ethiopian would perceive such a luxurious dwelling, how a sixteenth-century monarch would view my small wooden abode, and so on, I increase my understanding of the transcendent house. Although each new cultural interpretation is still sifted through *my* understanding, it adds to the overall experience of the house, and the *degree* of my participation in the transcendent community is altered. Clearly, I do not have access to the Ethiopian's horizon of experience. My experience will never be "how an Ethiopian views the dwelling," but rather "how I view an Ethiopian viewing the dwelling." Such a realization, however, is not a problem for our project. Suppose I am standing in front of the house and see a person on the roof. I wonder what it is like to see the house from his perspective, so I climb up on the roof and sit where he was sitting. Of course, I do not have the perspective he had, I only have my own perspective from the roof. There is an approximation to his experience, however, and my experience of the whole is therefore richer. The same holds for cultural perspective. I can never completely adopt another perspective, but I can gather as many approximations as possible and realize that the rest is apperceived.

Finally, we want to suggest that such apperception involves the notion of pairing that was developed above. This is to say that other cultural perspectives, and thus a notion of the transcendent community, are necessary for me to have an understanding of my own cultural perspective. Just as the Ego required the notion of the Other, and thus a community, so our culture requires the notion of other cultures, and thus a transcendent community. There is always the mutual transfer of sense occurring: for me to understand fully my own cultural experience of a house it is important for me to understand other experiences of a house and to realize that my experience is but one perspective on the whole, transcendent object.[15] Thus our critique of relativism is even greater; not only do we have a certain access to other perspectives, through an understanding of the transcendent, but such access is fundamentally necessary for the establishment of our *own* perspective.

CONCLUSION

Thus we have constituted the final level of community and brought our social ontology to a close, but to what end? What are the implications of having established this highest level of community, the transcendent community in which we all participate? Perhaps there are necessary ethical and religious implications. Perhaps Husserl's "social individuality of a higher order" can make sense only in such a context. Upon realizing our commitment to participation in a universal community, is there a "normative tug" to act accordingly, that is, to act as a member of such a community and not as an isolated individual? Do we attempt to reify the transcendent perspective suggesting that this is what we mean by God's perspective? Do we feel more comfortable talking about the possibilities of absolutes such as Truth since we have reason to believe that the objects of our consciousness are absolute-wholes in some sense? Such questions are important—perhaps the only valid reason for undertaking a project such as ours—but these implications we leave for another discussion.

NOTES

Epigraph is from *Husserliana* F I 28,189a–b as quoted and translated in James Hart, *The Person and the Common Life* (Dordrecht: Kluwer, 1992), 464n 40.

1. Edmund Husserl, *Cartesian Meditations*, trans. Dorion Cairns (Dordrecht: Martinus Nijhoff, 1960), 89. Hereafter cited as "CM."

2. Hart, *The Person and the Common Life*, 186.

3. Michael Theunissen, *The Other: Studies in the Social Ontology of Husserl, Heidegger, Sartre, and Buber*, trans. Christopher Macann (Cambridge, MA: MIT Press, 1984), 62.

4. Ibid.

5. Ibid., 63.

6. Ibid., 84.

7. Ibid.

8. At this level, however, it must be remembered that the Other's physical body is not yet taken as belonging to the Other, for we have not yet constituted him. We have distinguished a physical body but as of yet cannot assign ownership—indeed, the notion of ownership is basically meaningless at this level.

9. Michael Theunissen, *The Other*, 63.

10. Hart, *The Person and the Common Life*, 179. Failure to understand these notions and the basic nature of pairing has led to many misinterpretations and unwarranted critiques of Husserl's social ontology—most notably among them, Sartre's discussion of the topic in *Being and Nothingness*. Furthermore, a deep understanding of the pairing relation does away with the "bootstrap problem" of which comes first—the Ego or the Other.

11. This notion of human significance will, of course, become a key concept for Heidegger. It might even be argued that Heidegger begins his work accepting this third level of communalization as foundational.

12. By "system" we mean many possible things: culture, community, narrative, language, and so on.

13. Another question also comes to mind, namely, is there not an infinite regress beginning? If we need the notion of our community to understand the Ego, and we need the notion of a "community of communities" to understand our community, do we not need a notion of a "community of a 'community of communities'" in order to understand the "community of communities"? Our only response is that such further levels are not necessary, for although the argument appears to lend itself to the creation of a regress, this is not a logical necessity. The reason we needed a community of communities was not to parallel logically the earlier argument, but rather because the reduction to a sphere of own-communalness did not hold. If we were to attempt a reduction at the level of a community of communities, it would not be the case that there is assumed something larger and more inclusive—but this is a notion that we will touch on below. Since the community of communities is transcendent, there is no greater community.

14. Clearly, a discussion of *hyle* and "filling" would be appropriate here, but we leave this task for another day.

15. Much more could be said about the role of pairing at this level; suffice it to say that the argument runs fairly parallel to the earlier argument concerning the Ego and the Other.

CHAPTER 7

Circulation Unbound
Hegel, Heidegger, and the State

DAVID KOLB

Modernity means freedom, we say, and circulation let loose: commodities, technology, choices, the autonomous individual. In contrast to our free exchange, we imagine old traditional societies as regulated exchange along a network of posts defined by fixed roles. In those societies, identities and roles were experienced as naturally given. They were not experienced as constituted (and questioned) by the circulation among them, nor as exchangeable or substitutable one for another.[1]

The extreme opposite of that picture of traditional society would be a Baudrillardian flow of identities and signifiers none of which have any solidity. Or the Heideggerian *Gestell* where all identities are available for use and consumption, exchange and substitution in a depthless circulation of beings made indifferently available. In such a world our individual freedom can be trivialized by the circulation that we thought guaranteed it.

We picture our modern or postmodern selves as unbound from traditional social roles taken as fixed by nature. Have we then entered a realm of total exchange, a realm in which all is malleable, open for use and substitution? Is the circulation that surrounds us domesticated or monstrous?

In this essay I examine how Hegel and Heidegger envision the role of the state in binding up the unlimited flows of modernity. I begin with an overall summary, then look at several issues in more detail.

For Hegel, the state is the civic totality, encompassing and architectonically allotting space to differentiated subordinate spheres of life. The state

101

provides legitimation and security of function and meaning. It limits and binds together the circulation of goods and mutual recognition. The state is an end (but not a total end).

For Heidegger, the state is a kind of beginning (but not a pure beginning). In his *Introduction to Metaphysics*, the polis provides a place [*topos*] for life; it grounds and preserves all communal activities. The polis works in these and lets them work in its space.[2]

For Hegel, the state is a whole that is a process with a form. We do not judge a state according to how it was founded; we judge according to what form its constitution enacts.

> If we ask what is or has been the historical origin of the state in general, still more if we ask about the origin of any particular state . . . these questions are no concern of the Idea of the state. . . . So far as the authority of any existing state has anything to do with reason, these reasons are culled from the forms of the law authoritative within it. (PR §258)

For Heidegger, the state is an expression of a destiny, an event, and a task to which no constitutional or social form could be adequate. The beginning "stands before us. . . . [I]t awaits us as a distant command bidding us to catch up with its greatness."[3] Heidegger is fascinated by the "violent" act that founds a people or state in responding to that call. In "The Origin of the Work of Art" he speaks of the "state-founding Act" [*staatgründende Tat*] and its possible relation to the "essential sacrifice" [*wesentliche Opfer*] that act can demand.[4]

Even after his adventures in the thirties and forties, even when he plays down such heroic masculine rhetoric, Heidegger still talks of a beginning and a destiny to be retrieved. The Event bestows a meaning that is never captured by any particular institutional form. Although our current social forms are part of our response to the call of our regime of presence and possibility, the call does not legitimate those particular forms.

For both Hegel and Heidegger there is a sense in which the state has the function of binding and arresting a circulation that threatens to get out of hand. This is explicit in Hegel's discussion of the relations of civil society and state. The rational state legitimates limits. Circulation seems unbound in civil society, which gets its form from the interreplaceability of commodity circulation, but even there the universal lurks. It finally expresses itself in the state that binds circulation into the rational process.

We can see in Heidegger's political engagements a hope that a genuine response to the destiny of the folk might break the inauthentic spiral of technological *das Man*. Perhaps the political and social pessimism of his later writings reflects a conclusion that there is no vocation in the political that can limit that circulation. The step back that is thinking does not directly accomplish anything social, and it certainly does not legitimize particular limits or forms of social interaction.

There is a deeper point. In the end, Hegel's system binds exchange and circulation by showing that, despite its seeming universality, the circulations of goods and services and recognition within civil society and the state are only limited operations. They themselves exist within an ontologically fuller motion and circulation (of Spirit) whose "infinitude" includes self-defined limits.

Heidegger cannot accept this implied metaphysics of fullness. But his own notions about the conditions of the possibility of *das Gestell* insert that circulation within a "deeper" process (temporalization and our receptive relation to the Event) that has its own finitude and epochal limits.

Later thinkers revise the relations of these levels. In Baudrillard and others the deeper process is itself redefined as an unlimited circulation, so that the conditions of the possibility of ordinary events now open things up even further to exchange and substitution.

I turn now to examine several of these points in more detail. Although Hegel's analysis of civil society anticipates much of what has been discussed in more recent theories, there are crucial differences. In Hegel's system, Spirit's self-recognition circulates around and comes to itself, but signs and status do not circulate as freely. The "infinite" movement of Spirit puts limits on all other circulations.

Hegel analyzes commodities in terms of their use-value. Mutual need fuels civil society. But while this or that need can be satisfied, needs in general multiply.

> Particularity by itself, given free rein in every direction to satisfy its needs, accidental caprices, and subjective desires, destroys itself and its substantive concept in this process of gratification. At the same time, the satisfaction of need, necessary and accidental alike, is accidental because it breeds new desires without end, is in thoroughgoing dependence on caprice and external accident. (PR §185)

This multiplication of needs goes on ad infinitum (PR §191) with no qualitative limits (PR §195). In this circulation our needs become both more particularized and more abstract, as do our relations with other people: while particular life-styles and occupations are multiplied, I interact with you only in your role as a provider of food (PR §192).

Yet the circulation of particulars is not the whole story. "To particularity [the Idea] gives the right to develop and launch forth in all directions; and to universality the right to prove itself not only the ground and necessary form of particularity, but also the authority standing over it and its final end" (PR §184).

Heidegger describes a similar multiplied circulation of goods and meanings. He offers two basic descriptions of what he sees as modern total circulation: universal planning and universal use. Universal planning involves a

> guarantee of the stability of a constant form of using things up . . . it develops the completely equipped plan and certainty of all plans whatsoever . . . the encompassment of areas, the particular realms of human equipment necessarily become 'sectors' . . . the planning calculation of the guarantee of the whole of beings.[5]

This picture of a differentiated whole arrayed around a controlling center is not yet the full circulation in *Gestell*. Heidegger later thinks our world as a standing reserve for use without a central will or plan from which it can be organized. Everything is available. Everything is used. But there is no longer a center and an overall plan; there is only availability and use without end and without mutuality. This will be "the essence of modern technology—the steadily rotating recurrence of the same."[6]

In Hegel's view, such total leveling and exchange does not occur because the circulation of need and commodities within civil society develops its implicit limits. "The infinitely complex criss-cross movements of reciprocal production and exchange, and the equally infinite multiplicity of means therein employed, become crystallized, owing to the universality inherent in their content, and distinguished into general groups" (PR §201).

Civil society's circulation creates fixed posts within itself. Groups and functions come to occupy these posts whose identity cannot be easily exchanged away. Some of these derive from natural givens, others from the division of labor. The state helps to articulate civil society's movement by ratifying some of these institutions and roles and by creating others.

We can see Hegel creating such fixed posts in his treatment of the agricultural class that is to embody the spirit of the nation. Despite its historical becoming, the national spirit (a people's characteristic values, styles of acting, and sense of identity) is in the experience of its citizens an immediate given. This is especially the case for those citizens living an agricultural life. The life of agricultural people, Hegel says, does "not owe much to reflection," but is centered on planning and future storage, and an immediate sense of ethical substantiality, family, and trust (PR §203). In Hegel's state, agricultural capital and property cannot be sold. It must remain in the family line; in legal terms, it is entailed and cannot be alienated. This removes agricultural capital from market exchange. Similarly, the large agricultural landowners are given political position and power by birth. These maneuvers create a fixed point that is endowed with the national values and that exists outside the circulation of commodities and power.

It is tempting to view Hegel's treatment of the agricultural class as a pragmatic concession to the Prussian Junkers, but I see it as crucial to his theory. Hegel wanted farmers and landowners to embody an immediate unreflective sense of particular loyalty and values in order to anchor the community amid civil society's whirling circulation of goods and status. The state needs a basis in a feeling of particular identity that is not available for exchange. Without this, states lose their particularity and blend into a worldwide, anonymous civil society that reduces human identity to that of mere consumers and producers.

The role Hegel assigns to women provides a similar anchoring because women are to have a special loyalty to family values and rootedness in nature. Hegel's treatment of women has been criticized for (among other things) nostalgically romanticizing an oppressive regime. But, as with the farmers, the women fulfill a necessary function in the theory: they provide the moment of immediacy.

Hegel says that the foundation of states is agriculture and marriage. "Security, consolidation, lasting satisfaction of needs, and so forth—things which are the most obvious recommendations of marriage and agriculture—are nothing but forms of universality, modes in which rationality, the final end and aim, asserts itself in these spheres" (PR §203z). Universality asserts itself; for Hegel these fixed posts are not artificially introduced into the circulation, for they ultimately stem from Spirit's coming to itself through the dialectic of particular, universal, and individual identity. Of course, it is just these things, "security, consolidation, lasting satisfaction of needs," that thinkers from Heidegger to Baudrillard would say are impossible in that total circulation where there is no immediacy, where no form is stabilized, and where there is no ontological guarantee of self-return.

There are still other anchors that Hegel sees developing within civil society. The division of labor becomes institutionalized into the corporations (which are more like trade associations than what we think of as single corporations).[7] "One joins a corporation because of one's talent, birth, but especially one's individual particular will and desire, which receive their right, merit, dignity by this choice" (PR §206). Without being a member of a corporation a man lacks rank and dignity; without a corporation he

> has to try to gain recognition for himself by giving external proofs of his success in his business, and to these proofs no limit can be set. He cannot live in the manner of his class, for no class exists for him, since in civil society it is only something common to particular persons which really exists. Hence he cannot achieve for himself a way of life proper to his standing and less idiosyncratic. (PR §253z)[8]

The corporation provides a second family (PR §250f.), yet the corporation member "belongs to a whole which is also an organ of the entire society" (PR §253). The state realizes its own form in part by taking up these groupings from civil society: "only by being authorized does an association become a corporation" (PR §253z).

Hegel's corporation members are craft workers distinguished by their specialized skills. Hegel does discuss what he calls the rabble [*Pöbel*], which can be thought of as the beginnings of an urban proletariat. Hegel does not see these people as de-skilled workers, however, but rather as welfare dependents. The rabble is not a Marxist proletariat that circulates as raw labor. Their problem is that they do not circulate at all; they are outside the system and feed on its surplus.

"The sanctity of marriage and the dignity of corporation membership are the two fixed points around which the unorganized atoms of civil society revolve" (PR §255z). "As family was the first, so the corporation is the second ethical root of the state, one planted in civil society" (PR §255). Family and corporation provide ethical substance: ways of living and being that are not exchangeable. Social identities are to be chosen freely but do not circulate freely; the chosen becomes substantial. Yet our freedom is to be preserved. Substance becomes subject; the social can only exist through mutual recognition. It is the dependence of identity on mutual recognition (and the need for that process of recognition to possess particular content and a recognized external vehicle) that puts limits on circulation. We are not free-floating individuals facing some resistant structure imposed upon us. Modern society, for Hegel, involves mutual recognition of the rational structures that limit circulation in order to create social space for the exercise of civic and political freedom.

"[Plato] could only cope with the principle of self-subsistent particularity, which in his day had forced its way into Greek ethical life, by setting up in opposition to it his purely substantial state" (PR §185z). In the modern state the individual is educated into free choice of those rational roles that make up the state. Legitimated differentiations within the circulation provide "the process whereby [citizens'] particularity is educated up to subjectivity" (PR §187). When this happens, that freedom is achieved that is "having to do only with what it has itself produced and stamped with its seal" (PR §186z). The result is both a mutually free community and the legitimated circulation of power, status, and goods within a functionally differentiated whole. We are familiar with the problematic degree to which Hegel's state—or any state—can realize this goal.

We should not stop at the particular institutional arrangements that Hegel is promoting, however, for these stem from a deeper claim. The circulations of civil society and state lie within a larger motion that educates and tames them. Recall that for Hegel the state originates in a violent act and expresses a national spirit, but in the end it will be judged according to the form enacted in its constitution. States begin in violence and then achieve form. It is not the form-giving, but the form itself that is judged.

So it must be that Hegel has criteria for judging forms. But how? He cannot rely on a functional judgment because the larger functional ensemble is itself a form to be judged. Yet he needs teleology: the self-presence of Spirit to itself.

What is at stake is the being of form. A form is judged against the conditions of possibility of its being. Since being is to be thought as self-expression and self-return, the form will be judged against its possible enactment of that self-return and against its ability to express the process that gives it being. Is the form capable of holding the truth, of being a form of full community, of containing/expressing the life of Spirit?

As with Plato, Hegel's criteria for judging a form come from his notion of what constitutes full being. It is on this basis that Hegel can argue that some constitutional arrangements are better than others and that there may be a final rational state.

Although Heidegger has nothing similar to Hegel's recommendation of particular institutions, there is a parallel in Heidegger to the deeper Hegelian claim. Heidegger talks of stepping back to the context through which forms have their being. There is, however, no legitimation discourse in Heidegger.[9] In that sense, there is no foundation for judging political forms. Nor can modern exchange and circulation be confined by any social form. Yet it remains true that for Heidegger any ontic system of exchange is opened up by our relation to being and the Event, and we can ask to what extent communal arrangements help or hinder our recognition of our deep condition.

Our condition, however, is not to be moments in a grand Hegelian ontological circulation. Nor is the event of our relation to being infinite or self-returning. Paradoxically, if in the modern world the circulation of beings seems infinite and ontically unlimited, that is because of our ontological finitude. On the one hand, our entrapment in the infinite technological circulation of beings is our particular finite destiny, which involves a particular temporal structure (the collapse of the dimensions of time into bland availability). On the other hand, our fascination with infinite circulation stems in part from our forgetfulness and avoidance of our deeper ontological finitude.[10]

The most difficult thing in Heidegger is to keep the priority (the "nearness") of that ontological condition (so that we can find our authentic relation to being) while not letting the call or destiny in that condition become either purely formal or too particular. If the destiny becomes too formal, the finitude of temporalization is smoothed out into some kind of general ontological circulation. I think Heidegger would rightly complain that thinkers such as Baudrillard deny our finitude and undermine the relation of time and being. But if our destiny is not purely formal, it risks becoming a particular call of the sort that Heidegger thought he could discern in the 1930s. If you do not have Hegel's legitimating ontological process to provide a critical norm, can you safely talk about calls and destinies that are linked to our fundamental relation to being?

In this context, we might wonder whether it is really fair to say—as Heidegger would—that Hegel's foundational discourse offers only the ontic relation of a big being to other beings. Going beyond particular institutional proposals, we can make these comparisons between the "deeper" events of form in Heidegger and Hegel:

1. In Heidegger, the step back to the origin behind any ontic origins or definite forms takes us to the event of presencing in its finitude and withdrawal. In Hegel, the step back behind any empirical relation of entities to one another takes us to the event of the presencing of the belonging together of the logical categories.

2. In Heidegger, the event of presencing founds nothing; it offers no form. Any foundational relation or structure is

ontic. In Hegel, the event of presencing has its own form that is expressed in certain definite self-conscious structures.

3. In Heidegger, the event of presencing has its own dimensions. These give us some general "formal" restrictions on what can count as an economy of presence or a world. In Hegel, the logical categories and their mutual event define the structures of what must count as a fully self-present world.

4. In Heidegger, the step back provides no foundation and no detailed criticism, but it does question any claims to legitimacy that might be made by a particular form of society or state. In Hegel, the step back is both foundational and critical. It affirms a structure for the full being of community, justifying some institutions and criticizing others.

Note that this critical judgment is accomplished in Hegel by an act of letting be. We let the form develop and exhibit its limitations and its ties to its own context and to the fuller forms that ultimately make it possible. In Heidegger, too, there is a letting be. What is let be is, among other things, the process in which form has its being: but now that process is being's withdrawal in the Event. The process looks to the origin that withdraws, rather than to the goal that approaches. This can be read either as an affirmation of the finitude of the state or as the call that encourages us to obey.

In the event of form, for Hegel, historical becoming and earlier versions of the state are lifted up into the current form. In the end, history is wrapped up into a total present. For Heidegger, however, the appeal to origins is an appeal to a history that cannot be capsulized, an origin of possibility that does not reduce to a present field of alternatives however rich. The distension of time opposes the dialectic of time.

The past is not for Hegel an origin to be interrogated for fresh possibilities or deeper meaning. The beginning of thought and of the state do not remain rich with undeveloped possibilities. The founding act and the primitive or early forms of community make no calls to us now. History is differentiation, not retrieval. Legitimated differentiation blocks total circulation.

Heidegger distrusts differentiation; he prefers interpenetration, each in every, as in his Fourfold. Hegel mistrusts that kind of undifferentiated, unsystematic interpenetration; he thinks that it is a romantic escape. Hegel wants disruption followed by a coming together in rational mediation that maintains tensions within a totality. But in Heidegger's *Gestell* there is no way for it all to come together in a differentiated totality. It cannot come together that way because it has no form. *Gestell* has movement, it opens a way beings are present, but it has no overall form or system. It is not the result or cause of differentiation.

In Hegel and his successors, the immensely complex criss-cross movements of exchange and circulation can be contained because the system of exchange stands as a particular kind of interaction that has in-built movements toward universality and rationality. Ultimately this is because the current social differentiation is enclosed in a still larger movement of history and spirit.

So Heidegger's *Gestell* poses a challenge for differentiation theories influenced by Hegel (for instance, Jameson and Habermas) facing the postmodern world. For *Gestell* is not a totality. It is not differentiated, and it has no form. No social arrangements can be anything more than items of use within *Gestell*; they cannot mediate an overall movement the way political institutions do for Hegel. Yet we cannot lose sight of the fact that Heidegger does agree with Hegel that there is a deeper level of our relation to being than is obvious in the endless exchanges in modern society.

Those such as Baudrillard who go beyond Heidegger by rejecting his lingering metaphors of surface and depth make our ontological condition an unlimited circulation. In so doing they offer a perverse romantic organicism in which each and every thing is touching each and every thing. From a Heideggerian point of view, this is ontologically inadequate because it loses the finitude of our temporalization. From a Hegelian point of view, it is ontically misleading because it mis-describes the role that particularity and mediated immediacy play in individual and social life.

Although everyone we have been discussing would agree that there is no simple givenness or immediacy to our social roles and arrangements, I suspect that it is the Hegelian tradition that has the resources for talking about the strange situation of particular roles and values in our world today. Even though these ways of talking about mediated immediacy are obscure and can be used clumsily, as Hegel used them in the cases of farmers and women, Hegelian thought refuses to make us totally creatures of exchange and distance and irony. Heidegger avoids this too, but he can only speak in a global way about the destiny of the times. His more extreme followers can only turn everything into an ironic play at being itself.

Although I have not said anything about Derrida in this essay, I think that on the issues I am discussing he belongs more in the Hegelian camp. To put the matter briefly, Derrida never claims that the unlimited economy of signs can be instituted in actual social or economic relationships, while Baudrillard seems to say that commodity society has already done so.

Such volatility loses an important dimension in our situation. Many mininations and groups within nations are currently creating themselves. In their struggles to give form to themselves they are claiming some immediate basis in national feeling or group identity. The Hegelian tradition can speak of differentiation and insertion into larger processes (which themselves do not have an immediately given form), and this allows more ways to be self-critical when making or meeting such claims to group identity. The rhetoric of *Gestell* (and its successors) provides important warnings to these groups, but does it have much to say in detail? After he abandoned his talk about the destiny of this or that people, Heidegger felt he had nothing to say about concrete situations. Baudrillardian declarations that all these new/old identities are items within the flow of simulacra put the critic in the position of the Enlightenment intellectual who understands what is really going on and can criticize the natives for clinging to outmoded superstitions about the fixity of identity. This does not encourage dialogue about the particularities of concrete situations. A properly chastened Hegel and his successors have at least the possibility of meeting today's renewed concern for identity and givenness with a combination of immediacy and mediation that may hold both criticism and complicity.[11]

NOTES

1. I have argued elsewhere that this story about traditional society should be questioned and that it functions largely as a myth of origin for modern self-consciousness. See *Postmodern Sophistications: Philosophy, Architecture, and Tradition* (Chicago: University of Chicago Press, 1990), chapter 7.

2. Martin Heidegger, *An Introduction to Metaphysics* (Garden City, N.Y.: Doubleday, 1959), 12. References to the works of Hegel and Heidegger will be given in footnotes with the exception of references to Hegel's *Philosophy of Right* (PR), which will be given in the text by paragraph number from the Knox translation (Oxford: Oxford University Press, 1967). When references are given to both German and English editions of a work, they are separated by a slash with the German edition first. Several

Heideggerian terms are used frequently; *Sein* is translated as "being," *Ereignis* as "Event," and *Gestell* is left untranslated.

3. Heidegger, "The Self-Assertion of the German University," cited in Michael Zimmerman, *Heidegger's Confrontation with Modernity: Technology, Politics, Art* (Bloomington: University of Indiana Press, 1990), 67.

4. "The Origin of the Work of Art," *Holzwege* (Frankfurt am Main: Klostermann, 1963), 50 / *Poetry, Language, Thought* (New York: Harper & Row, 1971), 61.

5. "Overcoming Metaphysics," *Vorträge und Aufsätze I* (Pfullingen: Neske, 1967), 83ff. / *The End of Philosophy* (New York: Harper & Row, 1973), 103ff., §XXVI.

6. *Was Heisst Denken?* (Tübingen: Niemeyer, 1971), 47 / *What is Called Thinking?* (New York: Harper & Row, 1968), 109.

7. The state allows free choice of occupation, but the corporation arrangement militates against easy change. The model resembles the common European pattern of choosing or being measured for a status early in your life.

8. The corporation also educates members to a universal point of view. Hegel says: "the corporation [is the place] in which the particular citizen . . . emerges from his single private interest, and has a conscious activity for a comparatively universal end, just as in his legal and professional duties he has his social morality" (Encyclopedia [1830 edition] §534).

9. See Reiner Schürmann, *Heidegger on Being and Acting: From Principles to Anarchy* (Bloomington: University of Indiana Press, 1987), 89–91.

10. "Once, however, in the beginning of Western thinking, the essence of language flashed in the light of being—once, when Heraclitus thought the logos as his guiding word, so as to think in this word the being of beings. But the lightning abruptly vanished. No one held onto its streak of light and the nearness of what it illuminated. We see this lightning only when we station ourselves in the storm of being. Yet everything today betrays the fact that we bestir ourselves only to drive storms away. We organize all available means for cloud seeding and storm dispersal in order to have calm in the face of the storm. But this calm is no tranquility. It is only anesthesia; more precisely, the narcotization of anxiety in the face of thinking" ("Logos," *Vorträge und Aufsätze III* [Pfullingen: Neske, 1967], 25 / *Early Greek Thinking* [New York: Harper & Row, 1975], 78). Is total circulation another way to calm the storm? The call of the origin must not be reduced to something ontic related to something else ontic in an economy of presence.

11. "Without totality our politics become emaciated, our politics become dispersed, our politics become nothing but existential rebellion. Some heuristic (rather than ontological) notion of totality is in fact necessary if we are to talk about mediations, interrelations, interdependencies, about totalizing forces in the world" (Cornell West, "Interview with Cornell West," in *Universal Abandon: The Politics of Postmodernism* [Minneapolis: University of Minnesota Press, 1988], 270).

CHAPTER 8

Some Particular Limitations of Postconventional Universality

Hegel and Habermas

SHAUN GALLAGHER

In the mid-1960s, Jürgen Habermas outlined three interpretations of Hegel's political philosophy in terms of the relation between universality and particularity. First, conservative interpretations of Hegel make the abstract concept of universal right conform to the particular character of nationalist spirit [*Volksgeist*]. Second, liberal interpretations find in Hegel the primacy of universal right over particularistic national identity. Finally, left Hegelians (Habermas here cites Herbert Marcuse) object to what makes the conservative interpretation possible and the liberal interpretation unsure, namely, the threat (both in Hegel's texts and in reality) to universal principles posed by the "substantive morality" associated with nationalistic particularities.[1] Habermas himself adopts this third, critical view and blames Hegel's own particularism ("Hegel too was not able to transcend his time and his circumstances" [TP 194]) for his overemphasis of the particularities of national spirit.

In his more recent writings, and specifically in his attempt to explicate a concept of postconventional universality, Habermas continues his critique of Hegel. For example, in the texts of his recent debate with neoconservative German historians—a debate known as the *Historikerstreit* [historians' dispute]—Habermas works out the possibility of postconventional (postnational) identity in explicit contrast to Hegel's concept of national identity and its dependency on a self-conscious appreciation of national history.[2] In the context of this critique of Hegel, I will suggest some important limitations of postconventional universality without, however, returning to a conservative, liberal, or left-Hegelian position.

HEGEL'S PARTICULARISM

National self-consciousness, according to Hegel, is the internal reflection of the existing external institutions that constitute the nation in its particularity. "The self-consciousness of a particular nation is a vehicle for the contemporary development of the collective spirit in its actual existence: it is the objective actuality in which that spirit for the time invests its will."[3] As such, self-conscious political sentiment, necessary for the development of the nation-state, is conservative and lacks any hint of utopian tenor. Hegel summarizes nationalistic sentiment in one word: *trust.* It is an "assured conviction" and "a volition which has become habitual" (PR §268). "This sentiment is, in general, trust . . . the consciousness that my interest, both substantive and particular, is contained and preserved in another's (i.e., in the state's) interest and end" (PR §268).

For Hegel, however, national self-consciousness moves beyond the particularistic aspects of the individual nation. The nation itself embodies a universality that is expressed in the political constitution and reflected in the sense of national identity experienced by the citizen.[4] Still, it is important to note, this universality is not independent of the particularistic nature of national identity. The general principle for Hegel is that "the universal does not prevail or achieve completion except along with particular interests and through the co-operation of particular [modes of] knowing and willing" (PR §260). This principle is clearly exemplified throughout his analysis of the political individual, civil society, and the state. The individual, for example, conforms to universal law only while following his particular interests. In a similar fashion, the administration of universal rights within civil society continues to be limited by particularistic requirements and wills (see PR §§230, 231). Even in the most universal expression of the state, that is, in war, state rights "are actualized only in their particular wills and not in a universal will with constitutional powers over them" (PR §333). Thus, the force of international law, which is universal law, is limited by the reality of particular histories and conditions of nations. On this basis Hegel rejects Kant's notion that a perpetual peace may be attainable through a league of nations (PR §333).

Hegel concludes that the constitution of any particular nation, as the expression of universal principles, "depends in general on the character and development of [that nation's] self-consciousness" (PR §274). He offers the following clarification: "The proposal to give a constitution—even one more or less rational in content—to a nation *a priori* would be a happy thought overlooking precisely that factor in a constitution which makes it more than an *ens rationis*. Hence every nation has the constitution appropriate to it and suitable for it" (PR §274, Remark). The constitution is a historical entity. It is "the consciousness of rationality so far as that consciousness is developed [historically] in a particular nation" (PR, Addition to §274; also see PH 46). The elements of universality contained in national self-consciousness will always be limited by the particularistic aspects of the nation's history and identity. "A constitution," Hegel writes, "only develops from the national spirit identically with that spirit's own development, and runs through at the same time with it the grades of formation and the alterations required by its concept. It is the indwelling spirit and the history of the nation . . . by which constitutions have been and are made" (PM §540). Historically determined national consciousness, which rules over the formation of the constitution, limits the universality possible in any national identity.[5]

Hegel outlines two implications that follow from this concept of national-ist spirit. First, political critique, made possible in the freedom granted to public communication in the freedom of the press, is not really effective. In the face of the rationality of the constitution and the constancy of national sentiment, critique is rendered "innocuous" (PR §319). Critique, defined in opposition to trust, is made harmless by the maturity of the nationalist spirit in its constitutional expression.

Second, the nation-state has a claim over its citizens, even to the point of requiring their self-sacrifice in war (PR §§268, 324). For Habermas, this is the "core content of [Hegel's type of] nationalism," and it stamps national-ism's mentality.[6] This primacy of the state can be expressed dialectically in the unity of right and duty. For Hegel, duty subsists in a relation to the uni-versal. It is dialectically equivalent to right which is a particular expression of individual freedom. In the state, the individual's freedom is "put in corre-spondence with the universal" insofar as it conforms to national interests (PR §261). Hegel makes the state "the basis and centre of all the concrete elements in the life of a people: of Art, of Law, of Morals, of Religion, and of Science" (PH 49; see PR §261). This means that the universality of the state always turns out to be embodied in a particular nation-state. In this respect it is not difficult to understand why duties to self-sacrifice and "extraordinary exertions" (PR §268) suggest to some interpreters that Hegel's sense of nation lends itself not only to constitutional monarchy, as Hegel himself believed, but also to totalitarianism and fascism.[7]

Hegel's concept of nationalist self-consciousness can be summarized in four propositions.

1. Nationalist sentiment involves a trust in the existing constitution and in the institutions that constitute the nation.
2. Nationalist self-consciousness disarms critique.
3. Nationalism requires that the state have a primacy over the individual citizen.
4. The particularity of any nation's self-identity limits the universality embodied in its constitution.

HABERMAS'S POSTCONVENTIONAL UNIVERSALITY

Habermas proposes a theory of critical, postconventional, constitutional patriotism that contrasts point for point with Hegel's idea of national sentiment. In opposition to neoconservatives who would revise and neutralize history to promote the formation and normalization of a contemporary national identity, Habermas argues for a less trusting, indeed, a *suspicious*, self-reflection as the basis for citizenship (see NC 234–36). In order to promote social integration and a "conventional" national identity, neoconservative historiography fosters a trust in "a past that no longer causes concern" (NC 193) and a comfortable complacency with acceptable and positive "pasts that 'one can approve of'" (NC 210). In such interpretations, according to Habermas, "nationalism is as virulent as ever" (NC 193). In contrast, Habermas's enlightened patriotism calls for a suspicious self-reflection that takes the form of a historical self-consciousness ready to question the past in order to come to terms with it and to accept responsibility for it.

Habermas's concept of critique has always been understood in contrast to the absence of critique in the later Hegel. In his essays on theory and practice, Habermas laments Hegel's abandonment of the critical dimension of political theory and philosophy. In Hegel's early political-journalistic writings, critique plays the role of a "preventive reflection" that unmasks "merely pretended universality" and reveals "the decadence of the particular by confronting it with the mirror of the universal interests to which it still presumes" (TP 181–82). When the mature Hegel discovers the objective power of *Geist*, he gives up the notion of critique and concludes that philosophy cannot instruct the state on "what it ought to be; it can only show how the state, the ethical universe, is to be understood" (PR §11; see TP 178–79). Theory does not direct itself critically against the state, but simply describes what the state is. Habermas prefers the young Hegel who would grant philosophy a critical role, "almost in the sense of the Young Hegelians' . . . claim for critique as preparation for a revolutionary praxis" (TP 180).

Like Hegel's early journalism or Habermas's own participation in the *Historikerstreit*, critique, in the spirit of the Enlightenment, can be embodied in a "historical-critical discussion" or publicly conducted debate. Historiography can play a role in the accomplishment of critique only to the extent that the historian seeks a critical, detached ("third person"), enlightened objectivity rather than an ideologically biased or selective perception of the past (see NC 202, 217, 225, 226–27, 237). The proper role of the *Geisteswissenschaften* is to offer resistance to any easy (noncritical, conventional) social integration (see NC 254–55).

A conventional national identity corresponds to Hegel's trusting nationalist self-consciousness. Only a critical reflective practice can lead us toward a "postconventional" identity based on a "constitutional patriotism."[8] A postconventional identity is characterized by an attempt to embrace values, not because they are held as authoritative by some particular person, group, or nation, but because they are based on a universality and consistency—qualities to be found in a critical constitutional patriotism. Constitutional patriotism is directed to universal constitutional principles rather than to particularistic national qualities of citizenship. In this sense, the concept of a critical self-reflection is consistent with the Enlightenment concept of "world citizenship." Enlightenment determinations of legality, morality, and sovereignty "are best suited to the identity of world citizens, not to that of citizens of a particular state that has to maintain itself against other states" (CES 114). Habermas, in contrast to Hegel, seeks something akin to a Kantian internationalism. Again, in complete contrast to Hegel's proposition, constitutional patriotism demands that the universality embodied in a nation's constitution rule over and define the limits of the particularity of any nation's self-identity. For Habermas, "the imperatives of the self-assertion of national forms of life through power politics no longer simply dominate the mode of action of the constitutional state but find their limits in postulates of the universalization of democracy and human rights" (NC 256).

The move from conventional (national) identity to postconventional (postnational) identity entails a move from a pretended universality embodied in conservative "sociocentric" regimes and limited by a particular national consciousness to universalistic principles consistent with internationalism and gained through democratic constitutionalism based upon unforced, enlightened consensus. In this move, "identifications with one's own [national] forms of life and traditions are overtaken by a patriotism that has become more abstract, that now relates not to the concrete totality of a nation but rather to abstract procedures and principles."[9]

In contrast to nationalism's insistence on "the primacy of the *higher-level subjectivity of the state* over the subjective freedom of the individual" (PDM 40), Habermas insists that there are transnational, universal duties that rule over duties required by a particular state. Hegel's requirement of self-sacrifice in war, Habermas maintains, "has not withstood the development of weapons technology. Today anyone who actually uses the weapons with which he threatens another country knows that he is destroying his own country at the same moment" (NC 257–58). Constitutional patriotism always requires the citizen to question the particular decisions of his or her own nation from the viewpoint of universal principles.

THE LIMITATIONS OF POSTCONVENTIONAL UNIVERSALITY

I am inclined to follow Habermas's critique of Hegel's nationalism on three of the four points that I have outlined. These three points can be formulated as prescriptives for a postconventional patriotism.

1. The citizen ought to be more suspicious than trusting.
2. The citizen ought to employ a critical reflection in opposition to a noncritical, normalizing self-consciousness.
3. The citizen ought to be guided more by transnational, universal principles than by duties to a particular state.

Yet, these three prescriptives are complicated by a difficulty found in Habermas's fourth proposition. In the form of a prescriptive statement, this fourth proposition would read "The particular (that is, the nation) ought always to be limited by the universal (that is, the abstract procedures and principles of democratic constitutionalism)." This prescriptive clearly depends upon a principle that states that precisely this type of limitation is always possible and that the opposite type of limitation (of the universal by the particular) can be avoided. In contrast to Hegel's general principle, that is, that the universal is not actualized except along with and through the particular, Habermas allows for the possibility of a disconnection of the univer-

sal from the particular. Thus, particular national interests no longer dominate the universal aspects of the constitutional state, but "find their limits in
postulates of the universalization of democracy and human rights" (NC
256). What I find problematic concerns not the idea or even the desirability
of this limitation, but the possibility or impossibility of accomplishing it.
Moreover, if Hegel is right, if it is impossible to escape the limitations
placed on the universal by particularity, then a different type of limitation is
placed on the first three prescriptives and on the possibility of postconventional identity itself.

The difference between Hegel and Habermas on this issue concerns the
question of where one places oneself in relation to the particular. Hegel
stands within the particular traditions and institutions of a nation; from there
he attempts to see the universal aspects implicit within that nation.
Habermas attempts to stand outside of particular traditions and institutions
in order to develop a critique of the nation from the standpoint of a transnational universality. In both cases, a self-conscious reflection on one's particular history is required. For Hegel, this self-reflection is embedded within
the particularity of a nation's traditions and is thus limited. For Habermas,
self-reflection is a "gaze" that critically appropriates its history, picks and
chooses the traditions by which it wants to be educated, and, even while
accepting responsibility for them, responsibly rejects those traditions that
do not measure up to universal standards. Within the particular context of
the *Historikerstreit* Habermas writes: "After Auschwitz our national self-
consciousness can be derived only from the better traditions in our history, a
history that is not unexamined but instead appropriated critically . . . in the
light of the traditions that stand up to the scrutiny of a gaze educated by the
moral catastrophe, a gaze that is, in a word, suspicious" (NC 234).

The fundamental and critical question is: "To what extent can one
detach oneself from the particular circumstances of life?" Or, in other
words, "To what degree is it possible to attain the universal?" The critical
gaze is, as Habermas acknowledges, educated by its history. And he does
recognize the force of the particular in the realm of individual identity formation. On the level of an individual life, identity does not depend solely
on moral choice, a choice that requires orientation within a universalistic
framework.[10] There is another, more particular dimension involved in
deciding "who one wants to be."

> There is an indissoluble element of arbitrariness [*Willkur*] in the
> choice of a life project. This is to be explained by the fact that the indi-

vidual cannot adopt a hypothetical attitude toward his own origins and background, that he cannot accept or reject his biography in the same way as he can a norm whose claim to validity is under discussion. (TCA II 109)

Thus, the individual is embedded within *Sittlichkeit*, within a set of cultural values, within a particularistic collective identity, within a historical tradition. Nonetheless, on the level of the individual actor Habermas posits the ability to disconnect or to "detach" oneself from the particular in order to instigate a decision within a universalistic framework. Even if the individual is "the *product* of the tradition in which he stands, of the solidary groups to which he belongs, of socialization and learning processes to which he is exposed," he can also, at the same time, be the "*instigator* of his accountable actions" (TCA II 135). This disconnection is possible as the transition from the stage of conventional identity to postconventional identity.[11] On Hegel's view, in contrast, embeddedness within *Sittlichkeit* means that there is never the possibility of moral disconnection. Freedom, for Hegel, is conformity to the universal as it is embedded within and limited by the arbitrariness and contingency of particularity.

The problem can also be viewed in terms of the Habermas-Gadamer debate. Gadamer's position is similar to Hegel's in this respect: particularistic traditions will always limit universal aspirations, rather than the other way around. The hermeneutical situation is always constrained by the particular traditions that define the life of the interpreter. The historian's use or abuse of history, the individual citizen's appeal to transnational, universal rights and duties, and even critical reflection itself are all instances of interpretational practice. As such, they are always biased by the interpreter's own prejudgments. A constitution is the product of a particular hermeneutical and national situation. Its interpretation is always limited by the particular historical circumstances of the citizen-interpreter. Its universal aspects always take on the tenor of those situations. As Gadamer puts it, "[l]ong before we understand ourselves through the process of self-examination, we understand ourselves in a self-evident way in the family, society, and state in which we live."[12] While attempting to define the universal, the interpreter is already bound up within a particular system of national values, prejudices, and traditions. To the extent that Habermas's postconventional identity depends upon a detached, abstract, universal standpoint (see NC 225, 257, 261), it can be no more than a regulative idea that, by definition, can never be achieved. One can only approach the universal from within the particular, but without ever escaping the particular.

I propose that Habermas's fourth prescriptive for postconventional citizenship be replaced by the practical orientation of *phronesis* (*prudentia,* practical wisdom). On Habermas's reading, Hegel had abandoned *phronesis* even before he abandoned critique (see TP 126–29). Habermas himself, although concerned about retrieving a young-Hegelian concept of critique, remains content to leave the concept of *phronesis* behind. Yet *phronesis* is precisely a concept that clarifies the relation between the universal and the particular. On the model of *phronesis* we do not start with universal, context-independent rules and then apply them in a technical fashion to particular cases. Rather, we begin to discern the universal only from within the particular circumstances in which we find ourselves.[13] A *phronesis* that is both suspicious and critical would be the proper model from which to derive the prescriptives of constitutional patriotism.

The model of *phronesis* would imply that there are no universal prescriptives that can be legitimately formulated in advance of particular situations that call for judgment. Still, in response to the four prescriptives suggested by Habermas, one could tentatively formulate the following qualifications.

1. Although, in certain cases, the particular ought to be limited in some way by the universal, we ought to realize that the universal is always limited by the particular understanding that we have of it. This makes the procedures and practices of democratic constitutionalism less universal than the ideal.

2. Precisely for this reason the citizen ought to be more suspicious than trusting. But even suspicion is an imperfect matter, a matter of degree, limited by the particularities of language, education, and so forth.

3. The citizen ought to employ critical reflection, but at the same time realize that critical reflection is never perfectly emancipated from particularity. Therefore it never guarantees that we attain the universal in a complete or perfect manner.

4. The citizen ought to be guided more by transnational, universal duties than by duties to a particular state. But the citizen also ought to realize that transnational, universal duties are always interpreted within particular hermeneutical situations.

These qualifications make individual judgments and the practices of constitutional democracy more ambiguous and unsure. As such, they question the very possibility of a completely postnational politics and suggest that in the realm of politics the notion of postconventionality ought to be rethought. Perhaps a less idealistic conception of postconventional identity needs to be worked out in terms of a critical reflection informed by *phronesis*, that is, a reflection that always moves in the direction of the universal, but also remains aware that it always falls short of attaining it.

In one important respect Hegel is right: a constitution is more than an *ens rationis*; it is impossible to get to its universal aspects a priori. A constitutional patriotism can only be one in which we move toward the universal law without ever escaping the particular circumstances of language, tradition, nation, and history within which we find ourselves. To put it in terms of Habermas's position in the *Historikerstreit*, our involvement in such particular limitations accounts for the liabilities that we must critically appropriate in a responsible manner.

NOTES

1. Jürgen Habermas, *Theory and Practice*, trans. John Viertel (Boston: Beacon, 1973), 134–36; hereafter cited as TP.

2. The historians involved in this debate with Habermas include Michael Sturmer, Andreas Hillgruber, and Ernst Nolte. For a discussion that focuses on the concept of nationalism in this debate, see Shaun Gallagher, "The *Historikerstreit* and the Critique of Nationalism," *History of European Ideas* 16 (1993): 921–26.

3. Hegel, *The Philosophy of Mind* (Encyclopaedia, part three), trans. William Wallace (Oxford: Clarendon Press, 1971), §550; hereafter cited as PM. Also see Hegel, *The Philosophy of Right*, trans. T. M. Knox (Oxford: Oxford University Press, 1967), §265; hereafter cited as PR. And *The Philosophy of History*, trans. J. Sibree (New York: Dover, 1956), 43–46; hereafter cited as PH.

4. See PR §269; Hegel thus proposes that the integration of the modern state depends not on language or culture, but on "the spirit and unity of a common political consciousness" (*Schriften zur Politik und Rechtsphilosophie*, ed. G. Lasson [Leipzig, 1913], 24–25; cited and translated by Shlomo Avineri, "Hegel and Nationalism," *The Review of Politics* 24 [1962]: 466).

5. This position is taken to the extreme in the German Historical School of Jurisprudence (Savigny and Puchta). See Avineri's summary ("Hegel and Nationalism," 474ff.). Avineri is not wrong to say that Hegel conceives of

law as rational and universal and thus "the positive content of the law cannot be *derived* from any national characteristics" (477, emphasis added). But Hegel's position might be stated more precisely as follows: law in itself is universal, but in any real instance, for any particular law, it is *limited* by particularistic national characteristics.

6. Habermas, *The New Conservatism: Cultural Criticism and the Historian's Debate*, trans. Shierry Weber Nicholsen (Cambridge, Mass.: MIT Press, 1989), 257; hereafter cited as NC.

7. See, e.g., Karl Popper, *The Open Society and its Enemies* (Princeton: Princeton University Press, 1950), ch. 12; E. F. Carritt, "Hegel and Prussianism," *Philosophy* 15 (1940): 51–56; and A. Hacker, *Political Theory: Philosophy, Ideology, Science* (New York: Macmillan, 1961), 438–45. Hegel's own thought can easily be defended against any claim that it is fascist. Along this line, Habermas cites the work of Marcuse and Ritter (TP 193). See also Avineri, "Hegel and Nationalism," 461–84; Georg Lukács, "Der deutsche Faschismus und Hegel," in *Schicksalswende: Beitrage zu einer neuen deutschen Ideologie* (Berlin: Aufbau-Verlag, 1948), 37–67; C. J. Friedrich, *The Philosophy of Hegel* (New York: Random House, 1953), introduction; C. J. Friedrich, "The Power of Negation: Hegel's Dialectic and Totalitarian Ideology," in *A Hegel Symposium*, ed. D. C. Travis (Austin: University of Texas Press, 1962); Eric Weil, *Hegel et l'etat* (Paris: J. Vrin, 1950).

8. Habermas borrows the phrase "constitutional patriotism" from Dolf Sternberger (see NC 193, 227, 256). He borrows the distinction between conventional and postconventional identities from developmental psychology (Piaget and Kohlberg). See Habermas, *Communication and the Evolution of Society*, trans. Thomas McCarthy (Boston: Beacon Press, 1979), 79ff., 95–129; hereafter cited as CES.

9. NC 261; translation revised. Also see Habermas, *The Philosophical Discourse of Modernity*, trans. Frederick G. Lawrence (Cambridge, Mass.: MIT Press, 1987), 40; hereafter cited as PDM. Here Habermas proposes, in explicit contrast to Hegel, the model of uncoerced communicative reason.

10. Habermas, *The Theory of Communicative Action*, vol. 2, trans. Thomas McCarthy (Boston: Beacon, 1987), 97. Hereafter cited as TCA II.

11. At the postconventional stage, "only *universal* norms let themselves be distinguished as moral. . . . The ego can no longer identify with itself through particular roles and existing norms. It has to take into account that the traditional accustomed forms of life prove themselves as merely particu-

lar, as irrational; therefore it must retract its identity, so to speak, behind the line of all *particular* roles and norms." (Habermas, *Die Entwicklung des Ich*, cited and translated in Jerald Wallulis, *The Hermeneutics of Life History: Personal Achievement and History in Gadamer, Habermas, and Erikson* [Evanston, Ill.: Northwestern University Press, 1990], 75).

12. Hans-Georg Gadamer, *Truth and Method*, second revised ed., trans. Joel Weinsheimer and Donald G. Marshall (New York: Crossroad, 1991), 276. Although Habermas clearly recognizes this point (see, e.g., NC 217, 233, 259; CES 108), he maintains that critical reflection is able to escape the particularity of the situation in order to obtain the detached, objective, universal standpoint necessary for postconventional identity.

13. Gadamer explains the model of *phronesis* in hermeneutical terms: "it does not mean first understanding a given universal in itself and then afterward applying it to a concrete case." Rather, the actual understanding of the universal itself is constituted only through our understanding of the given case (see *Truth and Method*, 341). For further discussion see Shaun Gallagher, "The Place of *Phronesis* in Postmodern Hermeneutics," *Philosophy Today* 37 (1993): 298–305.

CHAPTER 9

"We," Representation, and War-Resistance

Some Para-Husserlian Considerations

JAMES G. HART

In the first part of this paper, I sketch the relationship between community, many features of which are implicit in the appropriate use of the first-person plural pronoun, and statist representation. Throughout this paper, when I refer to "the state," I primarily have in mind what Husserl would call an empirical (not morphological or exact) essence. For all practical purposes, however, I have in mind the modern liberal democratic form found in North America and Western Europe. How what I have to say would fit the now-dissolving "state capitalism" or "democratic centralism" of Eastern Bloc countries would require excursions that we here must neglect. In the second part of the paper, I propose the ethical response for one who shares my views on these matters. As one who leans toward pacifism, violent revolution is not considered to be an option. The fact that one's state is waging war (as was the case when this paper was first written) merely accentuates the urgency of the action that is called for; it does not change it essentially.

In Heideggerian terms, this paper is an analysis of aspects of *Alltäglichkeit*, that is, of how we are for the most part in the world with others in a pre-reflective way, to which few philosophers attend. It is "para-Husserlian" in the sense that the major concepts that undergird the theoretical aspects of the paper are derived from my research on Husserl.

In this regard, I believe Husserl's thought to "be alongside," if not strictly "on the same side" as mine.

Finally, it ought to be noted that although I believe that the state creates a basically inauthentic (in Husserl's technical sense of being an uninsightful and irresponsible) agency and social arrangement that contradict the moral imperative of community (that there is such a moral imperative I have tried to show elsewhere[1]), the prior moral task is to stop the violent deeds of the state. The task of the dissolution of the state might well be facilitated best through the state's cooperation. Such a concession to practical exigencies need not imply acknowledgment of the legitimacy of the state.

SOME HUSSERLIAN PRINCIPLES OF COMMUNITY

The basic issues of political philosophy are tied to the phenomenon of representation. Not the least of these issues is the moral legitimacy of the state. Husserl flirted with the idea that the state is an essential part of the categorial form of the pregiven world (*Nachlass* MS. A V 10, 1ff.).[2] Yet when he acknowledges that the state is an *imperium* from above (A V 10, 44ff.), he goes against his basic communitarian philosophy in which "we" arises not "from above" but "from below." For Husserl, the community to which we are exhorted, indeed which is a moral imperative, is one that already obtains in an incomplete and restricted way in family outings, good discussions, forms of teamwork, and so on. This is a life in which

> we do not only live next to one another but in one another. We determine one another personally . . . from one I to another I. And our wills do not merely work on Others as the components of our surroundings but in the Others. Our wills extend themselves unto the will of the Other, unto the willing of the Other which at the same time is our willing, so that the deed of the Other can become our deed even if in a modified manner. (*Nachlass* MS. F I 24, 128)

For Husserl, "we" as the expression of community derives from the interpenetrating agency of individuals "who in binding themselves together penetrate one another in so far as the life of one is co-lived in the life of the Other and each shares in the Other's life. The I-ness of the one is not next to that of the Other, but lives and works in that of the Others.[3] Husserl contrasts the imperialist organization of will "from above," in which all of the individual wills are centered and to which they must voluntarily subordinate themselves, with the one that he espouses, namely, "a communist unity of wills" from below.[4]

I have argued elsewhere that the linguistic achievement of "we" is a performative in which the speaker both appresents, that is, apperceives in an empty intention, and represents the other members for whom he/she is speaking.[5] The representation is both a self-displacing presencing of those who are absent and an acting and speaking in their place. I claim that "we" also has features resembling the "quasi-indexical" in that the speaker refers to others as self-referring but also to others as implicitly referring to the speaker and thus empowering the speaker so that he/she can speak.

On the basis of these and other considerations, I argue that the "statist 'we'" is essentially inauthentic because another always speaks for each one. "No one at all has any choice but to be represented"[6] and each must rest content in this being spoken for. People speak, act, and think for me; they say "we" in a way that includes me, and in this context I have never had, nor ought I expect to have, a choice between being represented and acting for myself. Direct democracy and community are ruled out from the start. Thus, if I yield to the presumption of the "statist 'we'," I do not have a choice between participatory communitarian democracy and representation. Rather, the choice is between having someone say "I" for me and not acting for myself or not having someone say "I" for me and still not acting for myself.[7] Obviously, in both cases, "we" is jeopardized, if not emptied of meaning.

Representation in the absence of consent to representation is not legitimated by the fact that citizens do not throw bombs in protest. Casting a vote may well mean simply avoiding the greater evil among the candidates; it does not thereby legitimate representation. (With taxation, however, the issue is less clear as we will see presently.) Because the statist context never raises the issue of whether the citizen is to be represented, the issue of consent to representation has to do with a basic moral determination of the relationship between people and not merely with the details of the representative process. The reason why such representation is a moral configuration of interpersonal relationships is that people are determined in an inauthentic relationship to one another and to themselves. Each one, without being in a position of cooperating in this determination, finds that Others presume the right of making the determination. Thus, the issue of consent to representation has to do with a determination between people in which "there simply never is a choice between being represented or acting for oneself. There is only one between being represented and not acting for oneself, or not being represented and still not acting for oneself."[8]

The moral exhortation to vote, made by proponents of hierarchical representative "democracy," is ambiguous because it defines democracy in terms of that which already indicates a depleted sense of democracy, that is, ballot-box visits. The fulfillment of one's democratic responsibilities by a visit to the ballot box is endlessly removed from "government by the people, for the people, and of the people." For under the best circumstances, those of friendship—which are not typically the ones present in, say, the United States—it transfers one's mind and will to another in such a way that the other's mind and will are given a blank check or an antecedent endorsement. Such a trust is unwarranted even among friends in the determination of all of one's life. Furthermore, it is obvious that such a view of democracy regards participatory democracy as disruptive. In its emphasis on the visit to the ballot box, it creates an atmosphere of acquiescence and adds to the powerful social control that the prevalence of such a definition enables. Finally, voting for what is right is, as Thoreau noted, not doing it. "It is only expressing to men feebly your desire that it should prevail." Although it seems clear that it is not anyone's duty to spend his whole life eradicating just any evil that might exist, "it is his duty, at least to wash his hands of it, and if he gives it no thought longer, not to give it practically his support."[9] In the next section, I will show how we all practically give our support to what most of us regard as evils.

The mechanisms for this essentially hierarchical and representative form of "democracy" are political consultants, mass media, corporation-funded think tanks, public relations firms, polling, targeted mailings, and political action committees. Besides these, of course, we must include the "minatory" agencies of the police and legal system that lurk in the background if one strives to establish a form of self-rule by means of direct participation apart from the rules laid down by the state. There is a parallel here with the legitimate rule by majority, that is, government by the people and not mere majority rule. If this is to be founded on right and not might, if the will of the majority is not to be founded on only the expression of superior force by superior numbers ("rule of the majority and not rule by the people"), then there is presupposed a general disposition, under certain circumstances, toward rule of the majority. This disposition obtains when all of the members anticipate that in spite of their will to community and consensus there shall be occasions when consensus is impracticable and when particular points of view are not decisive and individual wills are unfulfilled. Therefore each (and on *this* point a consensus is assumed and the ideal of community is affirmed) wills in advance not to press his or her particular viewpoint, but rather to abide by what the majority prefers.[10] In the absence of consensus on this point, rule by majority is fundamentally despotic.

Similarly, representation without consent is a "choice not between democracy and anarchy but between democracy and despotism."[11] Since representation as a democratic form of procedure only makes sense as a development of direct democracy and since, from the start, representation within the state, the so-called liberal democratic state included, has functioned with indifference toward consent and direct democracy—because impossible by reason of the size and top-down nature of the state—the actual form of statist representation, like majority rule as the greater strength of greater numbers, is a rule of might.

The circumstance of being forced to make a choice between two alternatives that detract from community ("us"), that is, on the one hand, being represented without one's consent and, on the other hand, not being represented and not acting for oneself, cannot be said to be the result of an institution "we" establish for the sake of community and self-rule. Rather, as Buber put it, "the more a human group lets itself be represented in the management of its common affairs, the more it lets itself be represented from outside, the less communal life there is and the more impoverished it becomes as a community."[12] These considerations, aside from the facts about stateless communities,[13] would seem to be reasons that speak against the view that the state is compatible with the Husserlian ideal of a community of I's, a "we" constituted from below. They also are reasons why the state cannot be considered an a priori category of the social life-world.

Because democracy as government by the people, for the people, and of the people is essentially communitarian, democracy is compatible only with a form of centralization that resembles the polis, not the statist *imperium* imposed from above. Dewey put this nicely.

> Regarded as an idea, democracy is not an alternative to other principles of associated life. It is the idea of community life itself. . . . Wherever there is conjoint activity whose consequences are appreciated as good by all singular persons who take part in it, and where the realization of the good is such as to effect an energetic desire and effort to sustain it in being just because it is a good shared by all, there is in so far a community. The clear consciousness of a communal life, in all its implications, constitutes the idea of democracy.[14]

It is almost axiomatic among both the leaders and major theoreticians in the liberal representative democracies that the ideal of the polis is "impractical" (apparently in contrast to what this writer regards as the catastrophe of the modern megapolis and nation-state), that collectivities act by accepting leadership, and that the primary function of citizens is not to govern themselves, but to produce a government that will rule them. Joseph Schrumpeter has expressed well the *de facto*, if not the *de jure*, state of affairs of modern orthodox attitudes toward democracy: democracy is not the collective or communal deciding of an issue, but the "election of men who are to do the deciding." These "men" are served up to the citizens by parties that Schrumpeter defines as groups "whose members propose to act in concert in the competitive struggle for political power."[15]

In modern representative democracies, "we" is thus seemingly achieved by others for us. And if one consents to this, then "we" is typically achieved by *us* only in either the past tense, *ex post facto*, that is, after the initiative from above has been taken and the only possibility left is our consent; or in the future and future perfect tenses: we will think and do what our representatives will do; we will have thought and done what our representatives decide.

Of course, there are occasions when one may wish to be represented or must be represented. In such a case I am truly represented by another who thinks and acts in such a way as I would if I were fully awake, *sui compos*, "at my best." To authorize this on occasion, however, is not to sanction that someone else should create policies, goals, and ideals on my behalf. Furthermore, to be willing to be represented, as a habitual circumstance, in matters of great consequence for me and my neighbors is to renounce my life or to declare that I am "nobody," one who lacks a mind, a will, and a heart.

It must be noted that the attitude of trust that is essential in this discussion is often exhorted to in the interests of representative democracy—in other words, in the interests of the anonymous, bureaucratic, hierarchical, and competitive society of the modern liberal capitalist state. Trust has a basic place in community and in its rich political articulation in the democratic polis, but it has little legitimacy or foundation in a society founded on competition and profit and governed at least indirectly by a ruling economic elite.[16]

RESISTING THE STATE THROUGH TAX-RESISTANCE

The general drift of these considerations is familiar to anyone versed in the anarcho-communist tradition. Many in the European eco-pax movement, some feminists, the Greens, the regionalists, the communitarians, and those concerned with "appropriate technology" and decentralization are saying similar things. Most eloquently, perhaps, we find it in the writings of thinkers like Murray Bookchin, Rudolf Bahro, Vandana Shiva, Lewis Mumford, Noam Chomsky, and even, in some respects, Hannah Arendt, for example, in her passages esteeming workers' councils [*Rätesystem*]. Therefore, I do not think that the moral dilemma that this thinking poses, especially in time of war, is uniquely mine. I wish to develop it, however, and to point to a response.

If the state is morally ambiguous, then our allegiance to it is also morally ambiguous. If it commits crimes in our name, then our cooperation is criminal. We cooperate willy-nilly in many ways. Many of these ways, but surely not all of them, are harmless. It is obvious that we can and must, of course, protest on the streets, do civil disobedience, write letters to editors and to our alleged representatives, and vote for new candidates. For reasons given above, of course, these do not get to the heart of the matter.

Of foremost moral importance in regard to the crimes that the state commits is the consideration that we cooperate by making possible the material conditions for the crimes. Thoreau clearly saw this connection.

> Those who, while they disapprove of the character and measures of a government, yield to it their allegiance and support, are undoubtedly its most conscientious supporters, and so frequently the most serious obstacles to reform. Some are petitioning the State to dissolve the Union, to disregard the requisitions of the President. Why do they not dissolve it themselves—the union between themselves and the State—and refuse to pay their quota into its treasury?[17]

The state has no strength and soon loses its apparent legitimacy if it has no power for action. This occurs especially when it loses its ability to exercise violence on its subjects as well as on its declared foreign enemies. The liberal-democractic state claims to acquire its legitimacy by means of the participation of the citizens in the rituals of legitimacy, that is, those rituals that indicate the consent of its citizens. In criticism of this, the Left in each generation has pointed out that "the public," to a large extent and much of the time, is a creation of the state and of the corporations for which the state works. There are, of course, important exceptions, for example, the present debates on pro-choice versus pro-life, as well as the controversies and demonstrations during the time of the Civil Rights Movement and the anti–Vietnam War protests. These more genuine democratic impulses indeed cloud the issues, give hope to educators, and defy dogmaticians. Nevertheless, it remains true, for the most part because of the nonparticipatory nature of government in the United States, that the "the public" is often little more than "the collectivity of individuals each rather passively exposed to the mass media and rather helplessly opened up to suggestion and manipulation that flow from these media."[18]

A related point is made by Hannah Arendt when she draws a distinction between representation of action and thought and the representation of interests. In a modern representational democracy the "special interest groups," lobbies, and so forth, are effective vehicles of influence in which some segments of the society can put forth and realize their wishes at the expense of others. This is a form of blackmail exercised by individuals or private groups and accompanied by a total indifference to the common good.

> The most the citizen can hope for is to be "represented," whereby it is obvious that the only thing which can be represented and delegated is interest or the welfare of the constituents but neither their actions nor opinions. In this system the opinions of the people are indeed unascertainable for the simple reason that they are non-existent. Opinions are formed in a process of open discussion and public debate, and where no opportunity for the forming of opinions exists, there may be moods—moods of the masses and moods of the individuals, the latter no less fickle and unreliable than the former—but no opinion.[19]

The state has diminished power for agency if its guise of legitimacy is removed from it. But even if its legitimacy becomes obscure and ambiguous, the state still has power if the citizens act in a way that makes its agency possible or if it still has power to make the citizens act in such a way. Milton Fisk urges us to look at the economy and not at institutions as the theoretical grid in which to view events such as oppression, injustice, war, poverty, and sexism.[20] Whether this is the correct perspective or not, at least this much seems clear: the link between the state and the economy is so close that not only will the state do everything it can to promote the economy, it will do everything it can to secure revenue to facilitate its functioning. This means that the source of the actual being of the state is less the rituals of legitimacy—as important as these are—than the tax revenues. The fuel for the state is the money that the taxpayers pay. The entire power of the state, even its means of procuring its legitimacy through the media, hinges on this.

Taxes are a way, to put it in Husserl's terms, that the wills of the essential strangers of the modern, liberal, capitalist society can live with one another, thereby creating a common will toward a common purpose. Of course, this will is not "from below," but orchestrated and initiated "from above" by the central authorities. Still, this common will is an act of will by each, binding each and all to the central will of the governmental agency and to its goals. Protest as we might about the government, carry on as we may about how removed its ideals and will are from our own, if we are paying taxes, our wills are present in all of its nefarious activities.

Again, Thoreau saw this clearly. The only way that most of us meet directly, indeed constitute, the government in a face-to-face encounter is when the IRS says to us in April: "Recognize Me." And

> the simplest, the most effectual and, in the present posture of affairs, the indispensablest mode of treating with it on this head, of expressing your little satisfaction with and love for it, is to deny it then. . . . Let your life be a counter friction to stop the machine. What I have to do is to see, at any rate, that I do not lend myself to the wrong I condemn.[21]

I see this as a clear sense of collective responsibility. As Scheler once noted, the features of a life in common require the acknowledgment that if we were to imagine being summoned before a divine judge, no one would appear alone, but rather each would appear with all the others equally being heard; each would be judged along with each and within the whole; and the whole would also be judged in each. This view is echoed by Husserl when he maintains that the level of ethical value of the individual is dependent on that of others and that the community as a whole attains the level of value that correlates to that of the individuals who comprise it.[22] The compulsory cooperation of state taxation does not so much create a common life as it creates a common good arising from our own desires, insight, and will "from below"; but it is such as to effect a common will "from above" that still depends on the compliance of the individuals who pay taxes.

We tend to overlook how covetous of this power the state is and how encompassing it has grown. A good example of this was recently called to my attention by Mike Andrews.[23] Consider a cooperative enterprise in which no money is exchanged, as in the case where, in return for your help in establishing my garden, I do some work for you by building your house out of recycled materials. It is quite possible that the government would levy taxes on this exchange. Not only would there be the prior request of a building permit fee (tax), and the property tax go up because it now has a house on it, but the person would be taxed for receiving the "equivalent market value" of a friend's reciprocal labor (an "in kind" income) for one's own labor. These taxes are quite different from the taxes for water or sewage for which services are rendered. In fact, tax would be due even if the labor given by one of the friends was not reciprocated, that is, if it were a gift; it would still be considered to be taxable income under the legal fiction of equivalent market value. It is scarcely possible to live apart from the state's demand for revenues.[24] It is also true, however, that the state cannot live and kill without our revenues.

When the state is at war—which is only a difference of degree from when the state uses tax money for the building of forces of destruction and thereby does not use its resources to heal the warlike conditions at home such as poverty, a decaying environment, collapsing infrastructures, malnutrition, extraordinary incidences of crime and violence, a bulging per capita prison population (greater than that of South Africa), homelessness, addiction, illness, and AIDS—each taxpayer subsidizes the killing. If he or she is not for killing or is against a particular war, then he or she must bring to a halt his or her complicity in the killing. War taxes must no longer be paid.

For Husserl, a basic element of "authentic culture" is knowing what we are doing. A prime example of inauthentic culture (discussed already in his *Philosophy of Arithmetic*[25]) is exemplified in the way we learn multiplication tables by rote without really knowing what we are doing. Even though it lacks the authentic insight of seeing that $1 + 1 + 1 = 3$, this procedure becomes automatic, is convenient, and works. For Husserl, modern scientific-technological-capitalist culture is one in which we do not know what we are doing, even though we live within self-perpetuating and self-legitimating frameworks of agency that are, to a great extent, founded on criteria of technological success and on a short-sighted love of comfort and convenience.[26]

We cannot know what we are doing when we give a blank check to a stranger that allows him or her to represent our will and mind. And similarly, we cannot be said to know what we are doing when we are not in a position to know where our tax money is going. There is an analogous abdication of responsibility by repeatedly paying our taxes to someone who has been known to use it secretively, carelessly, and for criminal purposes.

My anarcho-communist proclivities make me inclined to reject all forms of taxation. Particularly objectionable, however, is the war and military tax. Finding out precisely what "war taxes" are is increasingly difficult when many seemingly nonmilitary funds, such as those allocated to research, are more or less directly involved in military projects. It becomes even more complicated when one grasps that much of this research and development wages an analogous but covert war against the environment and, therefore, against posterity. Today, as during the Vietnam War, the three percent federal excise tax on the telephone is a military tax and that tax is a target for withholding. Of course, there will be different interpretations on how much money is used directly for military purposes. After studying last year's budget, the War Resisters' League concluded that 61 percent of the federal budget goes for military and war purposes.

The War Registers' League has also prepared an alternative tax form, one copy of which may be sent to the IRS while the other is sent to the league. The withheld money is then relayed by the individual or by the league to agencies involved in alternative, nonmilitary purposes. Besides being one of the most direct ways of acting morally in a situation that is unconscionable as well as being one of the most effective ways of stopping the war—should enough people participate in the refusal to pay taxes—this action would also be very American. Recall that among the founding American revolutionaries the shibboleth of "No Taxation Without Representation" resounded. The converse of this is also true, that is, "No Representation Without Taxation." I cannot be represented effectively, nor can the state have the strength to prosecute its goals, if I refuse to pay taxes. When I refuse to pay taxes, not only do I declare, "You may not say 'We' and include me," but over and above the speech-act and its own deed of disavowal the effective cooperation of my will in the killing is stopped—albeit too late for many of the victims.

On 19 March 1991 Senator Mark Hatfield introduced a bill (S. 689) that provided taxpayers with alternatives to supporting war. This bill, although a step in the right direction, unfortunately seemed to move the money into bureaucratic channels, that is, it established a U.S. Peace Tax Fund and a Board of Trustees for this fund. More basic is the movement toward a self-directed income tax proposed by the Center for Energy Research in Salem, Oregon.[27] This is a nascent movement whose goals are to enable citizens never to have to pay for anything they do not believe in and to empower them to act directly in response to government policies with which they are in disagreement.

It would seem that, for an American, the most fundamental right is the right to be a conscientious objector with respect to any policy of violence and war. That right is denied by the present system of taxation. Consider that as a university professor or as an employee of a large corporation I find myself committed to a tax arrangement over which I have no say or control. The federal income tax is taken directly from my salary by the university or corporation. The university is bound by Circular E ("Employer's Tax Guide") not to honor my request that on the W-4 Form (Employee's

Withholding Certificate) I may be permitted extra allowances because of war tax resistance.

What, then, am I to do? If the calculation of the military monies is over 50 percent of my tax, then, to circumvent the employer's ruling—by law I need not explain my allowances to the employer—I would have to claim several extra allowances, presupposing legitimate exemptions, and so on. This action, in the eyes of the government, places me in the "willfully fraudulent" category, for which I am probably going to be fined $500.00 for filing a "false" W-4. Theoretically I am liable to up to a year in jail and a fine of up to $100,000.[28]

A moral difficulty connected with the action of claiming extra allowances must be addressed. The W-4 defines allowances in terms of head of household, dependents, spouse, and so on. Thus when I sign that I am entitled to X number of allowances, *I* mean that I have a right to refuse to pay war or military taxes. The *government*, it is clear, will take my signature to mean that I have other children or dependents. Because the government has forced me to participate in war and because it has not left room for my dissent, the moral course would seem to be to claim the extra allowances and, having notified the IRS of my intentions, to send the withheld tax to some other place such as the Alternative Revenue Service, the American Friends Service Committee, or the U.S. Catholic Bishops Relief Fund.[29]

If my act of claiming extra allowances is to be more than a courageous gesture by an isolated individual and if it is truly to help to bring the killing to a halt, then the movement would have to become widespread. How widespread it would have to become is not clear. If or when this form of resistance becomes popular, it could conceivably spread like wildfire and the wheels of destruction would stop turning.

The way in which the planning of such a protest would build up communities as a foil for the state would be of no small importance. This would not occur through the single, isolated acts of war tax resisters, in anonymous solidarity with all the others, whoever they might be, scattered throughout the land, and cheered on by a central War Resisters' League (as wonderful as this is), because such anonymity and solo heroism responds to the government's "divide and conquer" strategy. What is needed instead, or at least over and above this, is concrete preparation for the inevitable response of the government. The government would doubtlessly strive to persecute individuals in order to provide an example for the rest of the citizenry who might be tempted to participate in such an action. Thus, it would be imperative for citizens to form communities that would be committed to cushioning the state's terrorizing actions. This would include making arrangements to take care of the financial losses, to parent the children of those arrested, and to comfort those who are either imprisoned or rendered poorer by reason of the state's penalties. As the laws now stand, failure to pay taxes and fines results in the confiscation of the withheld money, or seizure of resources, and the addition of penalties for the delinquency. The penalties accrue according to the amount of tax that is withheld. This hardship could be alleviated by communities forming contingency plans, pooling savings, and providing legal counsel.

A community of communities that has decided to stop the killing and that has resolved to strive to live an authentic moral life in the context of the morally ambiguous state could find the initiated hostilities—at the writing of this piece, it was the Gulf War—occasioning the beginning of "a New World Order," or at least of a more humane America. If tax resistance became popular, then it is possible that basic democratic dignity and empowerment would be discovered and the seemingly inevitable future wars would be nipped in the bud. This kind of agency within a finite community is also and inseparably an awareness and expression of concern for universal humanity. Through it we are responding, as Husserl would put it, to the inkling of an absolute ought that is in the form of an overarching idea,

> a universal ethical synthesis in which each I lives in an effective ethical manner and thereby realizes his best possible life in such a way that this life concomitantly realizes the best possible life for the Others; and in such a way that this life is lived not external to but within the Other (that is, that each life wills its own will and makes its estimations through the will and estimations of the Others) and in the unity of will and joining with the Others it effects a community of agency in which the joined I's as a joined subjectivity become a "synthetic pole" of community action. (*Nachlass* MS, Archival Signature, F I 24, 132–33)

Such are my belated thoughts on a matter of great consequence. What is missing is the action that will lift the sense of inconsistency, if not hypocrisy, that weighs me down whenever I think and talk about these matters.

NOTES

1. See my *The Person and the Common Good: Essays in a Husserlian Social Ethics* (Dordrecht: Kluwer, 1992).

140   *James G. Hart*

2. This is the signature of the Husserl Archives in Louvain. I wish to thank Professor Samuel IJsseling, Director of the Archives, for permission to quote from Husserl's *Nachlass*.

3. Edmund Husserl, *Zur Phänomenologie der Intersubjectivität. Texte aus dem Nachlass*. Zweiter Teil: 1921–1928, ed. Iso Kern, Husserliana XIV (The Hague: Martinus Nijhoff, 1973), 179.

4. Edmund Husserl, *Aufsätze und Vorträge (1922–1937)*, ed . Thomas Nenon and Hans-Reiner Sepp, Husserliana XXVII (Dordrecht: Kluwer, 1989), 52–53.

5. See my "I, We and God: Ingredients of Husserl's Theory of Community," in *Husserl Ausgabe und Husserl Forschung, Phänomenologica*, vol. 115, ed. S. IJsseling (Dordrecht: Kluwer, 1989) and, at greater length, in chapter 3 of *The Person and the Common Life*.

6. See the very important article of A. Phillips Griffiths, "How Can One Person Represent Another?" in *Aristotelian Society* supplementary vol. 34 (1960): 202–3; hereafter referred to as HCOP. For a learned and insightful discussion of Husserl's concept of the state, see Karl Schuhmann, *Husserls Staatsbegriff* (Freiburg/Munich: Alber, 1988). Compare also chapter 5 of *The Person and the Common Life*.

7. See HCOP.

8. See HCOP, 202–3.

9. Henry David Thoreau, "Civil Disobedience," in *Walden & Civil Disobedience: The Variorum Editions* (New York, Washington Square, 1971), 349.

10. J.-J. Rousseau, *On the Social Contract*, ed. Roger D. Masters, trans. Judith R. Masters (New York: St. Martin's Press, 1978), 52; also, R. B. Perry, *A General Theory of Value* (New York: Longmans, Green and Company, 1926), 672–73.

11. Griffiths, HCOP.

12. Martin Buber, *Paths in Utopia* (New York: Beacon, 1965), 133.

13. For a discussion of how the state is a grotesque aberration peculiar to only certain societies, see Pierre Clastres, *Society Against the State* (New York: Zone, 1989).

14. John Dewey, *The Philosophy of John Dewey*, vol. II, ed. John McDermott (New York: Capricon, 1972), 622–23.

15. Joseph Schrumpeter, *Capitalism, Socialism, and Democracy* (New York: Harper & Row 1950), 269ff.

16. For the distinction between the polis and the community see the writings of Murray Bookchin, especially his *The Rise of Urbanization and the Decline of Citizenship* (San Francisco: Sierra Club, 1987).

17. Thoreau, "Civil Disobedience," 350.

18. C. Wright Mills, *Power, Politics, and People* (New York: Ballantine, 1963), 187ff., 336ff., 571ff.

19. Hannah Arendt, *On Revolution* (New York: Viking, 1962), 272.

20. Milton Fisk, *The State and Justice: An Essay in Political Theory* (Cambridge: Cambridge University Press), 143ff.

21. Thoreau, "Civil Disobedience," 352, 351.

22. Husserl, *Aufsätze und Vorträge (1922–1937)*, 48; see note 4.

23. I wish to thank Mike Andrews for his careful readings, and for the many improvements he made in this text.

24. Mike Andrews calls attention to the importance of this type of taxation in the disintegration of subsistence economies, peoples, and civilizations through expansion of the state power. If members of a basically subsistence nonmonetary economy are required to pay taxes with money, they are forced to leave their home areas and to go to urban centers to work for money in order that the taxes on the village property, homestead, and so forth, can be paid. Within a short space of a few generations, there are few people following the ancient ways, the way of life is pervaded by money, commodities, and "market forces," and most have moved to the urban ghettoes in order to reap the rewards of full membership in the nation-state.

25. Edmund Husserl, *Philosophie der Arithmetik*, Husserliana Vol. XII, ed. L. Eley (The Hague: Martinus Nijhoff, 1970), 348–50, 372.

26. See Husserl's *Aufsätze und Vorträge (1922–1937)*, 117–18.

27. Center for Energy Research, 333 State Street, Salem, OR 97301; Tel.: (503) 371-8002. This information is gathered from *The Peace Taxpayers' Newsletter*, #6, P.O. Box 383, Lexington, KY 40585.

28. The War Resisters' League reports that to date only two persons have been severely dealt with for such resistance.

29. In clarifying my mind on these matters I have been helped greatly by the recent essay, "Controlling Federal Tax Withholding," published by the National War Tax Resistance Coordinating Committee, P.O. Box 85810, Seattle, WA 98145.

PART III

Gadamer's Experience of Truth in Tradition

CHAPTER 10

Gadamer's Alleged Conservatism

HOLLY L. WILSON

The central position that Gadamer has assigned to tradition in his philosophical hermeneutics has provoked a number of commentators to criticize
his entire enterprise as "politically" conservative. This critique gathers
force in light of Habermas's analysis of the idealogical, dogmatic, and
authoritarian tendencies of tradition. If tradition prejudices us and creates a
systematic ideology that blinds us, then we need an emancipatory philosophy, not a hermeneutical philosophy, that will give us distance from tradition
or ideology in order to critique it.

Two recent attempts have been made to defend Gadamer's hermeneutics
against this alleged conservatism. Neither attempt does full justice to
Gadamer's hermeneutics and for that reason neither attempt furthers our
understanding of it. These defenses fail to succeed because they provide no
clarity concerning the ambiguous use of the word "tradition" in the allega-
tion itself. Georgia Warnke has attempted to defend Gadamer by claiming
that his conservatism is inessential to his hermeneutics.[1] Gary Brent
Madison has taken the strategy of defending the emancipatory, and therefore
revolutionary, element in hermeneutical theory against the claim that the
preservation of tradition is politically conservative in nature.[2] Although he
does not claim to be representing only Gadamer's position, but merely the
ideal of hermeneutical theory, Madison does refer to Gadamer often.

Neither of Gadamer's advocates, however, ever question the assumption
that tradition is a unitary phenomenon, nor do they stop to analyze precisely
in what way Gadamer's hermeneutics preserves tradition, as Gadamer's critics maintain. I would like to take up Gadamer's defense by putting the dis-

cussion on new ground. First, I will show that Warnke's and Madison's defenses fail because both presuppose a monolithic notion of tradition that blinds them to the different ways in which Gadamer uses tradition. Then I will analyze a passage in which Gadamer shows us explicitly how the hermeneut relates to traditions. We thus will see clearly that the type of preservation that occurs has nothing at all to do with political conservatism and that it is, therefore, not dogmatic and uncritical.

Warnke, in the section entitled, "Gadamer's conservatism," argues that Gadamer is conservative with respect to tradition because of his disagreement with the Enlightenment's critique of authority and because of his claim that authority, with its superior knowledge, is sometimes legitimate. She writes:

> Gadamer's thesis here is the fundamentally conservative one that since we are historically finite, since we have no concept of rationality that is independent of the tradition to which we belong and hence no universal norms and principles to which we can appeal, we ought not even to attempt to overthrow the authority of that tradition.[3]

Warnke also detects political conservatism in Gadamer's doctrine of the pre-understanding, because first, understanding provisionally begins with tradition; second, it is questionable when and how this provisional understanding is to be abandoned; and third, she finds politically conservative tendencies in Gadamer's preference for mediation as opposed to distantiation. Gadamer, she writes, "attacks Habermas for taking the side of methodical science against hermeneutics and thus the side of 'distantiation' or alienation [*Verfremdung*] against hermeneutic mediation."[4]

There is truth and confusion in each one of these points. The confusion can be cleared up, however, by determining more precisely what Gadamer means by tradition in each one of the instances. In critical theory, authority is that which maintains a social tradition, that which unconsciously binds and dominates people. For Gadamer, on the other hand, it is not authority that preserves tradition, but the rational act of the interpreter.[5] Gadamer argues that personal authority and sanctioned tradition and customs, which have a nameless authority, have a legitimate claim to respect because of the inability of the finite human being to know everything (WM 285; TM 281). The acknowledgment of authority by the finite human being, however, is always a rational act. To reject all tradition because of its claim to authority is no better than to accept uncritically all tradition. Gadamer does not want to repeat the mistake of the Romantics, who opposed the Enlightenment's

abstract notion of reason by embracing an abstract, ambiguous, and preju-
diced notion of tradition. To the Romantics, "tradition [*Tradition*] is still
viewed as the abstract opposite of free self-determination, since its validity
does not require any reasons but conditions us without our questioning it"
(WM 286; TM 281). On Warnke's account, Gadamer would be no more critical than the Romantics from whose position he is explicitly distancing himself. The "unconditional antithesis between tradition and reason" is a false
dichotomy (WM 286; TM 281).

Gadamer, however, is not attempting to renew any particular claim that
tradition makes. He is arguing that tradition in fact does give us a starting
point for reflection, not that it ought to. He is not advocating the superior
authority of tradition; he is only claiming that the authority of tradition is
based on an act of reason, an act of acknowledgment (WM 284; TM 279). In
other words, the causes of dogmatic consciousness must be located some
place other than in tradition. It is not tradition itself that causes dogmatism,
but rather the attitude that one takes to tradition.

Warnke's second point, that the interpreter begins with a pre-understanding, can be clarified further. Scholars are influenced by tradition, but
Gadamer does not mean to imply that tradition is a unitary phenomenon
influencing all interpreters equally. He explicitly refers to a plurality of traditions when he asserts that scholars find themselves "situated within traditions [*in Überlieferungen stehen*]" (WM 280; TM 276). Scholars who
approach traditional texts find themselves in a multiplicity of traditions, and
they find themselves addressed by multifarious voices in a variety of texts.
In a revealing passage, Gadamer writes: "Our historical consciousness is
always filled with a variety of voices in which the echo of the past is heard.
Only in the multifariousness of such voices does it exist: this constitutes the
nature of the tradition [*Überlieferung*] in which we want to share and have a
part" (WM 289; TM 284).

For the human scientist or scholar, tradition is clearly not monolithic;
there are many conflicting and contrary traditions to which the scientist
must be open. Every scientist, scholar, or reader begins with a fore-meaning
from a tradition. Those who are conscious of their hermeneutically effected
situation are able to be aware of this and, at the same time, are able to distance themselves from this prejudgment in order to be receptive to what is
being said in the text. There is nothing particularly conservative about this
process unless the scholar refuses to let herself be spoken to by the text. In
this case she would unconsciously preserve the fore-meanings or ideology
that a particular tradition has bequeathed to her. As Gadamer stresses, "it is

the tyranny of hidden prejudices that makes us deaf to what speaks to us in tradition [*in der Überlieferung*]" (WM 274; TM 270). It is precisely because some Other is speaking to us in a living way that we become aware of the weight of tradition that prejudices us.

Finally, Gadamer cannot prefer hermeneutic mediation to distantiation, since there is no mediation without distantiation.[6] Hermeneutic consciousness "is aware that its bond to this subject matter does not consist in some self-evident, unquestioned unanimity, as is the case with the unbroken stream of tradition [*fortlebende Tradition*]" (WM 300; TM 295). The direct stream of tradition is already broken by the unfamiliar. In fact, mediation is only possible on the presupposition of the openness and preparedness of the interpreter to hear what the Other has to say about a subject matter. Hermeneutic work "is based on a polarity of familiarity and strangeness . . . here too there is a tension [*Spannung*]. It is the play between the traditionary text's strangeness and familiarity to us" (WM 300; TM 295). It is the scientist who approaches the text as an object that makes no truth-claim and refuses to let her prejudices be called into question that ultimately preserves an unreflected tradition or ideology. The hermeneut always interprets in the tension or span [*Spannung*] between the past and the present. Tradition spans or bridges the past and the present.

Madison's characterization of hermeneutical theory is misleading when applied to Gadamer in particular, for it fails to recognize the unique way in which Gadamer relates to tradition, a way that is not necessarily oriented toward preservation or emancipation as explicit political ends. I will first show why hermenuetical theory cannot be emancipatory in the sense that Madison proposes. Madison hypostatizes the tradition of metaphysics and then opposes it to the tradition of finitude or freedom. He creates a false dichotomy in which one either critiques the tradition of metaphysics or merely repeats metaphysics. Gadamer, however, does not fall prey to this repetition of metaphysics, for he does not conceive of tradition as a unitary phenomenon whose essence we can know and oppose, but rather as a multiplicity of traditions. As a counter-proposal to Madison, I will illustrate how Gadamer's philosophical interpretation takes place in the encounter with a multiplicity of Others or Thous. In the section entitled, "Language as Medium and its Speculative Structure," Gadamer exhibits concretely his hermeneutical method and, in addition, points to the particular tradition that is currently blinding interpreters.

According to Madison, hermenuetical theory is untraditional because it critiques metaphysics and the concern for foundations, as well as modernism and the prejudice against prejudice.[7] These emancipatory elements can be found in Gadamer; he has appealed to them himself, in a dialogue with Derrida, as common ground between hermeneutics and deconstruction.[8] The difficulty arises, however, when we remember that Gadamer also claims that tradition gives us the basis of the possibility of critiquing tradition. If tradition is conceived of as ideologically slanted and unitary, and if our understanding is completely formed by historically effected tradition, then we have no basis of critique and no basis of emancipation from our prejudice. This seeming impossibility rests, of course, on an ambiguous use of the word tradition. Although Madison seems to recognize this fact by his title, in which he places "the" in brackets, he nevertheless does not make the ambiguity explicit. Thus he falls into the trap of hypostatizing tradition.[9]

In postmodern interpretation, Enlightenment ideology perceives tradition and freedom to be incompatible. Those who continue the Enlightenment project must conceive of tradition as a unitary phenomenon from which one can become free. Gadamer, on the other hand, does not conceive of tradition as a unitary phenomenon because he defines it as anything that is written and handed down [*überliefert*]. Tradition should rather be spoken of as traditions; we encounter a plurality of traditions in our encounter with the multiplicity of texts that have been handed down to us. It is interesting to note that Gadamer most often uses the phrase *in Überlieferung stehen* [standing in the handed-over], rather than the Latin term *Tradition*, when he is explaining the genuine activity of the interpreter.[10] He uses the concept of *Tradition* pejoratively more often than not or else he uses it to refer to the ground of an authority's validity (WM 285; TM 281).

According to Madison, there are only two traditions, that of "metaphysics" and "teleology" and that of "finitude." According to him, hermeneutics has reinstated the tradition of finitude and critiqued the hubris of metaphysics. If Madison is right, then when hermeneutics sets itself up as a critique of metaphysics, it falls prey to the critique of relativism, although Madison dismisses this charge as inapplicable. Madison's defense is not convincing and the spector of relativism is certainly not so easily banished. He provides us with his own type of metaphysics by asserting that history is without goals and that freedom is the "basic constitutive value of the West."[11] We are certainly liberated from relativism, but we are back in the metaphysical position from which we will then need to be liberated.

I would suggest that, in this false dichotomy of tradition and freedom, we end up with a dialectic of emancipation in which we have the tradition of metaphysics, on the one hand, searching for foundations, and the tradition of finitude, on the other hand, trying to outrun all foundations. They would each, in turn, liberate each other. They would, in Kant's terminology, present an antinomy of reason. Derrida recognizes that critiquing metaphysics could easily lead to the projection of a new metaphysics. He, therefore, has refused to characterize his position as a position, but rather points to deconstruction as a method or program.[12]

Gadamer transposes us from this dialectic because he does not define tradition in any monolithic or dialithic fashion. Tradition is the act of handing down [*Überlieferung*] and is all that is written: "Everything written, is in fact, the paradigmatic object of hermeneutics" (WM 398; TM 395). To see through substance metaphysics, which may well be a pervading presence, and overcome its dominating influence is not to combat it with another metaphysics, but to understand the questions that metaphysics is meant to answer. Gadamer approves of Heidegger's critique of metaphysics because it seeks to understand the questions motivating the genesis of the project of metaphysics. In *Reason in the Age of Science*, Gadamer poses the issue in terms of the logic of the question and answer: "If one understands the question, What is Metaphysics? in the sense that one asks what happened with the beginning of metaphysical thinking, then the Heideggerian question first acquires the force of its provocativeness and is disclosed as an instance of the new notion of interpretation."[13]

The questions motivating the development of metaphysics are genuine human questions, but two observations make the answers that "traditional" metaphysics provides questionable for us today: (1) the answers that Plato and the medievals proposed may not be adequate answers for us today; and (2) the questions that we are asking today may well be different questions. In this critique of metaphysics we are still free to see the truth of metaphysics, that is, the truth in the answers of Plato and the medievals. We also are able to see the limitation of these answers for us, since their questions are not fully our questions.[14]

The Gadamerian hermeneut is prepared to hear the truth in traditions because she is sensitive to the text's alterity (WM 273; TM 269). At the same time, because the hermeneut has the comportment of questioning texts, she knows the answers that will satisfy the question for her situation today better than any past author could intend. This is how Gadamer defends the traditional hermeneutic and critical insight that we can understand the author "better than she understands herself."

We can gain insight into Gadamer's encounter with traditions by analyzing in detail a passage in which we become aware of the question that
Gadamer wants to answer and of the way in which he finds an answer in traditions. Gadamer's question concerns how human experience is an experience of the relationship between language and the world. For this reason,
much of Western philosophy, but specifically Plato, Hegel, and medieval
philosophical theology, proves to be an appropriate place to inquire further
since there the question of language was also posed.

The effective history of these traditions has influenced Gadamer to take
up this question as a question. This is the influence of traditions on
Gadamer, the interpreter. Traditions not only propose answers, they also propose questions. The question of language, however, has been posed in many
ways, not all of which will lead to satisfactory answers for us today: "That
human experience of the world is linguistic in nature was the thread underlying Greek metaphysics in its thinking about being since Plato's 'flight into
the *logoi*.' We must inquire how far the answer given there—an answer that
lasted until Hegel—does justice to the question we are concerned with"
(WM 460; TM 456). Various interpretations of the common and pivotal concepts of hearing-speaking, dialectic, speculation, and finitude show us how
traditions assert their truths and limitations. In the section "Language as
Medium and its Speculative Structure," Gadamer wants to present a new
perspective on language that both critiques Platonic, medieval, and modern
views and recognizes their truths. The complicated way in which he affirms
the truth and denies the limitations of particular interpretations of these
concepts in various tests and traditions shows us the complexity of traditions
and Gadamer's relation to them.

In this section, he presents us with a notion of language, that is, as speaking and hearing (or responding), that is founded in Christian tradition,
although it is not articulated conceptually within the Christian tradition of
philosophy. At the basis of this view of language is the image of the listener
who hears and responds to what the traditional text has to say to her: "The
hermeneutical experience also has its own rigor: that of uninterrupted listening" (WM 469; TM 465). Gadamer partly has the concept of the Christian
incarnation in mind when he writes, "The mode of being of tradition . . . is
language" as event (WM 422,467; TM 418,463). The word of tradition happens or comes into being; "But the actual occurrence is made possible only
because the word that has come down to us as tradition and to which we are
to listen really encounters us and does so as if it addressed us and is concerned with us" (WM 465–66; TM 461). In other words, the *verbum* is not

revealed in its true being in the external word without becoming the internal word, that is, the word that means something to the hearer (WM 424; TM 420). Clearly, Gadamer has in mind the repeated Christian image of God speaking to His people, the Israelites, through his prophets, of His people not listening to Him, and of his need to send His son to speak His message of redemption (which some hear and others do not).[15] This is the primary image behind Gadamer's notion of tradition speaking truth to us. It is always a Thou that speaks to us and addresses us and our prejudices.

The notion of the speaker and hearer is found in the rhetorical tradition and in Aristotle, but it is not developed in this way. The act of hearing is universal for Aristotle because, unlike the act of seeing, one cannot turn away from hearing (WM 466; TM 462). In Aristotle, however, we do not find the peculiarly Christian sense of being spoken to personally under the claim of having to respond to the call of conscience or to God. From the Greeks, Gadamer recovers a different notion of dialectic as opposed to the Hegelian notion, although he continues to preserve the notion of reversal in Hegel (WM 469; TM 465). The concept of dialectic that occurs in dialogue is preferable to a dialectic that occurs through the conceptual strivings of one philosophical mind, but the Hegelian reversal is preferable to the Platonic notion of an approximate approach to the ideas. Dialectic is peculiarly Greek, not Christian. But again, Gadamer develops the notion of dialectic here in a peculiarly Christian fashion. It is the questioner who brings a question to a traditional text, who ends up coming into question, just as the Pharisees and Scribes question Jesus and Jesus turns the question into a claim on them to live a righteous life, which thereby throws them into question.[16] Yet the Socratic notion of dialectic is preferable to dialogue, since it makes explicit the question-answer structure of our coming to understanding. The Socratic dialectic is preferable here to the Hegelian dialectic because in it the listeners, the young malleable men of Athens, are drawn into the discussion only to have their opinions confused; thereby they are made to question their notions of truth and justice (WM 468; TM 464). Neither dialectic, however, will suffice since the Socratic dialectic is negative and the Hegelian dialectic is directed to complete knowledge, a point at which all reversal is overcome and infinite knowledge is reached (WM 469; TM 465).

A desire for infinite knowledge would be inappropriate for a finite human being, that is, for a human being who is not a creator, but a created being, one who is dependent on supersensible powers, God, or language, as well as on tradition, which is not created by one person. The recognition of our finitude is a uniquely Christian idea. For the Christian, human beings are dependent on God. There will never be a point at which human beings will be independent or self-creating, even if they pretend to be God as Lucifer did. The image of the willful being who poses as self-sufficient is the image behind Gadamer's account of modern science; herein lies, in part, his critique of modern science. Modern science does not recognize its dependence on our normal everyday use of language, in which the whole of the world becomes meaningful for us through the ordering of experience and orientations in the world.[17]

We have to recognize that much of *Truth and Method* is a critique of the modern attempt to separate subject from object and to locate truth in subjectivity. From the perspective of subjectivity, everything else becomes an object to be manipulated or used (atoms or molecules rearranged at our whim). Modern science has, in spite of itself, perpetuated its Greek ancestry insofar as mathematics has come to be the primary metaphor of nature (as it was for Plato) (WM 463–64; TM 459–60). This orientation to the world does not respect the dignity of things. Thus Gadamer goes back to the Greeks and the medievals in order to recover a notion of this dignity, that is, of the intrinsic "belonging" and meaning of things within a human world that is dominated by ends and not means (WM 466; TM 462-63). All things have a relationship to the human being in a world; things belong, even as the human being belongs, to a world. All things have their being in language, not in ideology. In other words, the hermeneutical perspective is already critical of a certain ideology, namely, that of modern science. When asked where "emancipatory reflection [is] effectual" in his work, Gadamer responds, "everywhere" (TM 570).

When the orientation of modern science is extended to the human sciences, we begin to view human beings as means, as things to be used or as dominated by means. If we recognize, on the other hand, that in the human world all things are related to ends, then all things are seen to have their meaning in relation to ends in a world. All the experiences we have of the world gain their meaning (or being) in relation to ends. The influence of this teleological tradition is evident when Gadamer speaks of a text as a "Thou."

At the same time, Gadamer does not want to "revive the classical doctrine of the intelligibility of being" (WM 465; TM 461). He goes beyond the medieval notion of belonging that refers to belonging to an intelligible world order (one that unfolds itself teleologically in its fullness) by developing the notion of belonging in another sense that is also derived from the Christian tradition. There is another dialectic of the word, which accords to every word an inner dimension of mulitiplication: every word breaks forth as if from a center and is related to a whole, through which alone it is a word. Every word causes the whole of language to which it belongs to resonate and the whole world view that underlies it to appear.[18]

This means that every word is an event and carries with it what is unsaid, "to which it is related by responding and summoning" (WM 462; TM 458). Language preserved in writing is humanity of the past speaking to us and making claims on us. Writing is an alienation of speaking and it must thus be revitalized and brought back into speech; but to the one who listens, the truth can be heard. The medievals thought that the word was a reflection of a pre-given order of being and that there was a logical development of the word from that order, without reference to human subjectivity. We see, however, that tradition speaks to us in our situation, that is, in the finite situation in which we find ourselves. The word "that comes down to us as tradition and to which we are to listen really encounters us and does so as if it addressed us and is concerned with us" (WM 465; TM 461). Language is the medium in which experience becomes experience, in which finite human beings try to make sense of their experience, try to order their values and commitments, try to communicate who they are to others, and try to understand who others are. Language binds human beings to one another and to things in a primordial way. What human beings learn through their experience, they preserve through the language and the written texts that make up their tradition; thus they hand down their insights and the progress made to the next generation.

We don't have to reinvent the wheel every generation; we can learn from the previous generation. Language is the medium in which this takes place. It is like the earth itself that we take for granted, but that we now know must be preserved in order for human life to continue. Language is our dependence, the record of our finitude. In it is preserved the forming and developing that has taken place in human history (WM 461; TM 457).

This means for Gadamer, then, that emancipation from what embondages us can come from some other aspect of tradition. The contemporary domination of the scientific orientation has influenced the human sciences in their comportment toward texts and traditions. Texts become objects and lose the sense of a subject or a Thou who speaks to us. By going back to tradition (in its multifariousness—Greek tradition, medieval tradition, modern tradition), Gadamer attempts to recover a way of thinking that would preserve the human possibility of dialogue, speculation, and listening. He does not have a theory of emancipation, but he exhibits how an interpreter who is freed from the spell of prejudices can go to traditions more freely.

From the Greek tradition we inherited the supposition that we could speak all that we know, that we could make Being present. (That is the heritage of modern science.) From the medieval tradition we have the idea that we are not able to speak the whole of the world. We may be aware of the whole, but it is not totally expressible. We know from our own speech that we can make statements about ourselves and not tell the whole truth. Nonetheless, we seek words that will say what we mean and communicate what we cannot completely say. We speak in conversation what we think we mean. But in true conversation, we often reverse what we say if we think our meaning will become clearer.[19] In the midst of the event of understanding in conversation, language is only the medium for expressing a whole that can only be dialectically mediated. The Hegelian reversal is crucial for staying with the movement of understanding. We seek to express the whole and find just the right word at the right time, but, at the same time, we can never express everything. So we have to reverse our statement. This shows us the speculative dimension of language that exceeds all verbal statements. All understanding is linked with speech, even as all understanding is tied to application, but understanding exceeds speech.

Gadamer may well have said too little when he termed this event the "fusion of horizons," if this is taken to mean "agreement." There is no horizon without a ground on which a person stands, a situation in which a person is located. If there is to be a "fusion of horizons" in true conversation, then the two conversants have to find a common ground on which to stand. "Standing on common ground" means that the interpreters share the same questions or share the recognition that these questions are significant. They do not necessarily have to agree about the answers. Finding common ground is one of the main tasks of true conversation.[20]

The Hegelian interpretation of speculation and dialectic must be superseded because it subordinates language to the "statement" (WM 472; TM 468). The new sense in which speculation should be understood is as the "realization of meaning, as the event of speech, of mediation, of coming into an understanding" (WM 472–73; TM 468). It is the sense of making oneself intelligible to another. The speculative dimension of language is the distance we have from things and texts such that we seek to find the right words to express them. We seek to say who we are and make ourselves understandable not through statements, but through our meaning that holds together what is said and not said in a unity of meaning (WM 473; TM 469). Gadamer values the poetic word here since it brings a whole world to the fore and not just a part of a world. Gadamer presupposes the part-whole metaphor as the basis of human speech. This part-whole is both the teleological and organic part-whole, as well as the part-whole of the beautiful. Beautiful speech gives the correct measure in the part through which a whole then resonates.[21] The part attempts to express the whole. When we communicate with others, it is essential that we try to communicate the whole; if we don't, we will be misunderstood. Since we are finite, we can never communicate or understand the whole without interpretation. We are constantly involved in interpretation when we try to express ourselves and understand others.

In conclusion, there is no attempt in Gadamer to preserve tradition ideologically, because he is also highly critical of certain traditions. He does succeed, however, in preserving certain questions that he has received from various traditions. He has extended and widened "the possibilities of significance and resonance" (WM 466; TM 462) that we now hear in the questions and in the answers of those traditions. Gadamer has shown that he interprets traditions by means of other traditions; this means that he uses concepts in one tradition to conceptualize the subject matter of other traditions. He can do this because he does not conceive of tradition as a unitary phenomenon, nor of his relation to it as a monologue. Gadamer has many dialogue partners in tradition who speak to him. He is playing out "the content of tradition" (WM 466; TM 462) because it is playing him out.

NOTES

1. Georgia Warnke, *Hermeneutics, Tradition, and Reason* (Stanford: Stanford University Press, 1987), 134ff.

2. Gary Brent Madison, "Hermeneutics and (the) Tradition," in *Proceedings of the American Catholic Philosophical Association*, 62 (Supplement, 1989): 165–73.

3. Warnke, *Hermeneutics*, 136.

4. Ibid., 137.

5. Hans-Georg Gadamer, *Wahrheit und Methode: Grundzüge einer philosophischen Hermeneutik* (Tübingen: J. C. B. Mohr [Paul Siebeck], 1986), 283–87, abbreviated WM; *Truth and Method*, trans. by Joel Weinsheimer and Donald G. Marshall, second revised edition (New York: Crossroads, 1989), 277–84, abbreviated TM.

6. Gadamer writes, "A person who is trying to understand a text has to keep something at a distance . . . " WM 469; TM 465.

7. Madison refers to a passage in which Gadamer is discussing Hegel's teleological account of the development of political freedoms from the Orientals, to antiquity, and finally to the Christian world where all human beings are free. Gadamer's point is not that from the value of freedom (that is, political freedom) we can derive all other values, but that if we want to understand history, reason can find no higher principle than freedom. Contrary to Madison's intention, this represents a teleology, where an ideal end of free human beings is projected into the future as the end toward which history is heading. Gary Brent Madison, "Hermeneutics and (the) Tradition," 167.

8. Hans-Georg Gadamer, "Text and Interpretation," in *Dialogue and Deconstruction: The Gadamer-Derrida Encounter*, ed. D. Michelfelder and R. Palmer (Albany: SUNY Press, 1989), 21–57.

9. Paul Ricoeur in *Time and Narrative*, vol. III (Chicago: University of Chicago Press, 1988), 227, differentiates rightly between (1) traditionality, (2) traditions, and (3) tradition. Traditionality, in the first sense, is equivalent to Gadamer's *Überlieferung*, which makes the handing down of various traditions (the second sense) possible. The third usage of tradition refers to the ground of validity of the truth-claims made by traditions or authorities passing on those traditions.

10. *Überlieferung*: WM 274, 280, 285, 286, 289, 465, 494; TM 270, 276, 280, 282, 284, 461, 490; *Tradition*: WM 285, 286; TM 281, 282.

11. Gary Brent Madison, "Hermeneutics and (the) Tradition," 172.

12. See the discussion of this in Josef Simon, "Good Will to Understand and the Will to Power: Remarks on an 'Improbable Debate,'" in *Dialogue and Deconstruction: The Gadamer-Derrida Encounter*, ed. by D. Michelfelder and R. Palmer (Albany: SUNY Press, 1989), 162–75.

13. Hans-Georg Gadamer, *Reason in the Age of Science*, trans. by Frederick G. Lawrence. (Cambridge, Mass.: The MIT Press, 1981), 102.

14. Plato and the medievals seem to be asking the same question about the essense of being, about "what is," and for that reason we can characterize them both as doing metaphysics. They both place language at the center of their answer. Yet there are significant differences in their understanding of language and dialectic.

15. Any number of references can be given, but the passage at Matthew 13:13 is perhaps the clearest. Jesus explains to his disciples, "This is why I

speak to them in parables, because seeing they do not see, and hearing they do not hear, nor do they understand."

16. See Matthew 21:23–27 and Matthew 15:1–3.

17. Compare WM 449 and 463; TM 445 and 459.

18. WM 462; TM 458.

19. Consider how often one says something carelessly and suddenly realizes that the other might take it differently than it was meant. This realization is often followed by "I didn't mean that the way you are taking it." In reversal, we reflect back the image that is presented to us. WM 477; TM 474.

20. The Gadamer-Derrida encounter is a good illustration of two interpreters who could not find common ground, although Gadamer tried. See *Dialogue and Deconstruction: The Gadamer-Derrida Encounter.*

21. Compare WM 463 and 485; TM 459 and 479.

CHAPTER 11

The Imaging of Truth in Philosophical Hermeneutics

JAMES RISSER

Was aber schön ist, selig scheint es in ihm selbst
—Mörike

It seems ironic that in a book entitled *Truth and Method* little is said in the book itself *about* truth.[1] This is not to say that Gadamer does not speak *of* truth. To take but one example: in describing art as the transformation of play into figurative structure [*Gebilde*], Gadamer writes: "What we experience in a work of art and what invites our attention is how true it is, that is, to what extent one knows and recognizes something and oneself."[2] Presumably, what is intended by the title of the book is conveyed by this experience of truth that is found in the work of art, where truth is no longer tied exclusively to methodological procedure.[3] And insofar as the experience of art is simply a form of hermeneutic experience in general, it would appear that Gadamer will let his analysis of the hermeneutic phenomenon obliquely present the thematic of truth.

Such a tactic can certainly be justified. According to Jean Grondin, the fact that Gadamer does not have a systematic theory of truth is essential to the message of *Truth and Method*. An explicit theory of truth in its inevitable distance from the concrete experience of truth would consolidate the methodological approach that hermeneutics seeks to undermine.[4] Nevertheless, this justification does not obviate the need to bring to a level of philosophical clarity what supports and what is entailed in this concrete experience of truth that occurs not just in the work of art, but in all aspects of hermeneutic experience. It is precisely here that commentators, for the most part, want to recognize Gadamer's indebtedness to Heidegger. They thus supplement the interpretive context of the hermeneutic experience of truth by pointing out resonances with Heidegger's own analysis of truth as *aletheia*.[5] Here too we find the experience of truth as something beyond methodological procedure and, if we take Heidegger's "The Origin of the Work of Art"[6] into consideration, as something adjoined to the work of art.

Richard Bernstein, for example, acknowledging the affinity with Heidegger and yet not wanting to limit the hermeneutic experience of truth to this affinity, accounts for the hermeneutic experience of truth in the following way: Gadamer appeals to truth in order to distinguish philosophical hermeneutics from a historicist form of relativism, and the nature of such truth comprises a blending of motifs that have resonances in Hegel and Heidegger. Like Hegel, Gadamer understands truth to be revealed in the process of experience, in the dialogical encounter with the very tradition that has shaped us. Like Heidegger, Gadamer seeks to recover the notion of *aletheia* as disclosedness and unconcealment. But, Bernstein insists, unlike Hegel, Gadamer does not regard truth as the whole revealed in science; and, in relation to Heidegger, Gadamer is hesitant to follow his meditations in the way that Heidegger himself would.[7] In this blending of motifs, Bernstein thinks that what Gadamer is appealing to is a concept of truth that comes down to what can be validated argumentatively by the community of interpreters who open themselves to what is "handed down" to us.[8]

In opting for this Rortyan-pragmatic line, however, Bernstein shows more prejudice than insight into the character of the hermeneutic event of truth.[9] Bernstein's description is hardly sufficient to account for what goes on in the transformative unfolding of dialogue; moreover, it does not help to explain the connection between truth and art. Bernstein simply never pursues what the particular unconcealing character of truth is for Gadamer. He fails, in other words, to make explicit the thematic of *recognition* as the particular eventing character of hermeneutic truth.

This thematic is itself supported theoretically by the analysis of the metaphysics of the beautiful that occurs at the end of *Truth and Method*. There Gadamer is actually more explicit about the character of hermeneutic truth—albeit in an oblique fashion—than Bernstein admits. What I want to do in this paper is, first, to situate more precisely the question of truth—as Gadamer himself would have us do—from within the analysis of the beautiful. In doing so, we will then be able to see that the experience of truth in philosophical hermeneutics entails undergoing the experience of an image play. Second, following the title of this paper, I want to provide an interpretation of this image play that will help us make sense of the thematic of recognition that characterizes the specific dimension of truth in hermeneutic experience.

THE BEING OF THE BEAUTIFUL

Gadamer begins the last section of *Truth and Method* by summarizing his just completed analysis of language in relation to hermeneutic experience as a whole. Everything that is language, Gadamer insists, has a speculative unity whereby that which comes into language is not something pre-given before language. This means that the being of language is self-presentation. In order to explicate the self-presentational character of the being of language, which means here the dimension of self-showing in hermeneutic experience whereby the claim to truth has its force, Gadamer introduces the classical conception of the beautiful as analogous to the specific character of the event structure of understanding.

What appeals to Gadamer in the classical conception of the beautiful is precisely its relation to the structure of being. Nowhere is this classical conception better illustrated than in the myth of human destiny in Plato's *Phaedrus*. To the soul, whose vision is clouded and that has, at best, a fleeting memory of true being, is given the experience of the beautiful as the means of rejoining the ascent to the vault of the heavens. Beauty, we are told, is the one *eidos* that preserves something of the former lustrousness of an Idea; it shines forth in the visible stimulating love in us: "For the beautiful alone this has been ordained, to be most manifest [*ekphainestaton*] to sense and most lovely."[10]

The special status afforded the beautiful means that the beautiful functions to mediate between the intelligible and appearance. It can do so precisely because shining forth constitutes the being of the beautiful in such a way that being present belongs decisively to the being of the beautiful. The beautiful itself, as an *eidos*, rises above the flux of appearances; and yet, it is itself that shines forth in the appearance. As that which is most radiant [*ekphainestaton*], the beautiful is the appearance itself.[11] The distinctive feature of the beautiful, then, in contrast even to the good, is that of itself it presents itself; it makes itself immediately evident. But this means, at the same time, that the beautiful does not simply mediate between intelligible and appearance. It collapses the distinction between the difference; it collapses the distinction between the illuminated and the illuminating. It is the condition of the *eidos* itself to shine, to present itself, and thus it is not something that exists through something else.

How then is this illuminating character of the beautiful analogous to the event structure of hermeneutic experience, to an encounter with something that asserts its own truth? Gadamer's claim is that the beautiful, in connection with the comprehensibility of the intelligible, is *einleuchtend*. Literally, a "shining in," its meaning is conveyed in the expression "an enlightening experience." The enlightening refers to the fact that something has come to light in the sense that something becomes *clear*. Such clarity does not result from methodological procedure. Thus it stands in contrast to Cartesian certainty that marks the outcome of methodological procedure. The clarity of *einleuchtend* comes upon us, perhaps even surprises us. Gadamer thinks that one finds this notion of clarity in rhetoric. The art of rhetoric, which ties itself to the immediacy of its effect, advocates a claim to truth that defends the probable, the *eikos* [verisimile], and that which is convincing to ordinary reason (WM 460; TM 485). The true has the mark of "true shining" [*Wahrscheinlich*], asserting itself of its own merit, rather than certainty: an argument may have something true about it even though we may argue against it. The way in which what is true is compatible with the whole of what we consider to be correct is left open. Similarly, the beautiful engages us and charms us, without being immediately integrated into the whole of our orientations.

In this dimension of shining we already begin to see the connection, which was always evident for Plato, between beauty and truth. The enlightening as clear has something true about it; the shining in is a shining forth [*aletheia*]. What is most intriguing for us here, however, to go back to what was said earlier, is the manner of the shining forth. For the beautiful, it makes no difference whether it itself or its image [*Abbild*] appears. For Gadamer, this unique situation has a distinctive consequence: the being of the beautiful, this self-presentational shining forth, must always be understood ontologically as image [*Bild*] (WM 462; TM 487).

The whole issue of the shining forth of the self-presentational character of being (and ultimately the question of truth) turns on Gadamer's understanding of image [*Bild*]. Clearly, in this context, image is no longer the distorted copy that appears as semblance, an image with something behind or beneath it. But precisely how image is to be understood requires that we retrieve an analysis that Gadamer presents much earlier in *Truth and Method*.

In discussing the ontological valence of the picture [*Bild*], Gadamer is quick to point out that the problematic character of a picture is derived, as it was for Plato, from the problem of the original picture [*Urbild*]. The concept of a picture, linked to the concept of (re)presentation [*Darstellung*], is a form of imitation. What Gadamer wants to show is that the presentation of the picture, as in a framed painting, is related to the original in a different way than the relation of the copy to the original.

Gadamer has already been able to show that for the performing arts the mimetic presentation is not a mere copy. In drama, "the world that appears in the play of presentation does not stand like a copy next to the real world, but is that world in the heightened truth of its being" (WM 131; TM 137). A transformation occurs in dramatic play: what is meant is intrinsic to the presentation and only in a secondary, critical stance do we ask about the identity of the player or the quality of the production (those comparative questions that force a distinction between copy and original).

What is ontologically true of the performing arts is true of the work of art in general: every production is a self-presentation having its *telos* within itself. Such a claim is hardly striking at all if one recognizes, as Gadamer does, that this presentational character of art is what is expressed by the original concept of *mimesis*. Originally, the concept of mimesis has little to do with the imitation of something that is already familiar to us. Rather, it pertains to the way in which something is presented such that it is actually present in sensuous abundance.[12] The mimetic character of the presentation, the "copying" character of the presentation, is simply the appearance [*Erscheinung*] of what is presented. And even more so, "without being imitated in the work, the world does not exist as it exists in the work" (WM 131; TM 137). Consequently, it is possible to say in some sense that the work of art does not refer *to* something because the presence of what is presented stands in its own right as a completed whole in the presentation.

The question now is whether the same analysis can also be applied to the picture [*Bild*]. It would appear that with respect to a picture, copy [*Abbild*] and original [*Urbild*] are quite distinct, since the original picture, unlike dramatic play that has its real being in being performed and thus produced, resists production as self-presentation. But here too the image/original structure collapses. Notice what is entailed in the nature of a copy. Its function is to announce the original by resembling it. The measure of its success is that one recognizes the original in the copy. That is, although a copy exists in its own right, its nature is to cancel out its independent existence by pointing beyond itself. An ideal copy, then, would be the mirror image "for its being can effectively disappear; it exists only for someone who looks into the mirror, and is nothing beyond its pure appearance" (WM 131; TM 138). But in truth it is no picture or copy at all, for it has no existence for itself. And yet, that we speak here of a mirror *image* and not a copy is not insignificant. "For in the mirror image the entity itself appears in the image so that we have the thing itself in the mirror image," whereas a copy "must always be regarded in relation to the thing it means" (WM 131; TM 138).

A picture is not itself a copy since it is not intended to be canceled out. Similar to the mode of being of performance, the picture itself is what is meant; thus one is not directed away from it to some anterior or posterior presentation. This feature of presentation is the positive distinction of being a picture as opposed to being a mere reflected image.

And yet, as presentation, the picture is not the same as what is presented. According to Gadamer, "even today's mechanical techniques can be used in an artistic way, when they bring out something that is not to be found simply by looking [*Anblick*]" (WM 133; TM 140). Of course, such a picture remains limited by the original, but the relation to the original here is quite different from a copy-original relation. In the case of the picture, the relation is *no longer one-sided*. Since the picture has its own reality, one can say that the original presents itself in the presentation. In the case of the copy, the original is always inferred and has its semblance in the copy. The presenting in the picture is no incidental occurrence; it belongs to the picture's actual being. Every picture is an ontological event that in its presentation produces an increase in being. In a sense the picture is the original's emanation.

This conception of presentation in which the picture stands in a unique relation to the original is not novel. Gadamer thinks we find this same mode of being in the concept of *Repräsentation* [representation] in canon law. *Repraesentare* means to make present, and for canon law this meant legal representation. But "the important thing about the legal concept of representation is that the *persona repraesentata* is put forward and presented [*Vor- und Dargestellte*], and yet the *Repräsentant*, who is exercising the former's rights, is *dependent* upon him" (WM 134; TM 141). This concept of *repraesentation* suggests something even more about the relation of image and original. Now we can say that the picture has an independence that effects the original, "for strictly speaking it is only through the picture that the original actually becomes original [*Ur-bilde*]" (WM 135; TM 142). The religious picture is a good illustration of what is meant here. The appearance of the divine acquires its picturalness [*Bildhaftigkeit*] only through the word and the picture. The religious picture is not a copy of a copied being, "but is in ontological communion with what is copied" (WM 136; TM 143). The pictural image is thus not an imitative illustration, but allows what it presents to be for the first time what it is.

If we take this analysis of the pictural image as indicative of what Gadamer means by the self-presentational character of being, as an event by which the world comes into being, then self-presentation can be described as a play of image. And what is true of the visual image would also be true of the word, for the word is not simply a sign, but more like an image [*Bild*]. Consistent with Gadamer's claim that as living language the being of language is in conversation, this means that the structure of being, the intelligible, is not simply copied in language. Rather, in language the intelligible forms itself.[13] In the word, as in the beautiful in its shining forth, there is a showing forth.

Thus, in words, too, there is an image play. Insofar as every body of words is but a phase in the execution of a communicative event, the image play is nothing less than a site of performance. This site is such that, consistent with the character of living language, there is no first word, just as there is no last word. Most decisively then, in the same way that we are caught up in our speaking, we can say that the image play, the site of performance, is something in which we find ourselves entangled. At the end of *Truth and Method* Gadamer writes:

> When we understand a text, what is meaningful engages [*einnimmt*] us, just as the beautiful engages us. It has asserted itself and engaged us before we can come to ourselves and be in a position to test the claim to meaning that it makes. What we encounter in the experience of the beautiful and in understanding the meaning of tradition really has something of the truth of play about it. In understanding we are drawn into an event of truth and arrive, as it were, too late, if we want to know what we are supposed to believe. (WM 465; TM 490)

In such entanglement, we are not simply bound to an image play, we are also bound to the mimetic field in which the image play is located.

But precisely how is this mimetic field to be understood, this sphere of replay and repetition that has entered into the collapse of the image/original distinction? The answer to this question allows us to make a connection between the positions of Gadamer and Derrida. Gadamer would want to recognize the paradox of mimesis that Derrida finds lying within Plato's metaphysics, namely, that the origin of truth (which is beyond imitation) cannot be understood without the mimetic activity of repetition (in the form of recollection).[14] Philosophical hermeneutics itself escapes the paradox by refusing to posit an origin of truth beyond imitation. Consequently, Gadamer recognizes that the act of figuration [*Gebilde*] can no longer rest on the priority of the imitated over imitation. This is precisely what the "truth of play" is all about: an image play, whether conversation or drama, is essentially a performance that has no being, no substantiality, outside the performing.

At the same time, however, Derrida's own deconstruction of mimesis takes it in a direction that Gadamer cannot follow. For Derrida, the mimetic field produces no upsurge of sense in the determination of real being. Following Mallarmé, Derrida likens mimetic action to a perpetual allusion that constantly displaces its referent. Mimetic activity must defer any reference to what lies outside the activity. It is thus understood to be a movement of *différance* that serves to undo all presence and centering. This means that it is not just the truth of *adequatio*, which structures the image/original distinction, that Derrida would undercut in the mimetic field. Derrida would also undo the truth of *aletheia* insofar as the mimetic field does not produce a presentation of the thing itself, a showing forth of being. But to accept this latter consequence of the mimetic activity would be to undo the point to which we have just been led by Gadamer's analysis of the image.

There is a question of truth in hermeneutic experience, but it is certainly not that of *adequatio* whereby there is an agreement between the re-presentation and the thing, for the character of the image play is no longer tied to the image/original distinction. Philosophical hermeneutics, in other words, is not engaged in a metaphysical quest of seeing truth itself instead of an image. Rather, in its own paradoxical way, it is engaged in precisely the inverse: of getting entangled in the image that entangles us in truth. It must be added that this is no simple reversal that would now subscribe to a priority of the imagination within the still constituted framework of truth as origin. Gadamer is not positing a transcendental imagination that would apprehend the original in intuition or suggesting that art is the productive transformation of nature, as in Kant's aesthetics. Gadamer is too Greek to be this Romantic. But philosophical hermeneutics is concerned with truth.

Thus, for Gadamer, the mimetic field, although endless by virtue of its practical performance, is not a house of mirrors without referent, an endless play of a copy copying a copy. Rather, to be caught within the mimetic field *is* to be caught in a play of truth. The question, which is the question with which we began, is that of the character of truth in the image play. Ultimately this is the question of the difference not only between Gadamer and Derrida, but also between Gadamer and Heidegger with respect to the question of truth.

THE IMAGING OF TRUTH

Without *arche* or *telos* extending beyond the mimetic field, the image play as a play of truth suggests that what transpires in language, art, and all of the other dimensions of hermeneutic experience is a constant entanglement of *thick* images in which the intelligible is itself entangled. Such entanglement is prescribed not only by the character of the image, but also by the character of hermeneutic experience that always begins with "a supporting mutual understanding" [*ein tragendes Einverständnis*].

> There is always a world already interpreted, already organized into its basic relations, into which experience steps as something new, upsetting what has led our expectations and undergoing reorganization itself in the upheaval. Misunderstanding and strangeness are not the first factors, so that avoiding misunderstanding can be regarded as the specific task of hermeneutics. Just the reverse is the case. Only the support of the familiar and common understanding makes possible the venture into the alien, and lifting up of something out of the alien, and thus the broadening and enrichment of our own experience of the world.[15]

We are, by virtue of our beginnings, already in the truth. We bear witness to our entanglement with truth when we find ourselves caught up in the effort of finding the common ground whereby what is said by the word or presented by the performance speaks in a new voice. In this effort at understanding, it is not a matter of disentangling the image play, of retreating from the entanglement and image, but of a working [*Wirken*] in which an imaging shines forth. This is not to say that truth can be simply identified with anything that makes sense, that state of being lifted out of the alien. In such a claim, the matter of truth amounts to nothing, and it does not fully take into consideration the critical analysis that is part of the movement between the strange and familiar. Even more so, we must be careful not to reinscribe a more sophisticated notion of *adequatio* into the movement between the strange and familiar. A correspondence will always require an alignment to a reference point, a correlation from which the measure of the thing is taken. But this account of truth is insufficient to account for the dynamic of the image that is always bound to the play of figuration within hermeneutic experience.

We can go farther, but certainly not without some reservation, in determining the character of the imaging of truth if we employ a metaphor appropriate to thick images, namely, depth.[16] A thick image is one with great
depth. In its depth, however, it can be dense in the sense of abundant or
muddy and obtuse. Following this metaphor, we can describe the moment of
truth in hermeneutic experience in two ways. First, in the moment of truth
there is something fitting. In the logic of question and answer in which we
are caught within the mimetic field, for example, we can speak of a fitting
response. In conversation we throw out statements along the way in a double
sense: we put statements forward, but we also discard or abandon statements
along the way since some statements are found to lead us nowhere. Fitting,
then, pertains to a certain disentanglement, a separating out in which something comes together, a moment of coherence not of wholeness, but that
forms a whole in coming together as it does. The right word, the word heard
by the inner ear, fits or rings true. The fitting pertains to the action of a text,
as the action of the image play in the mimetic field, upon the hearer.

   In this context, it is even possible to speak about a notion of falsifiability
in hermeneutic experience. An interpretation becomes false whenever the
Sache breaks through in conversation to show itself as other than it first presented itself. The *Sache*, though, is not to be understood as that which is self-
same within the multiplicity of interpretation. Philosophical hermeneutics
is not subscribing to a metaphysics of a plurality of essence, that is, the self-
same showing itself in many ways, as one could read in cursory fashion, for
example, Gadamer's notion of tradition. The *Sache* is the singular datum:
this text, this work, this spoken word. Therefore, the recognition within the
mimetic field of the image play is simply the recognition of what is presented
in its presentation. This does not mean that recognition is merely a matter of
seeing something that we have seen before. Rather, in recognition we cog-
nize something *as* something that we have already seen in our entangled
condition. According to Gadamer, the enigma of knowing lies entirely in this
"as" that, in the process of recognition, lets us see things "in terms of what is
permanent and essential in them, unencumbered by the contingent circumstances in which they were seen before and are seen again."[17]

   At the same time—and here we point to the second way of describing the
moment of truth—the thick image suggests that truth is played out within
the continuum of empty and full.[18] The mimetic field, we should recall, is
such that in the image play something comes forth in sensuous abundance.
Inasmuch as the work of art does not simply refer to something, because
what it refers to is actually there, its productive character can be described
as an "increase in being." The determination of truth in the work of art

appears to be pointed at this overflow; it has to do with the possibility of saying more as the landscape in a picture becomes more by being picturesque. Similarly, in the virtuality of living speech, we are "full up," so to speak, and yet always able to say more. When we say what we mean, we are at once holding together what is said "with an infinity of what is not said in one unified meaning" (WM 444; TM 469). We can see more precisely what is meant here by again noting how there is a notion of falsifiability at work in our interpretative efforts. Error coincides with the empty; it occurs when the interpretation comes to nothing.[19] In the case of the work of art, the empty is imitation in its usual meaning; imitative art is no longer alive. Of course, what constitutes being full—the moment of truth—is not determined by a quantitative mark, but occurs whenever the *Sache* speaks again in a new voice.

In both descriptions, the moment of truth—and the conception of error—is linked to whether or not something actually takes place, to the performance that occurs when one is drawn into the experience with the work or when one responds to the voice of the other. With this notion of performance, we should not forget the connection that Gadamer has already made to the tradition of rhetoric.[20] From this perspective, one could argue that in hermeneutic experience we come back to a richer notion of truth as *veritas* (to the notion of truth as real) and *verificare* (to the notion of affirming and attesting). In the presentation of art, for example, Gadamer suggests that the presentation intends to be so true that we do not advert to the fact that it is not real. The work of art is true because it is a real image. In undergoing an experience with art, then, we "verify" it. This is not a matter of confirming but of testifying to the real; it is a matter of bearing witness to what is by being drawn into the image play, of making the matter itself real through the practical performance of play.

This notion of truth is suggested by Gadamer in *The Relevance of the Beautiful* in response to the question of the meaning of truth in poetic language. Poetic saying, he tells us, "says so completely what it is that we do not need to add anything beyond what is said in order to accept it in its reality as language."[21] The word of the poet is autonomous in the sense that it is self-fulfilling, bearing witness to itself. It thus does not admit of anything that could verify it in the ordinary sense, for example, a confirmation by external authority. The poem is not judged against the world outside it; on the contrary, a world is constructed from within the poem itself.

What is true of poetic language could also be said of all speaking inasmuch as poetic language simply "stands out as the highest fulfillment of the revealing which is the achievement of all speech."[22] Gadamer himself notes that in terms of the living language of the early Greeks, truth has a double sense. In connection with speech, *aletheia* is openness where being open means to say what one means. In *telling* the truth, we say what we mean. This is supplemented by a further sense of truth in which "*something* 'says' what it 'means': whatever shows itself to be what it is, is true."[23] Thus when we say "real gold" we mean it is gold; it is true gold as the Greeks say *alethes*.[24]

In describing truth in this way, however, *alethes* is understood to be equivalent to its Latin translation; the true is *veritas*, not in its medieval determination as a kind of *adequatio*, but as simply the actual nature of the thing. Here the point of difference between Gadamer and Heidegger becomes most apparent. For Gadamer, it is certainly not a matter of thinking the withdrawal that demarcates the region of the open. Nor is it enough to say that for hermeneutic experience, truth is openness as this occurs when words stand forth and show things as they are. The matter of truth is rather a matter of the thematic of speaking itself that holds the question of truth within it in an unthematized manner. The early Greeks understood this quite well: without any concern for the structuring of the true, for what pertains to *aletheia* per se, Nestor asks in the *Iliad*, upon hearing the thunder of the running horses, whether he is wrong or "speaking the true [*e etumon ereo*]."[25] Nestor asks if he speaks a true thing, if the matter is true or real [*etios*]. The Gadamerian hermeneut repeats this gesture: one stands in the truth, verifies it, only when one finds the right word, only when one says what one means. One stands in the truth, bears witness to it, only when the thing, the art work, says what it means [*etumon ereo*]. In such standing, we bear witness to our own being as well; the image play entangles us in its entanglement.[26]

Thus, the imaging of truth for Gadamer is not about how things come to show themselves as they do. It is not about the conditions for the rupturing in the folds of being (as Heidegger takes up this project). It is rather about the art of saying. It is about what Cicero understood to be a task of the orator: *consule veritatem*, consider the etymology. But *veritatem* here is a translation of *etumon*.[27] The task of the orator is to consider the real being. That is all anyone can do.

NOTES

1. I am not the first commentator to make note of this fact. See, for example, Richard Bernstein, "From Hermeneutics to Praxis," in *Philosophical Profiles: Essays in a Pragmatic Mode* (Philadelphia: University of Pennsylvania Press, 1986); Jean Grondin, "Hermeneutic Truth and Its Historical Presuppositions: A Possible Bridge between

Analysis and Hermeneutics," in *Anti-Foundationalism and Practical Reasoning*, ed. Evan Simpson (Edmonton: Academic Printing & Publishing, 1987); Brice Wachterhauser, "Must We Be What We Say? Gadamer on Truth in the Human Sciences," in *Hermeneutics and Modern Philosophy*, ed. Brice Wachterhauser (Albany: SUNY Press, 1986); Francis J. Ambrosio, "Dawn and Dusk: Gadamer and Heidegger on Truth," *Man and World* 19 (1986): 21–53.

2. Hans-Georg Gadamer, *Wahrheit und Methode* (Tübingen: J. C. B. Mohr, 1960), 109. English translation, *Truth and Method*, second revised edition, ed. by Joel Weinsheimer and Donald Marshall (New York: Crossroads, 1989), 114. Hereafter WM and TM respectively. In the introduction to *Truth and Method*, Gadamer states hermeneutics' involvement with truth more generally: "[The experience of art, philosophy, and history] are all modes of experience in which a truth is communicated that cannot be verified by methodological means proper to science" (WM xxviii; TM xii).

3. There is nothing in *Truth and Method* that would suggest that Gadamer does not support the claim that method is also a place of truth. Paul Ricoeur, more than anyone else, is responsible for this confusion over the title of Gadamer's work when he writes: "The title of his work . . . confronts the Heideggerian concept of truth with the Diltheyan concept of method. The question is to what extent the work earns the right to be called 'truth *and* method,' or whether it should not be called 'truth *or* method'." "The Task of Hermeneutics," *Philosophy Today* 17.2 (1973): 112.

4. Jean Grondin, "Hermeneutical Truth and Its Historical Presuppositions," in *Anti-Foundationalism and Practical Reasoning* (Edmonton: Academic Printing and Publishing, 1987), 50. See also his *Hermeneutische Wahrheit? Zum Wahreheitsbegriff Hans-Georg Gadamers* (Königstein: Forum Academicum, 1982), 1–8.

5. The commentators who note the lack of an explicit account of truth in Gadamer's project are the same ones who insist that truth in philosophical hermeneutics is simply Heideggerian *aletheia* with some variation. See note 1 above.

6. Martin Heidegger, "The Origin of the Work of Art," in *Poetry Language Thought*, trans. Albert Hofstadter (New York: Harper & Row, 1971).

7. Bernstein argues, quoting from a text of Gadamer, that Gadamer is more concerned with what is feasible here and now rather than with that meditation on the cosmic night of the forgetfulness of being. See *Philosophical Profiles*, 106–7.

8. See *Philosophical Profiles*, 108.

9. The prejudice pertains to the emphasis on the community of inquiry, to the emphasis on conversation as such. Bernstein insists that "we can only seek to justify claims to truth by giving the strongest arguments that we can to show why something is true—and this is in fact what Gadamer himself does." *Philosophical Profiles*, 108. What needs to be seen is precisely how the event of truth is more than this.

10. Plato, *Phaedrus*, trans. H. Fowler, Loeb Classical Library (Cambridge Mass.: Harvard University Press, 1977), 250d.

11. Heidegger makes this connection between the beautiful and appearance in "The Origin of the Work of Art." The beautiful as shining forth, as coming to show itself, does not occur apart from truth as the unconcealment of being: "Appearance—as this being of truth in the work and as work—is beauty." *Poetry Language Thought*, 81.

12. In his essay "The Festive Character of the Theater," published in *The Relevance of the Beautiful and Other Essays*, trans. Nicholas Walker (Cambridge: Cambridge University Press, 1986), Gadamer writes: "All true imitation is a transformation that does not simply present again something that is already there. It is a kind of transformed reality in which the transformation points back to what has been transformed in and through it. It is a transformed reality because it brings before us intensified possibilities never seen before" (p. 64).

13. Gadamer writes: "To come into language does not mean that a second being is acquired. Rather, what something presents itself as belongs to its own being. Thus everything that is language has a speculative unity: it contains a distinction, that between its being and its presentations of itself, but this is a distinction that is not really a distinction at all" (WM 450; TM 475).

14. See Jacques Derrida, "The Double Session," in *Dissemination*, trans. Barbara Johnson (Chicago: University of Chicago Press, 1981).

15. Gadamer, *Philosophical Hermeneutics*, trans. and ed. David E. Linge (Berkeley: University of California Press, 1976), 15. The German text of the essay quoted from *Philosophical Hermeneutics*, "*Die Universalität des hermeneutischen Problems*," appears in Gadamer's *Gesammelte Werke*, Band 2 (Tübingen: J. C. B. Mohr, 1986), 230.

16. The reservation concerns the way in which the metaphor of depth could be construed as a reintroduction of origin and the notion of a recovery from oblivion. John Caputo, for example, insists that Gadamer's hermeneutics is simply a hermeneutics of retrieval of a deep truth. See *Radical Hermeneutics* (Bloomington: Indiana University Press, 1987).

17. The *Relevance of the Beautiful*, 99. Gadamer makes no further elaboration of the connection between recognition and the "as" in this context. One can only assume that were he to say more he would repeat the analysis of the as-structure that Heidegger gives in *Being and Time*, while at the same time collapsing the distinctions that Heidegger makes there. For Gadamer, the point would seem to be that recognition, which is the knowing appropriate to the universality of interpretation, functions in a similar way to the as-structure; namely, it constitutes the interpretation whereby something is explicitly understood.

18. This notion of a continuum of empty and full can be correlated to Gadamer's notion of empty and fulfilled time. See *"Über leere und erfüllte Zeit," Kleine Schriften III* (Tübingen: J. C. B. Mohr, 1972), 221–36. In *The Relevance of the Beautiful and Other Essays*, Gadamer considers these two fundamental ways of experiencing time in order to describe the kind of recurrence that belongs to the festival and the work of art in general. Empty time is time that is at our disposal ("I have time for something"). Such time has to be spent; it is empty and needs to be filled. In both "bustle and boredom" we fill our time. In contrast to this, time can be experienced as fulfilled or autonomous as in the case of the festival that fulfills every moment of its duration. "This fulfillment does not come about because someone has empty time to fill. On the contrary, the time only becomes festive with the arrival of the festival" (*The Relevance of the Beautiful*, 42).

19. "Indeed, what characterizes the arbitrariness of inappropriate fore-meanings if not that they come to nothing in being worked out (WM 252; TM 267)?

20. The connection between hermeneutic truth and rhetoric is also made by Gianni Vattimo in *The End of Modernity: Nihilism and Hermeneutics in Postmodern Culture*, trans. Jon R. Snyder (Baltimore: The Johns Hopkins University Press, 1988). See pp. 130–44. Vattimo supports this claim by quoting from Gadamer's essay on the Frankfurt School criticism of hermeneutics, *Rhetorik, Hermeneutik und Ideologiekritik*. This essay appears in translation as "The Scope and Function of Hermeneutical Reflection" in *Philosophical Hermeneutics*, 18–43. The passage Vattimo quotes makes essentially the same point that is made in the discussion of rhetoric in *Truth and Method* that we have already made note of above, namely, that the tradition of rhetoric advocates a claim for truth that would defend the probable. Vattimo's interpretation of this sense of truth, however, is not without its difficulties. He characterizes the common language that serves as the content for rhetorical persuasion as a "collective conscious-

ness" and suggests that the moment of recognition is the acceptance of this collective consciousness. Such an interpretation makes hermeneutics susceptible to the charge of being an apology for what already exists. Vattimo's reading seems to disregard Gadamer's own comments made in response to this Habermasian charge.

21. *The Relevance of the Beautiful*, 110.
22. Ibid., 112.
23. Ibid., 108.
24. It is interesting to note that Gadamer uses the same example as Heidegger does in his essay "On the Essence of Truth." For Heidegger, though, this example is used as a point of departure for the question concerning truth: "what is true about genuine gold . . . cannot be demonstrated merely by its actuality." "On the Essence of Truth," trans. John Sallis, in *Martin Heidegger Basic Writings*, ed. David F. Krell (New York: Harper & Row, 1977), 119.
25. *Iliad*, book X, 534.
26. In the end, for Gadamer, the truth of poetry—and one would infer that this would also pertain to all speaking that "verifies" through its power of realization—consists in creating a "hold upon nearness." At the end of his essay, "On the Contribution of Poetry to the Search for Truth," Gadamer describes what this "hold upon nearness" means:

> The word of the poet does not simply continue this process of *Einhausung*, or "making ourselves at home." Instead it stands over against this process like a mirror held up to it. But what appears in the mirror is not the world, nor this or that thing in the world, but rather this nearness or familiarity itself in which we stand for a while. . . . This is not a romantic theory, but a straightforward description of the fact that language gives all of us our access to a world in which certain special forms of human experience arise: the religious tidings that proclaim salvation, the legal judgment that tells us what is right and what is wrong in our society, the poetic word that by *being there bears witness to our own being* (emphasis added). *The Relevance of the Beautiful*, 115.

27. See *Harper's Latin Dictionary* (New York: American Book Co., 1907).

CHAPTER 12

Das Einleuchtende
The Enlightening Aspect of the Subject Matter

LAWRENCE K. SCHMIDT

A reading of *Truth and Method* clearly indicates why Gadamer does not consider the scientific method or any other method to be the primary means of
warranting truth. What is less clear is how philosophical hermeneutics
understands the establishment of hermeneutic truth by means of a discipline of questioning and investigating.[1] Also well-known are the epistemological quagmires that some interpreters have found in philosophical
hermeneutics. These range from accusations that philosophical hermeneutics is not deconstructive enough and so conceals a hidden foundationalism
to charges that philosophical hermeneutics is too relativistic and so cannot
legitimately speak about truth. For example, Richard Rorty classifies
Gadamer as a "weak textualist" as opposed to a "strong textualist."[2] The
weak textualist is said to be a "decoder" and "just one more victim of realism, of the 'metaphysics of presence'."[3] Similarly, John Caputo echoes
Joseph Margolis's charge that Gadamer is a "closet essentialist."[4] Caputo
concludes that Gadamer's positive move toward openness to the other is
"undermined by a metaphysics of the tradition inspired by Hegel and
German Romanticism and by a metaphysics of the dialogical soul inspired
by Plato."[5] Jacques Derrida suggests that philosophical hermeneutics has
not progressed far enough along the path of deconstruction due to Gadamer's
reliance on a particular description of experience in his work that Derrida
suspects of importing a metaphysical element.[6] On the other hand, Jürgen
Habermas, in his review of *Truth and Method*, charges that "Gadamer has

failed to recognize the power of reflection that develops in understanding"[7] and, therefore, has lost the possibility of criticizing an inherited but false tradition. E. D. Hirsch argues that philosophical hermeneutics does not present "a genuinely stable norm [so] we cannot even in principle make a valid choice between two differing interpretations, and we are left with the consequence that a text means nothing in particular at all."[8]

This paper advances the concept of the *Einleuchtende*, the enlightening, as that conceptual element within philosophical hermeneutics that can answer the question of how hermeneutic truth may be attested to or warranted within the event of truth. In the first part, I will review those elements of philosophical hermeneutics that have led me to this concept. In the second part, I will examine more carefully the concept of the enlightening. This will be done with reference to its Greek roots and to Husserl's concept of evidence. In the final section, I will briefly indicate how this concept may help one out of the above mentioned quagmires.

THE LEGITIMATION OF *VORURTEILE*

Das Vorurteil, the prejudice, is the central concept in hermeneutic understanding.[9] Gadamer initiates his discussion of the theory of hermeneutic experience by introducing this term as a replacement for Heidegger's "fore-structures" of understanding. Gadamer sees the task of hermeneutic understanding also to have been formulated by Heidegger, for he quotes the famous passage from *Being and Time* in which Heidegger states that the circle of understanding is not vicious and that positive possibilities of knowing exist

> only when, in our interpretation, we have understood that our first, last, and constant task is never to allow our fore-having, fore-sight, and fore-conception to be presented to us by fancies and popular conceptions, but rather to make the scientific theme secure by working out these fore-structures in terms of the things themselves [*die Sachen selbst*].[10]

The task of hermeneutic understanding is, therefore, to explicate how the interpreter is able to secure those fore-structures by grounding them in the subject matter or the things themselves. Having rehabilitated the concept of prejudice by demonstrating that there are legitimate prejudices that aid understanding, as well as illegitimate prejudices that hinder understanding, Gadamer poses the following two, basic epistemological questions: "Where will the legitimacy of prejudices find its justification? What differentiates legitimate prejudices from all those numerous prejudices whose overcoming is the unquestioned task of critical reason?" (WM 261; TM 246).

Therefore, the question of hermeneutic truth will be answered by examining the legitimation of prejudices within hermeneutic experience. Legitimation will occur when the prejudice is grounded in the *Sache selbst*. One may demonstrate that the prejudices that one receives in acculturation and in learning a language form one's horizon of possible meaning; that the fusion of horizons concerns the alteration of one's prejudices; that effective history influences understanding by means of propagating prejudices; and that the dialectic of question and answer concerns the examination of prejudices. Further, I believe it is clear how one's embeddedness within a temporal-linguistic horizon, that is, a set of prejudices, prevents any ahistorical or absolute position from which a final truth can be discovered. If so, what needs clarification for our theme is the relationship between prejudices and the *Sachen selbst* within language.

Examining the image [*Abbild*] and sign [*Zeichen*] theories of language using Plato's *Cratylus*, Gadamer concludes, that "language is something other than a mere sign system used to indicate a present whole. A word is not just a sign. In a sense difficult to comprehend it is also something almost like an image" (WM 393f.; TM 377). The rejection of these two theories concerning the relationship between a word and its referent is essential for this discussion, since it implies a rejection of two epistemological theories and indicates the direction from which an answer to the question of truth will come. For the moment, it will be helpful to consider a prejudice to be a word and the *Sache selbst* to be its referent.[11] In denying the sign theory, Gadamer is rejecting the traditional epistemological image that one is able to have a nonlinguistic cognition of the referent, the *Sache*, and then later attach a linguistic sign, or prejudice, to this cognition, either establishing or following a convention. In this theory of language, the question of truth concerns guaranteeing that the conventionally correct correspondence has been made between a nonlinguistic perception or cognition and a linguistic sign. In denying the image theory, Gadamer is rejecting the epistemological stance that language perfectly mirrors reality. In such a theory, there could be no significant epistemological question concerning the match between word and referent since language and reality would necessarily always correspond.[12] Anything said would be true.

Gadamer's positive theory of language includes elements of both of the rejected theories. As in the image theory, the word and its referent are intimately connected—language partially mirrors being. On the other hand, Gadamer's position is similar to the sign theory in that mistakes in the connection between language and its referent are possible. It differs from the sign theory, however, insofar as there is no nonlinguistic cognition of the referent to which some linguistic sign could correspond. So "Being, which can be understood, is language" (WM 450; TM 431). Referring to this statement, Gadamer notes that

> what was implied thereby was that that which is can never be completely understood. . . . That which is to be understood is that which comes into language, but of course it is always that which is taken as something, taken as true [*wahr-genommen*]. This is the hermeneutical dimension in which Being "manifests itself."[13]

Gadamer's discussion of Humboldt and Husserl help to clarify this temporal and finite interrelationship between Being and language, referent and word, the *Sache* and the *Vorurteil*. With Humboldt, Gadamer agrees that any specific language can only present a particular perspective of the world, that is, a linguistic perspective [*Sprachansicht*] is a perspective of the world [*Weltansicht*] (WM 419; TM 401). Gadamer differs from Humboldt in rejecting the idea of a common spiritual power that functions behind all languages and that could be discovered through comparative linguistics. Therefore, any human language at some particular time can only represent a particular worldview. In other words, any specific horizon of meaning as established by a set of prejudices is necessarily a perspective of a particular world, a particular perspective of the subject matter.

In Husserl's discussion of the perception of a table, each perception is a perspective modification [*Abschattung*] of the trans-phenomenal table. Gadamer argues that each particular linguistic perspective is analogous to Husserl's perspective modifications insofar as each presents only a perspective of the whole.[14] He differs from Husserl in rejecting a transcendental consciousness that is capable of constituting the intentional object (table). For Gadamer, there is no means by which one could hope to escape human finitude or the *Sprachansicht* and arrive at being-in-itself. One's linguistic horizon, however, is not a final limitation, since the linguistic horizon may change through the process Gadamer describes as the legitimation of prejudices in the fusion of horizons. This demonstrates, for our discussion of truth, that any "correct" and linguistically structured human cognition, since it is limited by the particular linguistic perspective of the interpreter at a particular time due to one's set of prejudices, is necessarily incomplete;

only a perspective of the subject matter, an *"Ansicht der Sache selbst"* (WM 448; TM 430), can be apprehended.

One more point needs to be mentioned before this section is concluded. The event of truth is experienced by the interpreter as a sudden crystallization of meaning. It is an experience in the primary and negative sense, that is, an experience that differs from our previous experiences. It is unexpected and, strictly speaking, cannot be repeated.[15] Gadamer compares this experience to Aristotle's image of an army in rout that turns and, in an unpredictable manner, comes to stand again as a whole (WM 335; TM 316). Gadamer also refers to another image offered by Aristotle who described "the freezing of a liquid when it is shaken as a *schlagartigen Umschlag*, a sudden reversal that comes like a blow from without. It is like this with the blowlike suddenness of understanding."[16] The event of truth occurs in an inscrutable manner and suddenly overcomes the interpreter. Further, the event of truth is a speculative act of self-presentation by the thing itself. A view of the subject matter is mirrored in the language of the interpreter. It is the subject matter coming-to-be-in-language (WM 450; TM 432). It is primarily an act of the *Sache selbst* rather than an act of the subject (WM 439; TM 421).

Gadamer argues that "understanding is never a subjective relation to a given 'object' but a relation to effective history, and that means it belongs to the being of what will be understood" (WM xix; TM xix). Gadamer discusses this idea in several images: the game that plays, our belongingness to history, the speaking of language, the speculative event, and the beautiful. Thus it is not the interpreter as subject who controls the process of legitimating prejudices. He or she does not and cannot determine or predict before the event of truth what will occur, "for we come too late" (WM 465; TM 446). Rather it is the *Sache selbst*, the subject matter, language, that speaks. The event of truth is linguistic and the ontological significance of language is that the subject matter presents itself and its truth only insofar as it is realizable as a perspective of itself. This does not imply, as has often been thought, that the interpreter has nothing to do and is at the mercy of tradition. The interpreter has the essential task of questioning the prejudices presented (WM 441; TM 422). Not only are the other's prejudices questioned in the light of one's own, but one's own prejudices must be questioned in the light of the prejudices of one's conversation partner. This is essential in establishing the conversation in its proper, human, I-you relationship (WM 343; TM 324). In describing the interpretive process from the point of view of the interpreter, Gadamer recognizes the legitimate role of interpretive methods in exposing meaning, that is, in opening a space for the event of truth (WM 437; TM 419). Methods, however, do not determine truth. Gadamer's thesis is that the use of any method can only occur within the historically bounded situation and that this situation is prior to and so prevents any claim to absolute objectivity by method (WM xvii; TM xvii).

How then does the interpreter come to recognize the correct expression of the subject matter? How is this expression as truth to be distinguished from other expressions that are false? How does the interpreter legitimate the prejudice by grounding it in the *Sache selbst*? How is the interpreter able to attest to truth?

According to my reading, the essence of Gadamer's answer to these questions is that the perspective of the *Sache selbst* is *einleuchtend* (enlightening). In other words, the self-presentation of the *Sache* in the event of understanding is something expressed by this concept "*das Einleuchtende*," which literally means "as light, to penetrate into something." Gadamer writes, "the *eikos*, the *verisimile*, the *Wahr-Scheinliche*, the *Einleuchtende* [enlightening] belong to a series that defends its own correctness against the truth and certainty of the proven and known" (WM 460; TM 441).

The concept "enlightening" has been adopted from the classical metaphysics of light, without any overtones concerning some type of transcendent source of light. It is the beautiful that shines forth of itself. It allows the illuminated to be seen. Gadamer attributes this power to language. It is "the light of the word" (WM 458; TM 440).

THE ENLIGHTENING

To understand better the concept of the enlightening, let me return to the above series of concepts from the rhetorical tradition. In classical Greek, "*eikos*" means "like truth, likely, probable, or reasonable." Gadamer refers to the use of "*eikos*" that means a reasonable justification [*eikos logos*] as opposed to a scientific or deductive one [*alethes logos*]; this is the sense of *eikos* used in the rhetorical tradition.

In his essay "Idea and Reality in Plato's *Timaeus*,"[18] Gadamer discusses the passage in which Plato, in introducing the discussion of the fashioning of this world, writes: "the accounts of that which is copied after the likeness of that Model, and is itself a likeness, will be analogous thereto and possess likelihood [*eikos*]; for as Being is to Becoming, so is Truth to Belief."[19] According to this passage, the possibility of knowing something about the generation of this world can at best be known by means of a likely account or justification, an *eikos logos*, that Gadamer describes as "not a religious one [justification] which relies on traditional authority; rather it is thought to be a matter of logical insight available to anyone."[20] In other passages,[21] Plato continually emphasizes that the justification presented can only be probable [*eikos logos*] and that still higher principles can only be known to a god or the man dear to god (53d). This positive sense of *eikos*, as the most reasonable account possible, is to be contrasted with the negative sense of *eikos*, the probable, according to which one accepts popular arguments and figures of speech where one could and should have employed deductive proofs, as could occur in the field of geometry (see *Theatetus* 162e). These two senses of *eikos* can be related to the positive and negative evaluations of rhetoric that Plato presents in the *Phaedrus* (260ff.).

Aristotle continues this positive sense of *eikos*, although he limits its sphere of application. In the *Prior Analytics*, he states, "a probability [*eikos*] is a generally approved proposition: what men know to happen or not to happen, to be or not to be, for the most part thus and thus, is a probability, e.g. 'the envious hate', 'the beloved show affection'."[22] In the *Rhetoric*,[23] Aristotle points out that rhetoric, as opposed to dialectic, primarily concerns things about which we deliberate and that could be otherwise, thus it concerns what is probable [*eikos*], for example, human actions. The application of the probable to the sphere of human actions links the probable with the enlightening by connecting it with the rationality of *phronesis*. One purpose of Gadamer's discussion of Aristotle's concept of *phronesis* in *Truth and Method* is to indicate that the logic and rationality of hermeneutic understanding is analogous to *phronesis* (WM 295f.; TM 278f.). The objects of concern for *phronesis* can be otherwise than they are and so are distinguished from those of *episteme* that are unchanging.[24] Also, the justifications of *phronesis* are not strict but probable and the conclusions can hold only as a general rule.[25] Aristotle does state[26] that the type of apprehending characteristic for *phronesis* is not the intuition of *nous*. Rather, as the perception of the correctness of what is to be done, it is similar to the mathematical perception that the triangle is the final figure. This seeing or grasping is not a matter of deduction, yet, as in the geometric example, it is also quite true. This perception is also not like sense perception that is more fallible. I would suggest that it is just this type of seeing or grasping of the correctness of what is to be done that is analogous to what is being expressed by the concept of the enlightening.

Aristotle's understanding of the concept of the *eikos logos* establishes the tradition of the correct but only probable arguments in rhetoric. In referring to Aristotle's use of *eikos*, Cicero[27] uses *veri similium* [seemingly valid]. So, although not proven with absolute certainty, the *eikos*, the *verisimile*, or the probable, is able to stand up to testing, is apparently true, and is the most rationally true possible in that area of investigation. It appears as truth or shines forth as truth, the *Wahr-Scheinliche*. Similarly, the enlightening is the shining forth of the probable or likely truth. It is as much truth as we may hope for as human beings. It is reasonably true and capable of withstanding a test.

Further insight into the concept of the enlightening can be attained by contrasting this concept with Husserl's concept of evidence [*Evidenz*]. In the *Logical Investigations*, Husserl identifies truth with an inwardly evident judgment. "*The experience of the agreement* between meaning and what is itself present, meant, between the actual *sense of an assertion* and the self-given *state of affairs*, is inward evidence [*Evidenz*]."[28] Husserl clearly states that he is not referring to a subjective feeling connected to this type of judgment when speaking of evidence. Following Hegel, who claims that consciousness can provide its own criterion since the notion and object are both present in consciousness, Husserl argues that consciousness can compare within itself and with absolute clarity the meaning, intention, or assertion with what is present, the self-given state of affairs. The fulfillment of an intention relates to the self-evident correspondence between the intention and what is presented. Inasmuch as an intention could only be partially fulfilled by the presented, Husserl speaks of "degrees and levels of self-evidence."[29] However, "the *epistemologically pregnant sense* of self-evidence is exclusively concerned with this last unsurpassable goal, *the act of this most perfect synthesis of fulfillment*, which gives to an intention, e.g. the intention of judgment, the absolute fulness of content, the fulness of the object itself."[30]

Tugendhat notes a certain dogmatism in Husserl's early account, which was just presented, but he finds it corrected in Husserl's *Formal and Transcendental Logic*.[31] In that work the concept of evidence is widened to imply future possible confirmation, so "all evidence is relative, but only in relation to new evidence."[32] Even apodictic evidence can be discovered to be in error, but this presupposes an evidence of a similar type upon which the former is seen to be in error.[33] This, Tugendhat argues, does not lead to an empty relativism, but to a historical relativity.[34] In the *Crisis*, however, Husserl bases all truth, including scientific truth, on the evidence present in the life-world. He writes, "the life-world is a realm of original self-evidences. That which is self-evidently given is, in perception, experienced as 'the thing itself' [*es selbst*], in immediate presence, or in memory, remembered as the thing itself."[35] And later, "Having arrived at the ego, one becomes aware of standing within a sphere of self-evidence of such a nature that any attempt to inquire behind it would be absurd."[36]

We may discover both similarities and differences between Husserl's concept of evidence and Gadamer's concept of the enlightening. As in Husserl, there is in Gadamer a close connection between the enlightening and the event of truth. Furthermore, the enlightening, like evidence, is not a subjective emotive state that accompanies truth. The major difference is that Husserl distinguishes two elements in consciousness, the subject's act as the intention and the "object's" act as the given state of affairs. In Gadamer, however, there is no such subject-object duality within consciousness since experience is necessarily already present in language. This is the speculative coming-to-be in language that is experience. Thus the so-called subjective and objective sides are already combined in experience. Therefore, the enlightening cannot refer to the absolute clarity of the conscious awareness of a correspondence or even partial correspondence between an intention and its fulfillment in the self-given state of affairs as it does in Husserl. What is enlightening in the event of truth is not a correspondence between two elements in consciousness. For Gadamer, the enlightening is itself an aspect of the experience. It is also clear that there is nothing in Gadamer's account analogous to the apodictic evidence of the transcendental ego that could function as the final foundation for all evidences.[37]

On the other hand, what is similar and important is the sense in which the enlightening is itself not questionable within the event of truth, as inner evidence is not questionable in the *Logical Investigations.* Even the later historical dimension that Tugendhat discussed is similar to Gadamer's in the sense that another or modified perspective of the *Sache selbst* may present itself as the true, enlightening one in a future event of truth, thereby correcting a previous enlightening perspective. Within one event of truth, however, the enlightening is not questionable: "As one who understands we are incorporated within an event of truth and come too late, if we wish to know what we should believe" (WM 465; TM 447).

The enlightening is the perspective of the *Sache selbst* that presents itself in the speculative event of the coming-to-be in language of the subject matter and is experienced by the interpreter. It is the sudden crystallization of meaning that legitimates a prejudice, distinguishing this correct prejudice from the other ones that have been called into question. As the enlightening, it is, for the moment, not questioned; it grounds the prejudice in the *Sache selbst*. As the enlightening, it is probable in the positive sense of being as much truth as we finite humans can have. The enlightening permits the probable and reasonable justification of a prejudice. It shines forth and is taken to be true within the linguistic, historical finitude of human being.

CONCLUSIONS

Let me return to the epistemological quagmires to explain how this analysis of the enlightening may help one to gain one's footing. First, let me consider the charge that Gadamer's position destroys any meaningful sense of truth since it cannot distinguish between true and false interpretations. It should be clear that the whole purpose of the enlightening, as I have presented it, is to distinguish between truth and falsity by grounding one's prejudices in the things themselves by means of the enlightening that suddenly overcomes one in the event of truth. Of course, this is not an eternal truth, but one bounded by the temporal linguistic perspective of a human being. This concept of the enlightening, however, does permit Gadamer to claim, in concluding *Truth and Method*, that a discipline of investigating and questioning can attest to truth, for what is enlightening permits a reasonable justification. This also avoids the charge of an uncritical acceptance of traditions, for the truth of traditional views may be questioned and these views rejected if another perspective appears as the enlightening in an event of truth.

Thus I would argue that Bernstein is incorrect when he claims that "it is extraordinarily misleading—and betrays his [Gadamer's] own best insights—to say that there is any discipline that 'guarantees truth'."[38] Bernstein reasons that "this appeal to the *Sache* is not sufficient to clarify the concept (*Begriff*) of truth. For the question can always be asked, When do we have a *true* understanding of the thing (*Sache*) itself?"[39] Bernstein's point is that no matter how prominent the *Sache* is in legitimating our prejudices, a true understanding must be "*warranted by the appropriate forms of argumentation*."[40] I would argue, however, that Bernstein has not noticed the role of the enlightening in the event of truth. The effect of the apprehension of the enlightening, that correct perspective of the *Sache*, is just to warrant that truth, that is, to guarantee it not absolutely, but to allow a probable and reasonable justification [*eikos logos*]. In this sense, the appeal to the *Sache* is enough, and it is not the case that one can then go on and ask, as Bernstein will, whether one has understood the *Sache* correctly. The enlightening just is the shining forth of the *Sache*. One could ask whether one had correctly understood only in another conversation, another event of truth, where one might come to see that one's previous experience was incorrect, but this implies a new legitimation of another prejudice as the enlightening.

What may appear to one as correct may not appear to another as correct, since their respective horizons of meaning, that is, sets of prejudices, may be different. But to come to agree in such a situation implies the initiation of a conversation concerning the subject matter in question. Although one may use arguments to support and to criticize the other's and one's own position, the resolution of the conversation and the establishment of the *sensus communalis* will depend on the apprehension of the enlightening by those involved in the conversation. I believe this situation of coming to agreement is analogous to T. S. Kuhn's discussion of the resolution of the crisis in a paradigm switch. Kuhn notes that at first only one person may come to accept a new paradigm. It appears "all at once, sometimes in the middle of the night."[41] One may then try to convince others to view the subject matter in this new way. Kuhn argues that the conversion of others is not primarily a matter of rational argumentation, rather it is like a gestalt switch;[42] and I would suggest that it is a coming to accept the new view as enlightening. Some will never question the old paradigm, that is, prejudice, and so will not join the new consensus.

From the other side of the swamp, the "deconstructive" side, Gadamer appears too conservative, not willing to go all the way, and dependent on some foundation. Rorty, in "Idealism and Textualism," places Gadamer in the camp of the weak textualist[43] who "thinks that each work has its own vocabulary, its own secret code . . . [who] is just one more victim of realism, of the 'metaphysics of presence', [and who] wants a method of criticism, and he wants everybody to agree that he has cracked the code."[44] It is clear that Gadamer does not think that there is one secret code, nor is he interested in a method for the human sciences; rather he is interested in what the subject matter has to say to us, whether texts or persons speak.[45] Rorty writes that science replaced religion, and then philosophy replaced science, and now literature has replaced the metaphysics of presence, and that "each in turn has managed, without argument, to make its point."[46] I wish to suggest that this may well have to do with a general experience of the enlightening aspect of that perspective, similar to the way Kuhn spoke of the adoption of new paradigms. Further, when Rorty worries about the moral implications of textualism and prefers the democratic and liberal to the elitist and transcendental, he does not see how to "back up this preference with argument."[47]

Perhaps there is a probable, legitimate rhetorical argument, an *eikos logos*, to which Rorty's writing is appealing and, in fact, using—a literary argument, if you will. Again, in "Method, Social Science, Social Hope," Rorty writes, "Dewey seems to me to have done it better, simply because his vocabulary allows room for unjustifiable hope, and an ungroundable but vital sense of human solidarity."[48] In what sense does Rorty mean unjustifiable and ungroundable? Clearly Gadamer rejects the idea of a final ground or final justification, especially by means of following a method ("correct rituals"). But that one could, or that the community could, arrive at a consensus concerning the preferable jargon for now, and that this could be attested to through the enlightening aspect of this way of thinking about our experience, may be a better way of saying what Rorty wants us to acknowledge.

Caputo, in *Radical Hermeneutics* argues that Gadamer "offers us the most liberal possible version of a fundamentally conservative idea."[49] He argues that Gadamer is conservative because he presupposes a set of eternal truths and that he is liberal because we can never have a final formulation of these truths.[50] He claims that Gadamer does not question the truth of tradition.[51] In one sense this is surely incorrect, for Gadamer has emphasized the importance of critique not only of oneself, but also of tradition or one's conversation partner. The questioning of one's own tradition is a necessary requirement for opening the space for the event of truth. In another sense, the important question is whether Gadamer presupposes a set of eternal truths that continually reappear in different guises in the various historical traditions. I would submit that the discussion of truth presented here has not required and does not require such a postulation of eternal truths. The subject matter of the conversation may also fluctuate or be in process. Caputo recognizes that he is coming close to philosophical hermeneutics when he speaks of there being "thin spots where the surface wears through and acquires a transparency which exposes the flux beneath."[52] Why, I would question, is this not the speculative event where the flux of the *Sachen* appears, disrupting the previous conceptual matrix? Radical hermeneutics is to "come to grips" with this, although, Caputo adds, not in the traditional hermeneutic sense of interpretive projection and finding meaning, but in "the particular way one has found of remaining open to the mystery and venturing out into it."[53] But how is this different from the truth of experience and openness to new possibilities that will enlighten us? In presenting one such spot where the surface wears thin, Caputo says he "is offering up an additional piece of evidence, or testimony, for the whole project of radical hermeneutics."[54] What is meant by evidence or testimony now? Could it not be the presentation of what has appeared to Caputo as being enlightening in his viewing of the underlying flux, the basic *Sachen*?

In his discussion of the postmetaphysical rationality, Caputo refers to Kuhn's discussion of the adoption of a new paradigm and quotes Kuhn's description of the sudden, and may I add enlightening, experience of the new paradigm.[55] Caputo concludes "whatever this inscrutable, midnight decision is, it is not Aristotelian *phronesis*."[56] I would suggest that Gadamer's discussion of *phronesis* was primarily concerned with the rationality and logic of the process; it did not depend on other characteristics of specifically ethical judgments, such as the age of the persons involved or the existence of a consensus concerning moral values in the polis. Caputo claims that hermeneutic "*phronesis* presupposes an existing schema, a world already in place"[57] and that "*phronesis* functions only within an existing framework, an established paradigm."[58] He concludes that hermeneutic understanding could not function in a community divided within itself. Using Caputo's example, I would argue that, although it may be very difficult for Athenian, Spartan, and Chinese wisemen to question the fundamental prejudices that separate them, it is not impossible. As humans, they still share many similarities. Gadamer's point would be that if they entered a conversation and truly questioned their own prejudices as well as the prejudices of the others, then the possibility for an event of truth would exist in which each would not remain what they were before and where the *Sache* would be able to speak as enlightening. With the concept of the enlightening, Gadamer's hermeneutics is not prevented from self-critique or from a critique of others; it remains open to the play of the flux, the play of the *Sachen.*

These remarks will not get us out of the swamp. Nor are they intended to stop the conversation. Rather they are to suggest some of the possible advantages of examining the concept of the enlightening as it functions in the event of truth in philosophical hermeneutics. I have argued that the enlightening allows the legitimation of prejudices in the event of truth. It illuminates the connection between the prejudice and the *Sache selbst*. Therefore, it is the key element in answering the two basic epistemological questions, for it permits the distinction between true and false within a linguistic perspective and thus avoids both the extremes of complete relativism and unchanging truth. The discussion of the *eikos*, the probable, suggested that this sort of justification is the best justification we can have as humans. So the enlightening truth can be attested to, *verbürgt*, as truth within the human context.

NOTES

1. Hans-Georg Gadamer, *Wahrheit und Methode* (Tübingen: J. C. B. Mohr, 1960, 4th ed. 1975), 465. English translation: *Truth and Method* (New York: Seabury, 1975), 447. WM and TM respectively will be used in referencing. All translations of Gadamer are mine unless noted.

2. Richard Rorty, *Consequences of Pragmatism* (Minneapolis: University of Minnesota Press, 1982), 153.

3. Rorty, *Consequences*, 152.

4. John D. Caputo, "Gadamer's Closet Essentialism: A Derridean Critique," in *Dialogue & Deconstruction*, ed. Diane Michelfelder and Richard Palmer (Albany: SUNY Press, 1989), 259. Caputo quotes Joseph Margolis, *Pragmatism without Foundations* (Oxford: Basil Blackwell, 1986), 76.

5. Caputo, "Gadamer's Closet Essentialism," 264.

6. Jacques Derrida, "Three Questions to Hans-Georg Gadamer" in *Dialogue & Deconstruction*, 53–54.

7. Jürgen Habermas, "Zu Gadamers 'Wahrheit und Methode'," in *Hermeneutik und Ideologiekritik* (Frankfurt: Surhkamp, 1971), 48. My translation. Compare Karl Otto Apel, *Transformation der Philosophie* (Frankfurt: Surhkamp, 1973), 1:47.

8. E. D. Hirsch, *The Aims of Interpretation* (Chicago: University of Chicago Press, 1978), 251.

9. I have argued that the other structures of hermeneutic understanding can be analyzed in terms of the *Vorurteile* in L. K. Schmidt, *The Epistemology of Hans-Georg Gadamer* (Frankfurt: Peter Lang, 1985).

10. Martin Heidegger, *Being and Time*, trans. Macquarrie and Robinson (New York: Harper & Row, 1962), 195; in *Sein und Zeit* (Tübingen: Max Niemeyer, 1972), 153. Quoted in WM 251; TM 236.

11. In the end it will be seen that this separation of language from its referent is an abstraction that is overcome in the ontological turn toward language.

12. In his discussion of the *Verbum*, Gadamer suggests that such a language could only be divine or God's, but clearly it is not our human language, WM 402; TM 385.

13. H.-G. Gadamer, "Text und Interpretation" in *Gesammelte Schriften* (Tübingen: J. C. B. Mohr, 1986), 2:334. Dennis Schmidt's and Richard Palmer's translation from "Text and Interpretation" in *Dialogue & Deconstruction*, 25. One should note that Gadamer does recognize prelin-

guistic experience, but limits hermeneutics to its communication in his "Replik" in *Hermeneutik und Ideologiekritik*, 291.

14. "In a similar sense as with perception, one can speak of linguistic perspective modifications which allow the world to be experienced in different linguistic worlds." WM 424; TM 406.

15. "If we have an experience of an object, this means that previously we did not see things correctly and now we know better." WM 336; TM 317.

16. Gadamer, "Text und Interpretation," in *Gesammelte Schriften* (Tübingen: J. C. B. Mohr, 1986), 2:357. Dennis Schmidt's and Richard Palmer's translation from "Text and Interpretation," in *Dialogue and Deconstruction*, 48.

17. Compare the important discussion of the speculative in Kathleen Wright's "Gadamer: The Speculative Structure of Language," in *Hermeneutics and Modern Philosophy*, ed. Brice Wachterhauser (Albany: SUNY Press 1986), especially 206–11.

18. Gadamer, "Idee und Wirklichkeit in Platos 'Timaios'," *Gesammelte Werke* (Tübingen: J. C. B. Mohr, 1985). English trans. Christopher Smith, "Idea and Reality in Plato's *Timaeus*," in *Dialogue and Dialectic: Eight Hermeneutical Studies on Plato* (New Haven: Yale University Press, 1980), 164.

19. Plato, *Timaeus*, 29cd, trans. R. G. Bury in the Loeb Classical Library, (Cambridge, Mass.: Harvard University Press, 1952), 53.

20. Gadamer, "Idee und Wirklichkeit in Platos 'Timaios'," 6:248; "Idea and Reality in Plato's *Timaeus*," 164.

21. See 48cd, 53d, and 55d in the *Timaeus*.

22. Aristotle, *Analytica Priora*, vol. 1, trans. A. J. Jenkinson (London: Oxford University Press, 1955), 70a4-8.

23. Aristotle, *Rhetorica*, vol. 11, trans. W. Rhys Roberts (London: Oxford University Press, 1955), 1357a2–30.

24. Aristotle, *Nicomachean Ethics*, trans. Martin Ostwald (New York: Bobbs-Merrill, 1962), 1139b20ff.

25. See, for example, Aristotle, *Nicomachean Ethics*, 1094b21 and 1104a1.

26. Aristotle, *Nicomachean Ethics*, 1142a25–30.

27. Cicero, *De Inventione* I. vii. 9, trans. H. M. Hubbell in the Loeb Classical Library (Cambridge, Mass.: Harvard University Press, 1949), 19.

28. Edmund Husserl, *Logical Investigations*, trans. J. N. Findlay (New York: Humanities Press, 1970), §51, 1:195.

29. Ibid., §38, 2:765.

30. Ibid., §38, 2:765.

31. Ernst Tugendhat, *Der Wahrheitsbegriff bei Husserl und Heidegger* (Berlin: Walter de Gruyter, 1970), 230ff.

32. Ibid., 235.

33. Ibid., 232, where he quotes Husserl, *Formale und transzendentale Logik*, 140.

34. Ibid., 235f. and 245ff.

35. Edmund Husserl, *The Crisis of European Sciences and Transcendental Phenomenology*, trans. David Carr (Evanston: Northwestern University Press, 1970), §34d, 127–28.

36. Ibid., §55, 189.

37. Concerning the circle of understanding, Gadamer writes: "I believe I have followed Heidegger's critique of the phenomenological concept of immanence, a critique directed against Husserl's notion of an ultimate transcendental justification. The dialogical character of language . . . leaves behind it any starting point in the subjectivity of the subject, especially in the meaning-directed intentions of the speaker." H.-G. Gadamer, "Text und Interpretation," in *Gesammelte Schriften* (Tübingen: J. C. B. Mohr, 1986), 2:335. Dennis Schmidt's and Richard Palmer's translation from "Text and Interpretation," in *Dialogue & Deconstruction*, 26.

38. Richard J. Bernstein, "From Hermeneutics to Praxis," in *Hermeneutics and Modern Philosophy*, ed. Brice Wachterhauser (Albany: SUNY Press, 1986), 99.

39. Ibid., 107n32.

40. Ibid.

41. Thomas S. Kuhn, *The Structure of Scientific Revolutions* (Chicago: University of Chicago Press, 1962, 2nd ed. 1970), 90.

42. Ibid., 150.

43. Richard Rorty, *Consequences of Pramatism* (Minneapolis: University of Minnesota Press, 1982), 153.

44. Ibid., 152.

45. Compare James Risser, "Rorty's Pragmatism as Hermeneutic Praxis," *The Modern Schoolman* 43 (May 1986): 275ff.

46. Rorty, *Consequences*, 155.

47. Ibid., 158.

48. Ibid., 208.

49. John D. Caputo, *Radical Hermeneutics* (Bloomington: Indiana University Press, 1987), 115.

50. Ibid., 111.
51. Ibid., 112.
52. Ibid., 269.
53. Ibid., 271.
54. Ibid.
55. Ibid., 219.
56. Ibid., 220.
57. Ibid., 210.
58. Ibid., 217.

PART IV

The Nature of Justice and Community

CHAPTER 13

The Sincerity of Apology
Levinas's Resistance to the Judgment of History

JAMES HATLEY

THE QUESTION OF HETEROGENOUS JUDGMENT

The failure of justice is, among other things, the failure of judgment. Judgment, by discerning which particular human circumstances are good or bad, beneficial or detrimental, glorious or ignoble, prepares the way for political actions that will either victimize or sustain specific human beings, those fragile, embodied creatures that populate the modern technological state. It is understandable, then, that both Levinas and Arendt are concerned that judgment be recognized for its crucial role in the securing of justice. Both thinkers are further convinced that, insofar as judgment justifies itself through an appeal to a theoretical mode of understanding, the criteria by which the judgment justifies itself is not in turn open to judgment. By an insistent recourse to theory, to a thinking of the systematic truth of a social or political situation, various institutions disenfranchise judgment by forcing it to speak with a single voice, to become univocal, harmonizing all the elements involved in the situation to be judged, as if they could be viewed from a single, all-encompassing perspective. The price of such a harmonization is the reduction of the plurality of particular persons to an anonymous, conglomerate being described in an impersonal discourse that speaks about oneself as if one were no different than any other. This judgment placed beyond judgment is no longer capable of responding to and being responsible for the plurality of incommensurable situations that one encounters when dealing with specific human beings who differ from one another in unexpected and novel ways. The justice of an impersonal judgment, forgetting the uniqueness of human beings, inevitably becomes a rationalization of their victimization.

It is precisely the discourse of an impersonal judgment lacking a judgment beyond judgment that both Arendt and Levinas find in Hegel's claim that *Die Weltgeschichte ist die Weltgericht*, that is, that history is its own judge. Hegel claims that history is an immanent theodicy in which the dynamic of progress revealed in historical events *justifies* the very events that constitute or articulate that dynamic. One need only pay attention to those individuals that embody the logic of such a dynamic to understand what justice the movement of Spirit in history has wrought. Thus Hegel can argue, "phenomena [for example, nations, political movements, technology, philosophical thinking, and even justice itself] have become real independently of our [particular] efforts, and all that we need to understand them is consciousness, a thinking consciousness."[1] Because history is concerned with the building up of these supra-personal, rationally articulated phenomena, Hegel also contends that "reason cannot stop to consider the injuries sustained by single individuals, for particular ends are submerged in the universal end" (WH 43). In turn, Hegel claims that the universal end has finally been revealed in the Idea of Freedom, the ultimate and controlling destination of historical progress. For Hegel, if one's own judgment is to have any meaning beyond caprice, a passion that is merely subjective, then one's judgment must reflect the movement of the articulation of this Idea that is already at work in history. Judgment does not accrue to the individual, except as an after-effect of the universal development of Spirit. Although Hegel may claim that such a development only makes sense in the particular, for Levinas and Arendt the Hegelian particular is ultimately anonymous; the meaning of the Hegelian particular is entirely exhausted by the manner in which it articulates itself as a part of the whole, that is, the Idea developed as Spirit.

Resisting such an account of an impersonal historical judgment, Arendt appeals to the labors of the single historian who "sits in judgment" over history in the very act of relating it.[2] In doing so, the historian is capable of opposing the outcome of history so that "the victorious cause pleased the gods, but the defeated one pleases Cato." Levinas as well argues that human persons not only have the capability to oppose history's anonymous judgments, but also have always already been given the responsibility, indeed the right, "to judge history in the name of moral conscience."[3] One can characterize both accounts of judgment as being heterogenous, that is, as attempting to judge justly with respect to other persons whose identity is not commensurable with one's own and whose judgments may come to resist one's own judgment.

THE DIVERGENCE OF LEVINAS AND ARENDT

Although Levinas and Arendt agree in their condemnation of Hegel and the impersonal form of judgment that his position exemplifies, there are wide divergences in their respective accounts of a heterogenous judgment that would offer an alternative to the Hegelian position. Arendt's account of judgment finds it to be eminently political, while Levinas finds judgment to be initially moral and only afterwards political. Thus, Levinas's account of judgment emphasizes the subjectivity, the inwardness of she or he who judges. Such terms are an anathema to the politically situated thought of Arendt. As George Kateb has pointed out, Arendt distrusts the notion that one can come to know oneself through an inward glance.[4] For Arendt, one's political significance is exterior to one's subjectivity. To look inward is to make oneself vulnerable to a morass of shadowy motivations resisting any possibility of revelation, either to oneself or to others. Only through a second, postbiological birth initiated by one's *acting* in regard to others can one acquire a self. This worldly or political self is given through the judgments that others make about one as they react to one's own judgments and actions, particularly in the form of stories.[5]

The Levinasian account of inwardness and how it leads the self to judgment also takes issue with any notion of the subjective that would characterize the human self as a looking inward in order to know itself, as if its nature or being were revealed to its own gaze. Like Arendt, Levinas finds any defense for the ultimate privacy of the self misguided. Thus, Levinas argues that inwardness is not a revelation of the being or nature of oneself, but the unique summons to be responsible to an other. The inward self of Levinas is not at all private, but is preeminently responsible for others, already in exile from itself.

It is important to note that even as it exceeds the notion of private existence, Levinas's inward self is also not quite yet a political self. Levinas insists on arguing for the inwardness of the self in order to acknowledge a dimension of human individuality that a purely political account, such as Arendt's, misses. From Levinas's viewpoint, if one is to give a justification for heterogenous judgment, then it is imperative that one explore the ethical dimensions of the self that are revealed in the inwardness of the human response to historical injustice. Only then can one justify the use of judgment in the political sphere. In order to assess the strength of Levinas's argument and to understand in what way it might be used to supplement Arendt's own account of judgment, the remainder of this paper will develop Levinas's notion of ethical judgment and then contrast it with Arendt's consideration of conscience as a preparation for political judgment.

HISTORY: THE ALIENATION OF WILLS

For Levinas, history is already a pluralism, an arena in which discrete wills, each seeking "to be at home with itself," come into contact with those other identities surrounding one's home.[6] To be at home with oneself is to be able to return to oneself as the same, to be what Levinas calls a "psychism," a capability of enjoying one's existence by appropriating what is other than oneself for one's own. Such a capability requires the transformation of a world indifferent and even vaguely hostile to human existence into a home in which one is sheltered and nourished, in which one can gaze with a modicum of security into the unanticipated developments that one's future might bring. One can think of this arena of existence as roughly similar to Arendt's notion of private life.

The very effort to gain control over one's environment requires that one labors, that one exerts a force in order to transform what is other to one into the same. Here one's will is still at home with itself, still in control of the vector of its intention. But one's labor is inserted into works, into material entities that are vulnerable to appropriation by other wills. The inevitability of this appropriation, which is signaled in one's own death after which one's works will fall into the hands of others, means that the efforts of one's will are destined "to a history that one cannot foresee" (TI 227).

Indeed, history does not even exist until one's will has disappeared, that is, until one, either through physical death or some form of victimization, has her or his works wrested away and used by others for their enjoyment. Until this moment of capitulation, each will has the capability of resisting its entry into history by actively asserting its ownership of and control over its works. Levinas assumes that each will is capable of making a judgment concerning its works that will lead to its enjoying its own works and to its being sustained by them.

For Levinas, historical judgment occurs when those who survive, inheriting the works left behind by the dead or victimized, are called upon to make a decision concerning their use and value. Such a judgment is quite problematic. Insofar as one stays within the order of history, that is, within a series of economic relationships in which human wills strive to gain control over the works of other wills, such a judgment will be merely self-serving. It will write a history that Levinas condemns as being only capable of recounting "the way the survivors appropriate the works of dead wills to themselves" (TI 228). Such a writing represses the individuality of the victims of history so that all that is truly left of them is their works now alienated from them in the will of the conqueror. Thus, the stories, the religious implements, and even the skeletons of Native Americans find their way into the museums of their European annihilators where they are viewed to satisfy the curiosity, intellectual or otherwise, about how other peoples once lived.

This vulnerability of the dead to the living becomes scandalous insofar as human beings turn away from the realm of history and demand yet another accounting, another judgment that exceeds a mere calculation of the value of the other's works. Such a judgment no longer concerns the ability of the surviving will to return to the same, to enjoy its existence. Instead, the survivor comes to recognize in the will of another a resistance to her or his historical appropriation that is of an entirely different order. One encounters an exteriority that entirely withdraws from history and that draws one with it. In this fashion, the interiority of the self is revealed as that aspect of the self that cannot be assimilated into the play of commercial exchanges characterizing history. But the revelation of this interiority is precisely the revelation of the infinity of the other, of her or his utter resistance to any attempt I might make to calculate her or his will or to take control of it. Such a resistance is not historical; it is ethical. That is, it does not stem from the other's use of force to resist my own application of force, but from my recognition that, where the other is concerned, I no longer am able to be able. I cannot will for her or him. To do so is already to have wrested control of the other's body from her or him and to have bent it to my own enjoyment. But enjoyment utterly misses the point. Although I might effectively destroy the body of the other, it remains a *moral* impossibility to do so, precisely because her or his body is also a willing that will never recur to me, that can never return to me as the same.

APOLOGY: THE CALL OF THE SELF TO JUDGMENT

The point of view adopted in the preceding analysis is an interpretation of Levinas's own discussion in *Totality and Infinity* where, in contrast to my account, the vulnerability of one's own will to usurpation by other wills serves as the perspective from which the notion of interiority is developed. In either case, the important turn in the analysis comes with the realization on the part of the self that his or her death can be "as a result of someone and for someone" (TI 239). Such a realization enables one to endure one's own death with a patient mastery over the suffering that it brings so that "the will breaks through the crust of its egoism and as it were displaces its center of gravity outside of itself" (TI 239). In this manner, the will transcends its own death not because its body or being will live another life beyond this one, but because it inevitably turns its works over to the survivor just as it has already inherited works in its own role as a survivor. Beyond the act of appropriation, beyond what is possible for oneself, comes the command for generosity, that is, for a masterful giving up of what is one's own for the good of the other, a good that cannot recur to oneself. Coupled with this command for generosity is yet another command that one be thankful for the works already given one by others for one's own good. Both of these relationships, generosity and thankfulness, are asymmetrical. They express a responsibility that one undertakes for others *without* the expectation that these others will reciprocate. These relationships must occur in this manner because the difference between oneself and the one to whom one is related is infinite. One is never capable of grasping the will of the other by whom one is summoned, accused. In being summoned infinitely, one assumes a responsibility, a "restlessness for the other, a cellular irritability"[7] that cannot be quieted.

In the wake of this summons to responsibility, the will finds itself commanded to judge history rather than to succumb to it. But the will's relationship to its own judgment of history is in turn highly paradoxical: to judge history is to find oneself called to judgment for the manner in which one has responded to the vulnerability of the other to victimization. Thus, the I becomes in its judgment an apology, that is, a willing of its own judgment.[8] Has one responded to the other's command for generosity and thankfulness? The singular "I," whose responsibility can recur to no other person, finds itself already accused in such a judgment. The death of the other bothers one with the suspicion of murder, just as the suffering of the other provokes the suspicion of one's own sadism.[9] More generally, any political judgment by the survivor in relation to the dead or the victimized carries the suspicion that his or her own judgment has become insincere. One fears that one has come to justify injustice by finally accepting the verdict of history, by forgetting or repressing the other's infinite resistance to one's grasp of her or his will, a resistance that can never be overcome. For this reason, one's judgment of history must remain subjective. One is engaged in a judgment against oneself, in which the *sincerity* of one's judgment is always at issue. Levinas emphasizes this point by speaking of judgment as being an ongoing *"responsibility increasing in the measure that it is assumed*; duties become greater in the measure that they are accomplished. The better I accomplish my duty the fewer rights I have; the more I am just the more guilty I am" (TI 244).

ARENDTIAN CONSCIENCE AND POLITICAL JUDGMENT

The Levinasian account of apology shows that one's moral conscience, one's questioning of one's actions, is ultimately commanded by the transcendence of another that one can never grasp.[10] How does this account of conscience compare to the one elaborated by Arendt? Further, in what manner "ought" or "can" conscience lead to political judgment, to a judgment that is no longer interior but that takes place between individuals?

For Arendt, conscience stems from the manner in which the thinking self is doubled over against itself. Thinking is forever taking a critical position against itself so that the meaning of what one claims to know might be explored. Such an exploration inevitably unsettles one's knowledge by showing the insufficiencies of the reasoning process that led to a given conclusion. In one's conscience, this innate tendency of thought to resist indefinitely its own closure comes to be recognized and fostered.

By providing a critical perspective on one's own grasp of one's knowledge, the activity of thinking also signals the insertion of "a difference into my Oneness" (LM 181). Thinking allows one to become one's own companion; it allows one, in Arendt's words, to "keep myself company," since in thinking, "I am both the one who asks and the one who answers" (LM 185). For Arendt, thinking becomes conscience insofar as one experiences the need that she who asks and she who answers in one's own thinking be concerned that each voice be consistent with the other. If the duality within oneself, the two-in-one as Arendt calls it, remains in unremitting contradiction, one becomes one's own adversary. This is something one cannot wish unless one wishes one's own destruction, since there is no way in which one can escape from an adversary who is oneself. Thus, conscience is the insight that one ought not to act so as to become an adversary to one's friendship with oneself. Arendt asks: "Who would want to be the friend of and have to live together with a murderer? Not even another murderer" (LM 188). From this insight comes Socrates's famous dictum that it is better to suffer than to do wrong. One avoids harming another because to do so would be to sentence oneself to live with one who victimizes, with one who is an adversary.

As Kateb has so convincingly argued, Arendt's account of conscience transforms the anguish that one feels for the wrong done to another into an anguish that one feels for oneself. Conscience becomes a form of self-interest. But in explaining conscience as self-interest, one fails to address how in one's encounter of a victim, "the anguish of those to whom wrong is being done" (HA 110) is precisely *not* one's own anguish. Kateb argues that in conscience one is commanded to imagine another's suffering *even as one does not suffer!*

Levinas would go even further. He would argue that even an act of imagination concerning the suffering of another ultimately fails to grasp the other's will, which is different than mine not only in its affect or circumstance, but also infinitely, that is, in a manner that no delimitation can discover.[11] Thus Levinas would find thinking's striving after meaning to be capable only of providing an ersatz conscience, one that progressively undermines one's enjoyment but does not submit one to a command that is *infinitely* irritating. For Levinas, conscience is an uneasiness for the other, an uneasiness whose asymmetry cannot then be reintegrated into the self as a concern for one's own self-interest. To attempt to do so would be to attempt to limit conscience, to cancel at some point the restlessness of its call to sincerity. The problem is not only whether one is really being friends with oneself. The problem is also whether one understands how, in being friends with oneself, one can exclude the other so radically that one has not even noticed one's victimization of the other. Only then can the problem of one's sincerity become of importance for one's thinking. Socrates's account of conscience remains blissfully unaware of a willed duplicity in which one chooses to remain ignorant rather than be aware that one has victimized.

Thus, Eichmann's claim not to have acted from the base motivation of wishing to kill anyone, even as he effected the genocide of the Jewish people, implies a failure beyond that of not critically questioning the meaning of one's actions. One can imagine an Eichmann who was capable of questioning the meaning of this or that defense for his actions that he might give, insofar as it showed flaws in the rational support of his already willed resolve to avoid an interior judgment. Such a mind could be continually critical of its own thoughts and continually concerned that one not become one's adversary, without once raising the question whether one had already ignored at a moment before thought, before conception, a claim upon one's thoughts that entirely transcends one's own authority to speak for oneself.

Eichmann's profession of guilt is utterly political. He claims to have been part of a political system that failed to exercise good judgment in regard to choosing those who would be singled out for glory, those to whom promises would be kept, and those to whom forgiveness would be granted. For this, he is guilty. But this profession of guilt shows no remorse whatsoever for Eichmann's own *particular* responsibility to those he had murdered administratively.

The lack of remorse signals the collapse of the Levinasian notion of apology and the refusal of a subjectivity to be judged in the first person, as a singular identity. Such a refusal allows Eichmann to "judge" his motivations objectively so that, no matter what accusations may be made concerning his actions, he can claim that his own intentions remain blameless. The collapse of the singular first person in Eichmann's discourse hints at the moral collapse of an individual who shows the inverse of Levinas's dictum, "the more I am just the more guilty I am." Eichmann, in his own mind, was so just that he could not become guilty. But such justice was measured by the fact that one carried through the political will of a state precisely by resisting one's own inclination to allow one's subjective feelings for the other to interfere with one's duty! Eichmann's claim of a guiltless motivation for his actions that only happened to become destructive because of what a political system came to will belies the unique interiority of the human will that is forever submitted to a judgment originating outside of history or politics.

Eichmann professes a state of mind in which the transcendent accusation of the self by the other is no longer acknowledged. His defense, which is never an apology, suggests the collapse of any effort to be sincere, because sincerity is irrelevant to a man immersed in a world shorn of moral interiority, a world in which one merely acts for the recognition one might gain from others. Although Eichmann's willingness to send millions of Jews to their deaths for the rather shallow honors to be gained in the bureaucratic world in which he found himself may be banal, his steadfast avoidance of the question of his own sincerity, a question that can only emanate from the inwardness of a person, is not. One might characterize evil in Levinasian terms as an "irreducible disturbance," a willed chaos, that refuses any singularity or any terminus of responsibility whatsoever.[12] It is not surprising that those who are touched by such a disturbance are left feeling hollow, impoverished of their own interiority.

Levinas's emphasis upon the interiority of judgment, however, does not exclude an Arendtian concern for a realm of public, nonsubjective life whose dynamic of heterogenous judgment involves the elaboration of a *sen-*

sus communis that is truly plural. Yet Levinas would object to Arendt's characterization of moral categories as being inherently dangerous to political discourse. For Levinas, there is no easy dividing of the political from the moral. Precisely because in the Levinasian notion of conscience one is submitted by oneself to a judgment concerning a particular other exterior to one's own being, one must also confront the political fact that no particular other can stand for all of the others that lie beyond that particular other. Inevitably, moral judgment calls for another moment of judgment in which the absolute difference between oneself and a particular other (what Levinas terms "proximity," OB 159) must now be brought into accord with the many others who would make diverging claims upon my responsibility. Now is the moment of vision or imagination in which one must begin to account for how what one does for another affects the others beyond this moment of intimate proximity in which I am summoned by the infinity of the particular other. Thus, although I must answer for my infinite responsibility for the other who faces me, this other "stands in a relationship with the third party, for whom I cannot entirely answer" (OB 157). With the intervention of what Levinas terms the third party, the question of moral apology escalates into the question of political justice. A disinterested "comparing" of infinitely plural perspectives leads to the "ordering" of the political sphere, that is, the sphere of a public world in which one judges and acts as others look on and judge one's actions. According to Levinas, such judgments cannot be "the subsuming of particular cases under a rule," since "the judge is not outside the conflict, but the law is in the midst of proximity" (OB 159). Thus, one's moral concern for the infinite resistance of the other to one's grasp of her or him also becomes a political concern for the particularity and novelty of the other's situation.

Arendt's own development of a heterogenous judgment that is worldly and political would be welcomed by Levinas at this level of his analysis. Like Arendt, Levinas would be suspicious of any spiritualization of political judgment that replaces one's concern for the victimization of worldly humans with a sublimated concern for one's own self-interest disguised as a theory of otherworldly responsibilities. Instead, justice always requires "a better justice" here and now. *The judgment enacting justice must continually become aware that its opposition to history continually falls back into history, that every judgment enacting justice also enacts a violence that requires yet more judgments and more social responsibility.* Justice is necessarily an "incessant correction" (OB 158) in which my responsibility to a particular, proximate other must be repeatedly compared to the responsibilities arising beyond this responsibility. Thus, Levinas argues that the institution of human rights within the liberal state serves to remind that state "that there is no justice yet."[13]

Arendt eventually came to value one's subjective faculty of conscience as an important, although simply reactive, check upon misguided political judgment. In her insistence that the source of political judgment was in the "wind of thought," that is, in a thinking initiating an insistent critique of its own thinking, however, Arendt failed to see that the faculty of conscience carries yet another characteristic that is just as important for political judgment, namely, that in conscience a judgment is made in respect to another *who transcends one's own thinking of him or her*. It is not the *doubling* of the thinking self in conscience that serves as an indicator of "the infinite plurality which is the law of the earth" (LM 186), but the *submitting* of the self to the claim of another that was made upon the self before the self could even have begun to think or to be. Only because there is another who resists infinitely any conceptualization one might have of her or him can thought become windy and sustain the insistent judging of judgment that Arendt argues *ought* to characterize political life.

NOTES

1. G. W. F. Hegel, *Lectures on the Philosophy of World History: Reason in History*, trans. Nisbet (London: Cambridge University Press, 1975), 43 (henceforth WH).

2. Hannah Arendt, *The Life of the Mind*, vol. I (New York: Harcourt, Brace, Jovanovich, 1978), 216 (henceforth LM).

3. Emmanuel Levinas, *Difficile Liberté* (Paris: A. Michel, 1983), 41.

4. See George Kateb, *Hannah Arendt: Politics, Conscience, Evil* (Totawa, N.J.: Rowman and Allanheld, 1983), 9 (henceforth HA).

5. See Hannah Arendt's discussion of the story and its place within the Greek polis in *The Human Condition* (Chicago: University of Chicago Press, 1958), 175ff., as well as George Kateb's analysis of Arendt's discussion of human identity (HA 9–13).

6. See Emmanuel Levinas, *Totality and Infinity*, trans. Alphonso Lingis (The Hague: Martinus Nijhoff, 1969), 226 (henceforth TI). The following discussion of history and apology relies heavily upon Levinas's discussion of the same (pp. 220–47).

7. Emmanuel Levinas, *Otherwise than Being or Beyond Essence*, trans. Alphonso Lingis (The Hague: Martinus Nijhoff, 1981), 143 (henceforth OB).

8. See Edith Wyschogrod, *Emmanuel Levinas: The Problem of Ethical Metaphysics* (The Hague: Martinus Nijhoff, 1974), 112.

9. See Emmanuel Levinas, "The Paradoxes of Morality," an interview published in *The Provocation of Levinas: Rethinking the Other*, ed. Robert Bernasconi and David Wood (Routledge: New York, 1988), 173: "In the Old Testament there is the sixth commandment, 'Thou shalt not kill.' This does not mean simply that you are not to go around firing a gun all the time. It refers, rather, to the fact that, in the course of your life, in different ways, you will kill someone. For example, when we sit down at the table in the morning and drink coffee, we kill an Ethiopian who doesn't have any coffee." Levinas seems to be arguing that the very act of living involves us in economic relationships in which others are victimized.

10. Levinas states, "Transcendence as such is conscience" (TI 261).

11. But Levinas does acknowledge the opposition to historical judgment provided by pathetic responses to the suffering of the other. Such responses would not in any way form a representation of the other but suffer the other as a sensation, a being-touched-by that escapes one's reciprocal grasp of him or her who touches. See TI 217.

12. See Levinas's discussion of evil in his *Collected Philosophical Papers*, trans. Alphonso Lingis (The Hague: Martinus Nijhoff, 1987), 179–86.

13. Emmanuel Levinas, "The Paradoxes of Morality," 178.

CHAPTER 14

Lyotard and the Question of Community

STEVEN HENDLEY

Jean-François Lyotard has described our "postmodern condition" in terms of an increasing inability to believe in the great narratives that have, since the Enlightenment, formed the basis for our modern self-understanding.[1] In particular, our efforts to identify, in one way or another, with the idea of humanity struggling toward the realization of its universal emancipation now appear bankrupt in the light of the differences that divide one ethnic or cultural tradition from another. Our attempts to speak with what we might call the universal voice of humanity have unraveled with the recognition of incommensurable differences between language games or genres of discourse that preclude the formation of such a universal voice. With the unraveling of that voice, we are confronted with the unraveling of our sense of who we are and with the splintering of our modern sense of identity that raises the question not only of how we may continue to understand ourselves, but of how we may continue to understand the status of the "we" that must raise its own identity as a question in this way. In questioning the modern basis of our self-understanding, we are forced to rethink not only the issue of who we are, but the very sense of what it means to be a "we" as well—the sense of what it means to be a community, a gathering that can be concerned with such things as the question of who we are.[2]

In this paper, I would like to examine Lyotard's somewhat tentative responses to this question and to suggest how we might construct a sense of community based on his work that does not simply reject what he described in *The Postmodern Condition* as the "outmoded and suspect value" of consensus,[3] but that reworks that value in a constructive way. Lyotard has done more than just about anyone else to undermine the sense of unanimity and consensus that is usually implied with the designation "we." But those very efforts at exposing the radical degree of conflict and division that is concealed beneath that unanimity suggest a way of rethinking what it means to be in a community, a way that might begin not with a dream of consensus that inevitably does violence to the heterogeneity of the social bond,[4] but with the reality of what is always dividing us from one another. In beginning here, with conflict rather than consensus, it may be possible to rethink what it means to "belong together" with others in a way that respects the heterogeneity of that belonging. By attempting to understand how we might belong together not in terms of an answer to the question of who we are, but in the maintenance and persistence of that very question, it may be possible to conceive of a mode of community that fosters a sense of identity precisely through the permanent deferral[5] of the completion of that identity, through a practice that keeps it forever up for discussion.

Lyotard confronts this issue most directly in an essay he wrote in 1985, "Universal History and Cultural Differences." He frames this essay in terms of the following question: "Can we continue today to organize the multitude of events that come to us from the world, both the human and the non-human world, by subsuming them beneath the idea of a universal history of humanity?"[6] As Lyotard points out, his question presupposes that we have tried to understand the world in this way, that is, in terms of a universal history that has always been, in one form or another, a history of human emancipation.[7] The telling of this history has, of course, taken many forms. Kant and the Enlightenment told it as the story of our emancipation from our own "self-imposed tutelage" to the authority of others. Marx told it as the story of our emancipation from the exploitation of capital. And every liberal democracy has recounted it in terms of our emancipation from arbitrary uses of power that deny us our "natural and inalienable" rights. In all of its forms, however, this universal history of humanity has always been the narrative of the realization not merely of this or that aspiration of this or that class or tradition, but the realization of human freedom as such. To this extent, we have presupposed an ability to recognize a human nature that is either fostered or oppressed in any form of life—a nature that binds us together, despite our cultural differences, in a destiny that remains common and so is capable of serving as a basis for a universal sense of community. We, who all together enjoy or are denied a common sense of freedom, are capable of recognizing each other as another like ourselves.

The construction of this universal narrative stands in opposition to what Lyotard refers to as "the multiplicity of the worlds of names."[8] By this phrase he means to designate the ways in which we learn of who we are through learning the name of the culture to which we belong as it is determined in and through the recounting of the great deeds and events that constitute "our" heritage, as opposed to "their" heritage. The project of modernity may be understood, then, as an attempt to replace "the multiplicity of the worlds of names" that define our identities in relation to a past that "we" share, but that "they" do not, with a sense of identity that defines who we are in relation to a future "we all" share. Replacing this multiplicity of distinct pasts for a common future,[9] however, has proved unrealizable. At an empirical level, Lyotard notes how the persistence of local and national divisions have wrecked the political prospects for universal emancipation.[10] At a more structural level, he has drawn attention to how the very project of modernity contradicts itself in its historical-political realization insofar as it draws on the very worlds of names it is meant to transcend. When, for example, the Declaration of the Rights of Man was authorized by the National Assembly of the French People in 1789, the passage to the universal, to the perspective of "man," remains haunted by a relation to the worlds of proper names in and through its reference to "the French People" who enacted that passage. As Lyotard notes, "man should have signed the Preamble of the Declaration," not the National Assembly of the French People.[11] But as a reference to the future, to a sense of identity that is not already real in relation to the deeds and events that define our narrated past, "man" remains an Idea that still needs to be realized and so cannot be present to authorize the passage to its own history, the history of humanity. Hence, there remains a structurally inevitable reference to a particular history that undercuts and dispels the illusion of universality that the Declaration inaugurates. One can never know whether one's struggles for the rights of man are struggles to make the world "more human" or merely "more French."[12] One can never completely disentangle the human history that dawns in the Declaration from the history of France in which it is enacted.

Lyotard speaks of this empirical and structural failure of the project of modernity as our "modern defaillancy"[13]—a sense of exhaustion that has overcome our attempts to transcend "the multiplicity of the worlds of names." With this failure or exhaustion of modernity, we are confronted with the question of how we might continue thinking of ourselves. If, as Lyotard supposes, we are unable to recognize everyone else as another like ourselves and to understand who we are from that universal perspective, but we have not yet forgotten the dream of that universal mutual recognition, we are left with two possibilities for the future. Lyotard speaks of the first possibility as a kind of "secondary narcissism" in which we mourn the loss of the object of modernity's desire (universal emancipation) by withdrawing that desire from it and by extending it toward *ourselves*. If the Idea of the universal history of humanity is impossible, this need not prevent us from vigorously continuing to pursue our own commitments and values. It only prevents us from speaking of this pursuit as a universal emancipation by making it impossible for us to justify it in the eyes of the others. Speaking bluntly, Lyotard gives the name of "tyranny" to this option and describes it in the following way: "The law which 'we' decree is not addressed to *you*, to you fellow-citizens or even to you subjects; it is applied to *them*, to third parties, to those outside, and it is simply not concerned with being legitimized in their eyes."[14] Nazism, for Lyotard, exemplifies this response to our modern defaillancy insofar as it was, as he puts it, "a terror whose reason was not in theory accessible to all and whose benefits were not to be shared by all."[15] With this first option, we continue what Lyotard calls modernity's "project of conquest" by pursuing our ideals to the exclusion of all others *as if* they were universal, but now only in the name of our own satisfaction, not in the name of freedom.[16]

The second possibility that Lyotard mentions picks up where the first leaves off. It might be described as the formal completion of the mourning for modernity that is begun in the first, but that is not brought to its conclusion. As Lyotard puts it,

> Another way to mourn the universal emancipation promised by modernity might be to "work through" (in Freud's sense) not only the loss of the object, but also the loss of the subject who was promised this future. This would not simply be a matter of recognizing that we are finite; it would be a way of working through the status of the *we* and the question of the subject.[17]

Here we extend our mourning over the failure of modernity from the loss of the object to the loss of the subject—to ourselves, in other words. And this, as he notes, is not simply to recognize our finitude. It is not merely to acknowledge the historical particularity of the various aspirations and ideals that form the basis for our sense of identity. It is to raise the question of what it means to be a "we," a subject that could be said to have such aspirations and ideals. This is what the first option neglects. In continuing to pursue our own ideals and aspirations as if they were universal, we take for granted what it means to be a "we" that could share such things. We abandon the object of modernity's desire, universal emancipation, by ceasing to concern ourselves with the justification of our ideals in the eyes of humanity, but we fail to recognize the loss of the subject that has been constructed in the light of the promise of that object. The grounds that have made it possible for us to understand ourselves as all together sharing a particular vision of human emancipation or human dignity lie in our belief that it is "our" vision only to the extent that it is "humanity's" vision. We are able to know ourselves in a particular way, as committed to the same ideals of freedom and dignity, *because* we know that humanity as such shares these ideals. Lacking this, we can no longer know what it means to say that "we" share a particular vision. We can no longer take what "we" share for granted since the guarantee of our "common humanity" has been taken from us.

It is for this reason that it is insufficient merely to recognize our finitude. For simply to recognize the historical particularity of "our" vision of human freedom and dignity is still to fail to confront the question of what it means to speak of sharing such a vision. We could, of course, speak of our common institutions and traditions. We could, as Aristotle does, speak of a common language introducing us to a common perception of what is good or evil and just or unjust.[18] We often say that such things form the "context" for a community's interpretation of the world. Stanley Fish, for example, has popularized the idea of "interpretive communities" bound together in a shared understanding of the world by virtue of a common set of institutional practices.[19] And Thomas Kuhn has made us accustomed to speaking of a shared paradigm as the condition for the possibility of a scientific community coming to share a "world" in which its investigations make sense.[20] This way of speaking seems to answer our question as to how a community might share a particular vision of human freedom and the like in terms of finite contexts that provide a common framework for a particular understanding of the world and of our place within it.

But, in fact, we only push the question back a step since we must now inquire into what it means for a community to share such a context. Although we always appeal to shared contexts in forming an interpretation of the world, this does not prevent these contexts themselves from being subject to interpretation. Just as no rule determines its own application, so no context of interpretation determines its own interpretation. There is always what Derrida refers to as an "indefinite opening" to every context that prevents its univocal determination.[21] A paradigm is, for example, always capable of coming apart at the seams as different scientists apply it in different ways.[22] And no institutional practice is ever immune from interpretive or experimental transformation. As Lyotard notes, "The limits the institution imposes on potential language 'moves' are never established once and for all (even if they have been formally defined)."[23] They are always the result of agonistic moves both within and without the institution that are perpetually renegotiating its boundaries.

We are never without a shared interpretive context inasmuch as we are never without a range of background beliefs and assumptions that permit us to make some sense of what we do and say in relation to one another. But it is insufficient to appeal to such a context in order to account for the determination of anything like a community's sense of belonging together in a shared understanding of the world. Every context opens up a multiplicity of interpretive horizons in which the determination of *what is shared*, or, better, what *ought* to be shared, is subject to question; that is, every context opens up the significance of a community's background beliefs and assumptions to a range of contestable interpretation. A shared context provides the basis for raising the question of how "we" ought to understand the world and our relation to it, but it does not provide the basis for a univocal resolution of that question.[24] No context is ever sufficiently determined to rule out differences in interpretation that might constitute genuine differences in how "we" envision the world and "our" place within it. Hence, there is the everpresent possibility of what Lyotard refers to as a "differend," that is, a conflict over how any finite context ought to be interpreted and, in that way, determined. Such conflicts cannot be settled by appeal to a common rule or standard shared by all insofar as they call into question the issue of what rules and standards we ought to accept, what sense ought to be made of our shared context.

Lyotard gets at this point, I believe, in his remarks concerning how the nature or the identity of "the social" is always deferred in any phrase that would present it. In his idiom, a phrase is any event that, in its occurrence, presents a universe in which an addressor, addressee, sense, and referent are situated in some relation to one another.[25] To this extent, every phrase is social. For it always presents a universe that is inherently social insofar as its addressor is always positioned in relation to another, his or her addressee, and they are always situated in relation to a sense and a referent that is positioned as common to both of them.[26] But every phrase is susceptible to a multiplicity of different modes of linkage with other phrases that reconfigure the poles of addressor, addressee, sense, and referent in unpredictable ways. And, in that way, the nature of the social bond, as it is presented by any phrase, is always being redetermined by its links with subsequent phrases that reconfigure its presented universe. It is always possible, of course, to regulate modes of linkage between phrases within some particular genre of discourse. For example, it is inappropriate within the scientific genre to follow up a question concerning the probability of a major earthquake along the New Madrid fault with a remark concerning how natural disasters are God's retribution for the sins of humanity. But there is nothing about any particular phrase that demands any particular genre of discourse and so nothing about any particular phrase that demands any particular sort of linkage with another. The determination of the nature and the identity of the social, as it is presented by any phrase, is, therefore, always deferred to an indeterminate fate as every phrase is launched into an arena of competing genres of discourse that determine how it may be followed by another in different ways. The identity of the social becomes the perpetual object of a differend as competing genres of discourse bring with them incommensurable standards and stakes for what constitutes an appropriate link between phrases and, consequently, what determinations of the social bond will dominate any particular discursive situation.[27]

To speak in an unproblematic way of a "we" that shares a particular vision of the world on the basis of a shared context is to assume that there is some one set of rules or standards that regulates the way in which the world is phrased in that context and how, on that basis, a "we" might come to be phrased there. It is to assume, therefore, a kind of incontestable priority on the part of some particular genre of discourse and to ignore the way in which every attempt to phrase the world, to present a universe in which a "we" is determined, always opens onto a differend between competing genres of discourse. But it is precisely that assumption that is rendered untenable with the loss of our belief in a universal history of human emancipation. For that loss is equivalent to the loss of a belief in a universally authoritative genre of discourse—a discourse of "humanity" that would subordinate the links between all possible phrases to the common stakes of universal human emancipation. Without the common stakes provided by that discourse, all our attempts to phrase "ourselves" must remain deferred to an indeterminate future in which the next phrase might reconfigure what is at stake within the first in terms of incommensurable stakes. Without the guarantees of that common discourse, we can never be assured that our attempts to phrase ourselves as, for example, a community that is committed to the ideals of human freedom and dignity might not be followed by other phrases that reconfigure those ideals in an unrecognizable way or that come to present them as ideological covers for self-serving colonial or imperial designs. Lacking a universally authoritative genre of discourse that would disqualify such links, any attempt to recognize ourselves, even in a relatively finite way, must remain contestable in a way that prevents us from ever taking "ourselves" for granted.

The loss of a sense of community that might be stabilized in some particular, determinate presentation, however, is not necessarily the death of community per se. In his reflections on Auschwitz, for instance, Lyotard briefly suggests that "the true *we* is never *we*, never stabilized in a name for *we*, always undone before being constituted, only identified in the non-identity between *you* . . . and *me*."[28] The fracturing of the identity of the "we" that prevents the identification of "you" and "me" in terms of "our" common ideals and aspirations may, in other words, make possible a different mode of communal identification, one that is sensitive to its own untranscendable dispersal. If we cannot identify ourselves on the basis of a preexisting identity or commensurability between "our" various perspectives, we may still come to identify "ourselves" with that lack of identity and lack of commensurability. It may be possible to identify a sense of community that would resist both a modern as well as a premodern stabilization in terms of either a common future that "we" all share on the basis of a common nature or in terms of a particular narrative tradition, a past that "we" share, but that "they" do not. This would be a sense of community that would not be found in terms of a particular answer to the question of who we are, of what knits us together in a common bond, but in terms of the maintenance of the question of who we are. This would be an identification with a "we" that remains undetermined by remaining up for question—a sense of "we," in other words, that does not attempt to transcend its loss of itself, but comes to identify itself with the question of the "we" that is posed in that loss.

Lyotard's analysis of "the deliberative politics of modern democracies"[29] is, I believe, as close as he has come to explicating this idea. As he conceives it, democratic politics may not be construed in terms of a particular genre of discourse with a particular set of standards. Rather, "deliberation is a concatenation of genres"[30] grafted onto one another in terms of the question, "What ought we to be?" The deliberation of this question must proceed by way of a multiplicity of different questions, giving rise in turn to different genres of discourse linked together by their varying relevance to that question. Cognitive genres, for example, are called on as one pursues the question of how best to realize any particular end. What we might call genres of "free association" are called on as the question of what we *can* do is raised and explored in terms of imaginary scenarios that present different possible futures. Rhetorical genres are called on as these different scenarios are debated, with competing parties attempting to persuade one another or some relevant third party of the advantages of their own scenario. Judgment follows, then, taking the form of "resolutions, of programs, or of ballots,"[31] and, finally, the legitimation of judgment in terms of norms and the enactment of laws.

Lyotard speaks of this concatenation as "paradoxical"[32] in that it *seems* to link incommensurable genres of discourse in a relation of consequence or implication to one another—the moment of decision concerning what we *ought* to be following enigmatically from considerations of what we *can* be, of what is likely to follow from that, of what *must* be done to achieve it, and of the number of votes that various proposals receive. But this can only lead us to put the question of what we ought to be up for question again inasmuch as it cannot be answered conclusively on the basis of the genres of discourse that are deployed in its deliberation. As Lyotard notes, "the general feeling is that a discussion . . . could do no more than put the we back into question."[33]

The sense of community fostered through a practice of democratic deliberation can never, therefore, be completed or taken for granted. Indeed, that is its principle political virtue. It is a sense of identity between "you" and "me" that is maintained only in terms of how "we" belong together in a deliberative practice that raises our lack of identity to the level of contention and debate. The nature of the social, the identity of the "we," remains deferred insofar as it is always put up for question in terms of a deliberation in which it cannot be conclusively resolved. To this extent, democratic deliberation fosters a sense of community that emerges only in and through an identification with an Idea[34] of community whose identity remains unresolved, "the Idea of a humanity," as Lyotard phrases it, "which is not the master of 'its' ends (a metaphysical illusion), but which is sensitive to the heterogeneous ends implied in the various known and unknown genres of discourse, and capable of pursuing them as much as possible."[35]

With this Idea, we are brought to the heart of the issue that continues to divide Lyotard from those who would stress the formation of a community through communicatively secured modes of consensus such as Jürgen Habermas or, in a more 'postmodern' key, Richard Rorty. It is not as if Lyotard has ever rejected the idea of consensus. Even in *The Postmodern Condition*, where he described consensus as an "outmoded and suspect value," he went on to emphasize the justice of "local" modes of consensus that remain provisional and "subject to eventual cancellation."[36] The point has never been that there is something unjust or inadequate about the idea of consensus as such, but only that, *taken by itself*, it presents an idea of community that fails to do justice to the modes of conflict that are always tearing apart any consensus in formation. In order to do justice to those conflicts, to that "dissensus" at the heart of every "we," one needs an idea of community that is always, as he puts it in *Peregrinations*, "in the process of doing *and* undoing itself."[37] But the idea of consensus speaks only to the first part of that need. It ignores the second.

To speak, for example, as Rorty does, of retrieving the idea of a universal history of humanity as a history *to be made* through mutual persuasion, rather than *assumed* in terms of a common human nature,[38] is not so much wrong as it is one-sided. It ignores the way in which the attempt to persuade another of the legitimacy of one's own perspective always threatens to run aground on the differends that make mutually convincing argumentation impossible. It, therefore, ignores the way in which the attempt to persuade always threatens to exacerbate differences rather than to heal them; it ignores how persuasion, as a practice, is always for that reason a "doing *and* undoing" of the community. To put the point somewhat differently, it ignores the way in which persuasion that is *not* sensitive to the differends that are always undoing the community is itself a form of violence,[39] that is, an attempt to impose a single regime or order on a community without respect for the potential limits of that regime's authority.[40]

There is a place, therefore, for the construction of communities through mutual persuasion in Lyotard's perspective and, in that sense, a place for the idea of argumentatively secured modes of consensus. Its role was touched upon when the importance of rhetorical genres of discourse in the practice of democratic deliberation was mentioned. Debate and argumentation are *one* of the ways in which a community puts itself up for question. For Lyotard, however, this drive to argumentatively secured forms of consensus is understood as a moment in a deliberative practice that always undoes that consensus by bringing any community *in formation* back to the question of its own identity. It is not, as it is for Habermas, an end in itself.[41]

"The only consensus we ought to be worrying about," Lyotard suggests at the end of *Peregrinations*, "is one that would encourage . . . heterogeneity or 'dissensus'."[42] The only adequate mode of consensus is, paradoxically, to be found in the recognition of our lack of consensus, just as the only adequate sense of community is to be found in the recognition of our lack of identity with one another—our inability to determine in what way "we" may all be said to belong together. We may speak of consensus as we may speak of community with Lyotard, in a sense that remains deferred. To insist on the deferral of community and consensus, however, is not to reject them. It is simply to insist on modes of belonging together that are realized through a practice that is always "doing *and* undoing" itself, forming a sense of community that cannot be taken for granted precisely because it only exists in and through a process in which it is kept permanently up for question.

NOTES

1. See Jean-François Lyotard, *The Postmodern Condition*, trans. Geoff Bennington and Brian Massumi (Minneapolis: University of Minnesota Press, 1984), especially, chs. 9–10.

2. See Jean-François Lyotard, "Universal History and Cultural Differences," in *The Lyotard Reader*, ed. Andrew Benjamin (Cambridge, Mass.: Basil Blackwell, 1989), 317.

3. Lyotard, *The Postmodern Condition*, 66.

4. See ibid., ch. 5, "The Nature of the Social Bond: The Postmodern Perspective" for a discussion of this point.

5. See Jean-François Lyotard, *The Differend*, trans. Georges Van Den Abbeele (Minneapolis: University of Minnesota Press, 1988), no. 195.

6. Lyotard, "Universal History and Cultural Differences," 314.

7. Ibid., 315.

8. Ibid., 319.

9. See Lyotard, *Le Postmoderne expliqué aux enfants* (Paris: Éditions Galilée, 1986), 80–83 for more on this temporal distinction between narrative and modern modes of communal identification.

10. Lyotard, "Universal History and Cultural Differences," 322.

11. Lyotard, *The Differend*, "Declaration of 1789 Notice 1," 145. Also see "Universal History and Cultural Differences," 322.

12. See Lyotard, *The Differend*, "Declaration of 1789 Notice 5," 146.

13. Lyotard, "Universal History and Cultural Differences," 322.

14. Ibid.

15. Ibid.

16. Ibid., 315.

17. Ibid., 317.

18. See Aristotle, *Politics*, 1253a.

19. See Stanley Fish, *Is There a Text in This Class* (Cambridge, Mass.: Harvard University Press, 1980), in particular, ch. 13, "Is There a Text in This Class?"

20. See Thomas Kuhn, *The Structure of Scientific Revolutions* (Chicago: The University of Chicago Press, 1970).

21. Jacques Derrida, *Limited Inc.*, ed. Gerald Graff (Evanston, Ill.: Northwestern University Press, 1988), 137: "the finiteness of a context is never secured or simple, there is an indefinite opening of every context, an essential nontotalization." This is, I believe, the upshot of Derrida's critique of the appeal to context in speech-act theory in "Signature Event Context" as well. See p. 310, where he states, "I would like to demonstrate why a context is never absolutely determinable, or rather in what way its determination is never certain or saturated" (in *Margins of Philosophy*, trans. Alan Bass [Chicago: The University of Chicago Press, 1982]).

22. See Kuhn, *The Structure of Scientific Revolutions*, 83, regarding the inconsistent applications that, in part, led to the dissolution of the Ptolemaic paradigm in astronomy.

23. Lyotard, *The Postmodern Condition*, 17.

24. Georgia Warnke makes something of the same point in her defense of Michael Walzer's work, "Social Interpretation and Political Theory: Walzer and His Critics," *The Philosophical Forum* 21.1–2, (Fall-Winter 1989–90): 204–26, in emphasizing that although a shared context of meaning is necessary even for disagreements within a community, there is no univocal interpretation of those shared meanings. The determination of better or worse interpretations must always be pragmatic (see, in particular, p. 217) and is, I would add, itself always contestable.

25. See Lyotard, *The Differend*, no. 111.

26. Ibid., no. 193.

27. See Ibid., no. 195.

28. Lyotard, "Discussions, or Phrasing 'After Auschwitz'," in *The Lyotard Reader*, 377.

29. Lyotard, *The Differend*, no. 210.

30. Ibid., no. 217.

31. Ibid., no. 215.

32. Ibid., no. 216.

33. Ibid., no. 210.

34. See David Ingram's discussion of this point in his "Legitimacy and the Postmodern Condition: The Political Thought of Jean-François Lyotard," *Praxis International* 7:3/4 (Winter 1987–88): 298–99.

35. Lyotard, *The Differend*, no. 253.

36. Lyotard, *The Postmodern Condition*, 66.

37. Jean-François Lyotard, *Peregrinations: Law, Form, Event* (New York: Columbia University Press, 1988), 38.

38. See Richard Rorty, "Le Cosmopolitisme Sans Émancipation: Réponse á Jean-François Lyotard," *Critique* 41 (1985): 575–76.

39. This is, I believe, at least part of Lyotard's point against Rorty in his response to his "Le Cosmopolitisme Sans Émancipation." See "Discussion entre Jean-François Lyotard et Richard Rorty," *Critique* 41 (1985): 582.

40. For more on Rorty's position see my "Putting Ourselves Up For Question: A Postmodern Critique of Rorty's Postmodernist Bourgeois Liberalism," *Journal of Value Inquiry* 29 (1995): 241–53.

41. See Jürgen Habermas, *The Theory of Communicative Action*; Volume 1: *Reason and the Rationalization of Society* (Boston: Beacon Press, 1981), 287, where he emphasizes that "reaching understanding is the inherent telos of human speech."

42. Lyotard, *Peregrinations*, 44.

CHAPTER 15

Derrida's Political Physics

From the Law of Force in the Book of Nature to the Force of Law in the General Text

JOHN PROTEVI

Derrida has tried to make sense of the nexus of force, violence, and law in writings from the 1963 "Force and Signification"[1] to the 1990 "Force of Law: The Mystical Foundation of Authority."[2] In the intervening years, essays on these topics such as "Violence and Metaphysics,"[3] "Différance,"[4] "Signature Event Context,"[5] "Declarations of Independence,"[6] "Devant la loi,"[7] "The Politics of Friendship,"[8] and "The Laws of Reflection: Nelson Mandela, In Admiration,"[9] also have appeared, as well as interviews like those of *Positions*[10] and the afterword to the new edition of *Limited Inc.*[11] In this essay, I will sketch a "political physics" that accounts for Derrida's emphasis on force in the context of law and justice. In the first half of the essay, I examine the relation of Hegel's book of nature and Derrida's general text; in the second half, the recent "Force of Law" essay and the notion of deconstruction developed therein.

DERRIDA AND HEGEL

Hegel's Book of Nature

As is often the case with Derrida, his confrontation with Hegel is instructive. Any talk of force and law naturally refers one to the chapter on "Force and the Understanding" in the *Phenomenology of Spirit*.[12] Here we encounter the failed attempt by natural consciousness to find unconditioned certainty in scientific laws of force. The attempt to find laws of force to explain all phenomena fails; in other words, the attempt to write the book of nature from the outside, nature as observed by consciousness, fails. In seeing how it fails, natural consciousness progresses in its curriculum on the way to absolute knowledge. Derrida knew this in 1963. In "Force and Signification" he writes: "Hegel demonstrated convincingly that the explication of a phenomenon by force is a tautology."[13] Derrida's next sentence is crucial in order to understand his differences with Hegel over force: "But in saying this, one must refer to language's peculiar inability to emerge from itself in order to articulate its origin, and not to the *thought* of force."[14]

As Derrida made clear a few years later in *Positions*, he is suspicious of the status of Hegelian discourse—suspicious, that is, of its very discursivity, its bookishness, its pretension to being a *pure thought* of force, a purity that relies on the previous work of language as the *Aufhebung des Daseins*, the canceling and lifting of existence into a pure thought-determination.[15] The *Phenomenology* is the gathering and ordering of these thought-determinations or shapes of spirit so that the successive failure to provide unconditioned certainty leads one to absolute knowledge, the standpoint in which the pure categories of thought can be gathered and ordered in the *Science of Logic*.[16] About the *Logic*, Derrida claims that:

> I have attempted to distinguish *différance* (whose *a* marks, among other things, its productive and conflictual characteristics) from Hegelian difference, and have done so precisely at the point at which Hegel, in the greater *Logic*, determines difference as contradiction only in order to resolve it, to interiorize it, to lift it up (according to the syllogistic process of speculative dialectics) into the self-presence of an onto-theological or onto-teleological synthesis.[17]

After the word "contradiction," Derrida appends a note in which he says:

> If I have more often spoken of conflicts of forces than of contradiction, this is first of all due to a critical wariness as concerns the Hegelian concept of contradiction [*Widerspruch*], which, in addition, as its name indicates, is constructed in such a way as to permit its resolution within dialectical *discourse*.[18]

Derrida continues the original passage:

Différance . . . must sign the point at which one breaks with the system of the *Aufhebung* and with speculative dialectics. Since this conflict-uality of *différance* . . . can never be totally resolved, it marks its effects in what I call the text in general, in a text which is not reduced to a book or a library.[19]

The realm of pure thought reached at the end of the *Phenomenology* and articulated in the *Logic* is a realm in which all opposition can be resolved precisely because of its posited character. It is the dream of a book, a book of nature in which the categories appropriate to thinking nature, force among them, find their proper positions. Derrida's suspicion about Hegel's law of force is not that it fixates an inherent flux, for Derrida knows as well as any Hegel scholar that there is a movement to Hegel's law of force. Derrida is worried, however, that this movement is regulated in a speculative economy of opposition and resolution that is made possible by the work of language and that turns a profit of meaning from each investment in a lost spiritual shape. This speculative economy is thematically treated in the section of the *Logic* entitled "The Determinations of Reflection" (to which the *Positions* quote alludes) and methodologically named *Aufhebung.* And indeed, the movement of "The Determinations of Reflection" in the *Logic*, from pure dif-ference to contradiction, does structure the "Force and Understanding" chapter from the earlier *Phenomenology of Spirit.* Hegel tells us there that the law of force is "universal difference," differing even from difference, as seen in the absolute flux of the play of forces and here repeated at the level of thought.[20] At the end of the dialectic of the laws of force, we read that the transition to the Concept, first recognizable in the move to self-conscious-ness, comes with the recognition that the structure of contradiction is now to be thought: "We have to think pure change, or *think antithesis within the antithesis itself*, or *contradiction.*"[21]

Reached through the speculative economy of the *Phenomenology*, in which the laws of force play their pedagogic role, Hegel's book of nature is the *Logic*, which arranges the reflexive categories that enable us to think the laws of force. These are then repeated in their externality in the Philosophy of Nature. The Philosophy of Nature comes second—not chronologically, to be sure, but systematically. As Hegel makes clear, his *Logic* is metaphysics: after physics in the order of knowing, but first philosophy in the order of being.

Derrida's General Text

When we return to "Force and Signification," we can see the basics of
Derrida's reading of Hegel—the reading of the general text as a field of force
and signification—in place years before *Positions* and *Glas*. Derrida writes:
"Force is the other of language without which language would not be what it
is."[22] This "other" is not oppositional, of course. Derrida continues, "Force
cannot be conceived on the basis of an oppositional couple."[23] How, then, is
it to be thought? Derrida does want to think it, although not in a pure
thought, but in a Nietzschean mode: "like pure force, Dionysus is worked by
difference."[24] Worked by difference—or as he will say in a few years, by *différance*, which as we have seen, "marks its effects in . . . the text in general."[25] So here is the distinction alluded to in my title: instead of the pure
thought of laws of force in the book of nature, Derrida writes of a differential,
signifying force in the general text.

Let us now consider the "Différance" essay for more details on the way in
which the general text is one of force *and* signification. Derrida begins by
insisting that we think *différance* in the "general structure of [its] economy."[26] He proposes the term "sheaf [*faisceau*]" to mark that: "the assem-
blage to be proposed has the complex structure of a weaving, an interlacing
which permits the different threads and different lines of sense [*sens*]—or of
force—to go off again in different directions."[27] On the basis of this passage,
let me advance this formula: *différance* "is" the interweaving of sense and
force in the general text.

Force reappears in the "Différance" essay in a thread that is, interest-
ingly enough, not mentioned in Gasché's treatment of the essay.[28] Derrida
names *différance* as the structure of the ever-shifting relations in the field of
forces described by Nietzsche. "Thus, *différance* is the name we might give
to the 'active,' moving discord of different forces that Nietzsche sets up
against the entire system of metaphysical grammar, whenever this system
governs culture, philosophy and science."[29] Nietzsche sets up *forces*, not
simply the thought of force, against metaphysical grammar. In hammering
away at metaphysics, the naming of force as *différance* is itself a force, a
countervailing force to metaphysical grammar, the thinking of force in
opposable, resolvable categories. In describing as differential what metaphysics would name as equal and opposed, there is a performative force,
challenging the interpretative structure that is metaphysics. This challenge
is not opposition, for the forces are not equatable, the discourses incommen-
surate to each other. The thought of laws of force might move through oppos-

able and resolvable categories, but *forces* are never equal, as Deleuze insists in his interpretation of Nietzsche. In the "Différance" essay, Derrida quotes Deleuze from *Nietzsche and Philosophy*:

> Quantity itself, therefore, is not separable from the difference of quantity. The difference of quantity is the essence of force, the relation of force to force. The dream of two equal forces, even if they are granted an opposition of sense [*sens*], is an approximate and crude dream, a statistical dream, plunged into by the living but dispelled by chemistry.[30]

A footnote by Deleuze refers here to passages not available in the English translation of *The Will to Power*, but found only in the French edition at II 86 and 87, where Nietzsche writes: "In the chemical world, the sharpest perception of the difference between forces reigns. . . . With the organic world imprecision and appearance begin."[31]

How are we to understand the claim by Nietzsche and Deleuze that an opposition of sense is but a dream? The economy of "sense" in modern Western European languages (for example, French *sens*, German *Sinn*, Italian *senso*) includes "directionality" and "sensibility" as well as "meaning." Sense is not simply reducible to "meaning" due to these other elements in its economy, for with directionality and sensibility sense is installed in a field of exteriority and force. A direction implies a space within which two points can be ordered, and a sensation implies a receptivity to the forceful action of that which is sensed. In fact, for Nietzsche, one could claim that meaning is the most superficial element in the economy of sense, that meaning is the effect of configurations of directional forces. On this view, meanings arise from the confluence of forceful vectors. But this means that forces can never be op-posed, because they are never posed. Since meaning and hence subjectivity arise on the basis of a field of forces, there is no meaningful subject outside the field of forces to do the posing. The dream of opposable sense is the dream of opposable categories isolated from a field of always oblique and never reconcilable forces. In other words, it is the dream of writing a book of nature, the dream of metaphysics. Naming the differential character of force and the force dimension of the general text dispels that dream for those that hear and understand that naming.

But dispelling the dream is not enough, for precisely what is to be understood is that understanding is not pure, that understanding and signification do not exhaust the general text. Bodies are in force in the general text. To quote Deleuze on Nietzsche from a few pages prior to the quote that Derrida selects: "every relationship of forces constitutes a body—whether it is chemical, biological, social, or political."[32] A body, as constituted by forces, is always in excess of pure meaning; it is always the overflow of sense in its full economy beyond the single moment of meaning. In *Positions*, Derrida claims that "There is [*il y a*] such a general text everywhere that (that is, everywhere) [metaphysics] and its order (essence, truth, sense, consciousness, ideality, etc.) are *overflowed*, that is, everywhere that their authority is put back into the position of a *mark* in a chain."[33] The overflowing of sense into the general text is its inscription in a field of forces, the directional forces or the vectors of the play of forces, that is relatively stabilized as meaning. Meaning is thus seen as the hegemonic formation of forces that guarantees the relatively stable identity of the intended object. The force field of meaning is why Derrida will claim in "Signature Event Context" that "an opposition of metaphysical concepts . . . is never the face-to-face of two terms, but a hierarchy and an order of subordination."[34] Conceptual opposition, opposition of categories posited in a book, is a dream; hierarchy is the way of the general text, the interweaving of force and signification.

The general text is an interwoven field of forces and significations. The interweaving of the field is named *différance*, while its elements are named "marks." The general text is a field of marks. Just as we have disabused ourselves of the dream of a book of pure signification, so we must beware of the temptation to think that we have arrived at a pure physics of force, for a mark is force *and* signification. Let me advance another formula to parallel our recognition that meaning is forceful. Let us acknowledge that force is a significant element of the general text. Writing, inscribing a mark, is a performative signifying and a meaningful performance—we could call it *making sense*. Making sense is the construction of a hegemonic formation of forces in which meaning arises from a formation of vectors.[35] In the general text force is interwoven with sense so that forces must make sense and making sense is forceful.

Force is not a ground closed off onto itself. Forces must make sense; they must be iterable in a mark that has a minimal identity over the time and space of the series of its iterated marks. A mark is thus a relatively stable inscription, never self-present, yet repeatable. On the other hand, making sense is forceful. I have noted above the force of Nietzsche's countering of metaphysics. We could also refer, in anticipation, to the primacy of the performative Derrida articulates in "Force of Law." Any constative is preceded by a performative affirmation: "Yes, I promise, testify, pledge, that this is true." Any constative is also performatively reinforced by a reading code that guarantees its legibility.[36] In other words, the reading of marks is institutionally enforced. Reading strategies outside the institutionally enforced reading code make no sense, as anyone who reads the bewildered responses to deconstructive readings can tell you.

Having been warned against the dream of a pure physics, we should, however, remember that in the academic/political culture still dominated by the metaphysical reading code, which commands us to ignore differential force and stress pure meaning, it is disruptive to stress force. But, of course, stressing force is a new way of making sense, one that possesses its own reading code. Reading meaningful force and forceful meaning is a way of reading the general text as the interweaving of force *and* signification.

The general text, we have seen, is a field of marks skewed into hierarchies. The hierarchies, which give themselves off as oppositions to a metaphysical reading, are pairs lifted from a differential reserve. As Derrida writes in "Plato's Pharmacy":

> [the pharmakon] is the *différance* of difference. It holds in reserve, in its undecided shadow and vigil, the opposites and the differends that the process of discrimination will come to carve out. Contradictions and pairs of opposites are lifted from the bottom of this diacritical, differing, deferring reserve. Already inhabited by *différance*, this reserve, even though it "precedes" the opposition between different effects, even though it preexists differences as effect, does not have the simplicity of a *coincidentia oppositorum*. It is from this field that dialectics draws its philosophemes.[37]

We must be careful here to note that the field is already inhabited by *différance*. That is, it is already structured by force. The lifting of opposites is always a skewing of them into new hierarchies, a twisting of them on the basis of previous hierarchies. Any hegemonic formation of meaningful force and forceful meaning is, however, never total, but has held in reserve the possibility of reinscribing its elements in different, disseminative, formations and contexts.

"FORCE OF LAW" AND DECONSTRUCTION

The Coup de force

The skewing force is the *coup de force* that establishes an institution, a new way of making sense. It is always a marshalling of force against force, a dif-

ferential shift of meaning by a shift of forces. The instituting event is a per-
formative-constative undecidable, in other words, one that interweaves performative force and constative signification. In several essays, Derrida
shows how any instituting event must grant itself, in advance, the right to act
with a force that will only be justified by the institution brought into force by
that act. In the 1986 redaction of a previous speech, "Declarations of
Independence," Derrida writes of the "fabulous retroactivity" of the *coup de
force* by which a people constitutes itself by signature in an undecidable
constative-performative.[38] The 1986 essay, "The Laws of Reflection: Nelson
Mandela, In Admiration," clarifies this difficult point. Derrida writes here
that the violent act of institution must at once produce *and* presuppose the
unity of the nation that is to be instituted.[39] In the case of South Africa, this
act *remained* a *coup de force* because its violence was excessive and deficient—it remained excessively visible because it enfranchised only the
European minority, yet it was deficient in that it was not violent enough, not
genocidal enough, in leaving behind too many African witnesses.[40] The
instituting *coup de force* is violent in the sense that it precedes the institution
of a state authority that can legitimately use force.[41]

It should be stated here that Derrida's reading is not, despite a certain
family resemblance, mere ideology critique. Critique finds the truth outside
the text. Critique would simply describe a higher-order law of force by
unmasking positive law as the instrument of forces that would remain foundational. Rather, force and law must be thought together as the force of law,
where the conceptual explication of the interweaving of force and signification reaches a limit. Derrida writes in the 1989 essay "Force of Law: The
Mystical Foundation of Authority" that

> the operation that consists of founding, inaugurating, justifying law
> (*droit*), making law, would consist of a *coup de force*, of a performative
> and therefore interpretative violence that in itself is neither just nor
> unjust and that no justice and no previous law with its founding ante-
> rior moment could guarantee or contradict or invalidate. . . . Here the
> discourse comes up against its limit: in itself, in its performative power
> itself. It is what I here propose to call the mystical.[42]

The discourse comes up against its limit: signification cannot fully explicate
the interweaving of force and signification.

As is so often the case, the German language is fortuitously undecidable
in helping to articulate this limit. *Gewalt*, as in the title of the Benjamin
piece, *Zur Kritik der Gewalt*, examined in the second half of the "Force of

Law" essay, means both violence and legitimate authority. For instance, *Gewalttätigkeit* is the word Kant uses to describe the violence of the state of nature,[43] while *Staatsgewalt* is a common expression for the authority of the state. The social contract tells us that individuals must delegate their natural right to violence to the state, which has a monopoly on the legitimate use of force. The delegation of natural *Gewalt* to the *Staatsgewalt* is the social contract. But, on Derrida's reading, the institution of the *Staatsgewalt*, the *coup de force*, cannot be located in this economy of violence/legitimate force.

This instituting event, even though it is irruptive and resistant to account, is iterable. In the terms of the Benjamin essay, its law-making violence is interwoven with a law-conserving violence. As Derrida says, "a foundation is a promise."[44] What is set up must be or ought to be repeated. The *coup de force* sets up the law in force here and now. The *coup de force* sets up a hierarchy by skewing differentially what went before. On that basis, it allows for the institution to continue. As Derrida makes clear, this continuation has the structure of auto-affection in which the law-conserving violence iterates the institution and keeps the skewed hegemonic formation of forces in force.[45] Derrida writes: "Iterability inscribes the promise as guard in the most irruptive instant of foundation. Thus it describes the possibility of repetition at the heart of the originary."[46] And again, a few pages later, "Iterability requires the origin to repeat itself originarily, to alter itself so as to have the value of origin, that is, to conserve itself."[47]

But iterability is also the basis of dissemination. In "Signature Event Context" we read of yet another force, the "force of rupture," that accompanies any mark and forbids the saturation of any context. In other words, the iteration of the institution is open to a force of rupture because the enforcing of the hegemonic formation of forces is never assured. It is never assured, because any mark is not self-present. Rather, a mark is spaced over the series of its iterations; in this series, the sameness of the mark is constituted from its different occurences. The *coup de force* is a writing, the inscription of a mark in the general text. The *coup de force* makes sense.[48]

Deconstruction: Reinscription and Incision/Decision

What, then, does deconstruction do? The skewing *coup de force* forces certain elements to bear the weight of the institution in force by forcing them into economically exploited, politically dominated, and culturally marginalized positions. This exploitation, domination, and marginalization is revealed in the concrete call for justice made by others forced into those positions. The enforcing of the law, the iteration of the institution, bears down on the point of tension. Reinscription in another context, the so-called "second phase" of deconstruction, is the unleashing of the force of rupture that makes an institution tremble along the incisions, the lines of force that traverse any institution along the skewing brought into force by the instituting decision. The incision follows the path of the decision. A quote from *Positions* makes this clear: "An incision, precisely, can only be made according to lines of force and forces of rupture that are localizable in the discourse to be deconstructed."[49] What is to be deconstructed is not simply a signifying discourse, as this quotation might seem to imply, but also the forceful institution that reinforces a certain reading of that discourse and that enforces the performance of the action dictated in the imperatives and performatives of the discourse.

The lines of force that call for incision are key undecidables that are forced, by decision, into positions that allow for the dominant interpretation of the institutionalized discourse. Forced into decided positions, they are prone to release forces of rupture when shown in their undecidability. Deconstruction is called for whenever one of the effects of institutional reading codes is to make hierarchies seem natural and not constructed, that is, to attempt, impossibly, to purify signification of contamination by force and thus to attempt to make the general text appear as a book of nature.[50] Since Derrida has written many times that deconstructive intervention is, in the words of "Force of Law," "a maximum intensification of a transformation in progress,"[51] we could identify at least three of the incisive lines of force and forces of rupture of our institutions as the denaturalization of gender, race, and class.

But *why* deconstruct, assuming that we have some decision here? In the name of what does deconstruction release its forces of rupture? Derrida answers: in the name of justice. Derrida's political physics looks like a "might makes right" position. And in one sense indeed it is, in the sense that might makes *droit*, that is, the fact that positive law can be analyzed in terms of social power. Derrida reminds us, however, that might does not make justice. Instead, "Force of Law" tells us that "deconstruction is justice."[52] Institutions, or sets of positive laws [*droits*], are deconstructible because they are not justice. Deconstruction is justice, that is, "deconstruction is already engaged by this infinite demand of justice."[53] Deconstruction also finds its "force, its movement or its motivation" in the "always unsatisfied appeal" to justice.[54] In the notion of justice that Derrida develops in "Force of Law" there is an aporetic structure in which a universal law commands the recognition of a singular case. The aporetic structure of law is justice. At this point Derrida mentions his debt to Levinas, to his notion of justice as the face of the other, always singular and hence infinite, to which Derrida "would be tempted to compare" his own notion.[55]

Although infinitely in excess of positive law, justice is not opposed to law. The law of law, the *loi* of *droit*, might be formulated as: always do justice to those who stand, singularly, before the law. Those before the law are also those whose concrete calling out for justice, interweaving the saying and the said, the primary and secondary affirmations of deconstruction, provoke the "transformation in progress" to which deconstruction responds with its "maximum intensification."[56] We might want to say here that *democracy* is the future, the "to come," of this transformation, intensifying itself to the point where instituted bodies that muffle or distort the calls of others are overflowed and reinscribed in other contexts. Deconstruction is democratic justice, responding to the calls from all others.

Democracy is not without institution, of course, just as justice is not without law. Justice demands that justice be done in the name of law, and law must be just. Yet, as Aristotle knew well, the universal law cannot always do justice to the singular case before the law. Thus, Aristotle would have us consult the intention of the lawmaker in order to do justice.[57] Derrida would have us do justice to those brought before the law (and that always means doing justice to "the third" always already there in these cases).[58] Doing justice for Derrida does not take recourse to a standard, as in Aristotle,[59] but it does articulate the impossible demands placed on judging. Judging is a trial, an undergoing of impossible tasks demanded by the aporetic structure of law. Derrida gives us three examples of the same aporia of the universal law to do justice to the singular case: (1) judging must be free and responsible, but not without rule or reference to previously established (positive) law;[60] (2) judging cannot be arbitrary, yet it cannot be mere calculation either;[61] and (3) judgment must have all the information, it must not rush to judgment, but justice cannot wait, justice must be served to those here and now before the law.[62] Judging must undergo these trials of the "undecidable," but judging cannot be decisionistic. Rather it must be bound to the other and to the third. Decisionism merely chooses one side of the paradox, opting out of the trial too soon, while calculation is merely its mirror-image. In deconstructive justice, the judge is always on trial; and one can never point to a just decision, for justice is always to come.[63]

CONCLUSION

The *coup de force* is iterable. Iteration occurs as auto-affection, timing and spacing, the turning space of time. Time exploded as spacing is the time of justice, the always past of responsibility, the infinite alterity of futural democratic justice. In this economy of exteriority, the supposed inside, signification, is turned out, opened up, to force, opened up from the inside. In this opening out, the construction of an institution of positive law and its deconstruction in the name of justice depends upon the opening of signification to force, the move from the law of force to the force of law, the turning of the book of nature into the general text.[64]

NOTES

1. Jacques Derrida, "Force and Signification," in *Writing and Difference*, trans. Alan Bass (Chicago: University of Chicago Press, 1978), 3–30.

2. Jacques Derrida, "Force of Law: The 'Mystical Foundation of Authority'," trans. Mary Quaintance, *Cardozo Law Review* 11 (1990): 919–1045.

3. Jacques Derrida, "Violence and Metaphysics: An Essay on the Thought of Emmanuel Levinas," in *Writing and Difference*, 79–153.

4. Jacques Derrida, "Différance," in *Margins of Philosophy*, trans. Alan Bass (Chicago: University of Chicago Press, 1981), 1–27.

5. Jacques Derrida, "Signature Event Context," in *Margins*, 307–30.

6. Jacques Derrida, "Declarations of Independence," in *New Political Science* 5 (1986): 7–15.

7. Jacques Derrida, "Devant la loi," trans. Avital Ronell, in *Kafka and the Contemporary Critical Performance*, ed. Alan Udoff (Bloomington: Indiana University Press, 1985), 128–49.

8. Jacques Derrida, "The Politics of Friendship," trans. Gabriel Motzkin, in *The Journal of Philosophy* 85.11 (November 1988): 632–45.

9. Jacques Derrida, "The Laws of Reflection: Nelson Mandela, In Admiration," trans. Mary Ann Caws and Isabelle Lorenz, in *For Nelson Mandela*, ed. Jacques Derrida and Mustapha Tlili (New York: Henry Holt, 1987): 13–42.

10. Jacques Derrida, *Positions*, trans. Alan Bass (Chicago: University of Chicago Press, 1981).

11. Jacques Derrida, "Afterword: Toward an Ethic of Discussion," in *Limited Inc.*, trans. Samuel Weber (Evanston, Ill.: Northwestern University Press, 1988), 111–54.

12. G. W. F. Hegel, *Phenomenology of Spirit*, trans. A. V. Miller (Oxford: Oxford University Press, 1977).

13. Derrida, "Force and Signification," 27.

14. Ibid.

15. Hegel, *Phenomenology*, 17.

16. Force appears in the *Logic* as well, in chapter 3 of section 2, book 2, the Doctrine of Essence.

17. Derrida, *Positions*, 44.

18. Ibid., 101n13.

19. Ibid., 44.

20. Hegel, *Phenomenology*, 90.

21. Ibid., 99.

22. Derrida, "Force and Signification," 27.

23. Ibid., 28.

24. Ibid., 29.

25. See note 19 above.

26. Derrida, "Différance," 3.

27. Ibid., 3.

28. Rodolphe Gasché, *The Tain of the Mirror: Derrida and the Philosophy of Reflection* (Cambridge, Mass.: Harvard University Press, 1986), 194–205.

29. Derrida, "Différance," 18.

30. Gilles Deleuze, *Nietzsche and Philosophy*, trans. Hugh Tomlinson (New York: Columbia University Press, 1983), 43; cited by Derrida in "Différance," 17.

31. Ibid., 204n5.

32. Ibid., 40.

33. Derrida, *Positions*, 59.

34. Derrida, "Signature Event Context," 329.

35. From the afterword to *Limited Inc.*, 145: "the semantic level [is not] . . . entirely semantic or significant." Derrida, speaking of the stability of interpretative structures, says he is not speaking of ahistorical "semantic structures," but of "stratifications that are already differential and of a great stability with regard to relations of forces and all the hierarchies or hegemonies they suppose or put into practice" (p. 144).

36. Derrida, "Force of Law," 969.

37. Derrida, "Plato's Pharmacy," in *Dissemination*, trans. Barbara Johnson (Chicago: University of Chicago Press, 1982), 127.

38. Derrida, "Declarations of Independence," 10.

39. Derrida, "Laws of Reflection," 17.

40. Ibid., 18.

41. On this point, see B. Honig, "Declarations of Independence: Arendt and Derrida on the Problem of Founding a Republic," *American Political Science Review* 85.1 (March 1991): 97–113.

42. Derrida, "Force of Law," 941, 943.

43. Immanuel Kant, *The Metaphysical Elements of Justice*, trans. John Ladd (New York: Macmillan, 1965), 72.

44. Derrida, "Force of Law," 997.

45. Here we see an opportunity to articulate Derrida's discourse with the Marxist issue of reproduction of the mode of production.

46. Derrida, "Force of Law," 997.

47. Ibid., 1007, 1009.

48. From the afterword to *Limited Inc.*, 148: "I say 'undecidability' rather than 'indeterminacy' because I am interested more in relations of force, in differences of force, in everything that allows, precisely, determinations in given situations to be stabilized through a decision of writing (in the broad sense I give to this word, which also includes political action and experience in general)."

49. Derrida, *Positions*, 82.

50. The relation between these "natural" relations and Hegel's book of nature is explored by Derrida in *Glas*. See Kevin Thompson's essay "The Indigestibility of Diversity," delivered at the 1991 annual meeting of the Society for Phenomenology and Existential Philosophy (SPEP).

51. Derrida, "Force of Law," 933.

52. Ibid., 945.

53. Ibid., 955.

54. Ibid., 957.

55. Ibid., 959.

56. See note 51 above.

57. Aristotle, *Nichomachean Ethics*, 5.10,1137b22ff.

58. Derrida, "Politics of Friendship," 641.

59. Kant is also hesitant to indicate a standard here. In the *Metaphysical Elements of Justice*, at the point where the universal law and the singular case come into conflict, he calls equity "a silent goddess who cannot be heard" (p. 40).

60. Derrida, "Force of Law," 961.

61. Ibid., 963, 965, 967.

62. Ibid., 967, 979.

63. The Kantian echo should be clear. A moral act can never be shown to have occured, as the *Grundlegung* makes clear.

64. I would like to acknowledge the provocation afforded my thoughts in this essay by the paper delivered by Simon Critchley at the 1991 SPEP meeting.

CHAPTER 16

Ghost Stories

Critical Remembrance and Justice in Derrida and Habermas

MAX PENSKY

In the *Dialectic of Enlightenment*, Horkheimer and Adorno write, "Mythic inevitability is defined by the equivalence between the curse, the crime which expiates it, and the guilt arising from that which in turn reproduces the curse. All justice in history to date bears the mark of this pattern."[1] Our response to this desperate insight will depend very much on which of these two conditionals of justice, "in history" or "to date," is taken as definitive, as nonnegotiable. For the former conditional, the oxymoronic notion of "justice in history" leads toward an encounter with a justice envisioned as absolute alterity and to be experienced at the limits of the possibility of the political; an impossible experience or experience of impossibility whose resonance might still be directed, somehow, into the heart of the present with a disruptive force. For the latter conditional, clinging to the "date" of justice that is promised within history and achievable at every individual moment, critique aims at laying bare the demand for worldly justice that is embedded within everyday practices themselves and seeks in this way to expose the essentially arbitrary state of affairs in which injustice is produced and reproduced.

Derrida and Habermas can be said to occupy these respective positions. In what follows, I would like to observe a number of parallels and divergences that arise between these positions as both attempt to present a philosophical account of the relation between justice and memory.

Derrida's reading of Walter Benjamin's early essay "Critique of Violence" leads to an unlikely pairing. The ultimate deconstructibility of law, that is, the inability of law to maintain a distinction between its own legitimacy and the physical violence through which this legitimacy is established, is matched against the ultimate *undeconstructibility* of justice. "Deconstructible" law is engaged in the perpetual attempt to ground its own authority in an originary act of force that, in turn, could only be justified by an appeal to the same law that it inaugurates. Once set in motion, such a devil's circle progressively reveals the unfoundedness of its foundation. The force of law is itself neither legal nor illegal. Instead, it transcends and violates our incessant legalistic and moralistic desires for preserving such a binary and effacing the sheer arbitrariness, the mythic gesture, through which law is violently established and violently preserved.

And yet, Derrida claims, the deconstructibility of law is "not bad news. We may even see in this a stroke of luck for politics, for all historical progress."[2] Deconstructive critique reveals the brute force that all legalisms work to cover over. Such an unmasking critique presumably is meant to mobilize a resistance against all of the efforts of legal systems to impose, by arbitrary fiat, a supposedly justified legal domination and to insist not just on the deconstructibility, but also on the negotiability, malleability, and transformability of legal systems themselves.

Derrida, however, does not pursue this. Instead, he observes that the deconstructibility of the law is met—runs headlong into—the *undeconstructibility* of justice. Justice is undeconstructible because it is not a part of the structured system of representations in which law is articulated and imposed. Justice is not the horizon of possibility toward which the law may orient itself; it is no *telos*. It exceeds and withdraws from—is older than and foreign to—the essentially calculative operations of legislative apparatuses. We may wish for justice to arise from the experience of the application of a law. But, for Derrida, justice itself could never be calculated by the application of a law, could not be delivered by the invention of a law, could not be evoked as the mythic representation of a law. On these terms, justice "is" incalculable, unrepresentable, undefinable, impossible, aporetic, *différant*. "A will, a desire, a demand for justice whose structure wouldn't be an experience of aporia would have no chance to be what it is, namely, a call for justice" (FL 94). A call for justice is a call for the oblique emergence of what occupies the narrow gaps between the laws. It is a call for justice that is never really present nor ever entirely absent, but that resonates in silence, as the missing note in the harmonics that "just" laws would have played. An impossible sound.

From here, it is a rather short step for Derrida to claim that "deconstruction is justice" (FL 945)—but a long step indeed for the reader, who may well confront this deceptively simple formula embedded near the opening of Derrida's text as another form of impossibility, as a Kafka-style parable of gnomic simplicity, perhaps even as a door meant only for the reader, through which the reader nevertheless finds herself incapable of passing. Still, rather than addressing this peculiar copula "deconstruction is justice" head-on, I would like to suggest instead that what Derrida wants to say is not that there is some intelligible relationship of existential or dialectical identity between the aporetic and unruly experience of radical alterity that he is calling justice and the critical strategy of reading known as deconstruction.[3] Rather, the copula expresses an *ethical* relation—the "is" is all that can be expressed of an impossible "ought." The copula is a call to establish a relationship to a text; a relationship that, for Derrida, establishes and maintains itself in the medium of *memory*. To say that deconstruction is justice is to say that a call for justice is heeded only by adopting the will to deconstruct. The will to deconstruct, in turn, is only to be sensed as itself a kind of remembrance.

For a very long time, Derrida has used the image of the ghost, or of haunting, to indicate the possibility of an absence—of trace, of *différance*—that nevertheless installs itself, through memory, within writing. Memory within the context of *un*deconstructed metaphysics is oppression. It consists of the claim to the pellucid and immediate re-presentation of the previously present. Writing in this sense is the medicinal poison, the "*hypomnemesis*," that acts as the supplement to this metaphysical memory. In his earlier writings, Derrida comes back again and again to the difficult point that, in the deconstruction of this opposition between spoken and written memory, we are referred to the infinity of *différance*: the trace is the "arche-phenomenon of memory,"[4] and the "living present" itself is thinkable as present only by the possibility of a retentional trace. The ethics of deconstruction reveals that one must take the side of *différance*; the trace, as writing, is what philosophy has from the beginning set out to efface. Moreover—and this is one of the most obvious continuities between Derrida and German Critical Theory— the history of philosophical systems is legible as the impossible project of effacing all that or all those who themselves act as traces, lacunae, disruptions, or aporias within the legalistic, self-calculating episteme of cognitive representations, the "belly turned mind," as Adorno called it. Philosophy dedicates itself to the suppression of the trace. This means that, as a phenomenon of writing, philosophy is no different than the process of Western history in which we impose an artificially grounded legality in order to define, master, and ultimately crush the other. This is accomplished according to that hopelessly familiar, grisly logic according to which the other is first posited as other, so that the oppression and ultimately the eradication of this other can be conceived as constitutive of the very concept of "otherness" itself.

"All reification is forgetting," the Critical Theorists say. The task, then, is the mobilization of an other memory, a different and hence critical memory, one that will act as a tool for the resistance to reification. The increasingly desperate search for just this memory ultimately led Adorno down the blind alley of aesthetic mimesis, and this failure was in large measure due to Adorno's unwillingness to give up the possibility that a conceptual mediation between subject and objects could be rescued from the operation of conceptual cognition. Derrida's celebration of the very dispersion of the former subject into the kaleidoscopic playground of *différance* may cause us to wonder who, exactly, is to be emancipated through criticism. But it does have the singular advantage over Adorno's negative dialectics in that it opens up an other way of talking about an infinite, ethical, critical form of remembrance. Infinite memory for Derrida is not the inherently teleological and appropriative *mimesis-anamnesis* of an aesthetic *theory* that, despite itself, replicates the moment of remembrance as the appropriation of the other back into the mourning hence narcissistic self. It is not *Erinnerung*, but the play of trace as it flickers between being and nonbeing, as it renders the very reflective certainty of being and nonbeing into a moment of undecidability.[5] The trace, as supplement or as absent but not really missing, is a ghost. Metaphysical texts are haunted by *différance*. Derrida does not mean this metaphorically. The *différance* that has been crushed by the metaphysics of presence lingers on, muttering, clanking, and slamming doors in the house of language; not quite visible, but nevertheless not really invisible; not really audible, but nevertheless generating the creaks and bumps that disturb sleep, the sounds of night that linger in the confusion of morning; not really there, but nevertheless never really gone.

Philosophical texts are haunted by the ghosts of the others who are killed but not eradicated. Deconstruction is a mode of remembrance in which the trace of the other is momentarily, imperfectly, and ironically indicated, while the tradition that contained it and consigned it to its spectral existence is allowed to fall apart.[6]

In the essay on Benjamin's "Critique of Violence," Derrida affirms that this Levinasian advocacy and "responsibility without limits" can be practiced only as the permanent "task of recalling the history, the origin and subsequent direction, thus the limits" (FL 953) of Western conceptions of justice and legality. We respond to the repressed call of the other by recollection; thus "the task of a historical and interpretive memory is at the heart of deconstruction" (FL 955).

The deconstruction of Benjamin's "uneasy, enigmatic, terribly equivocal text" (FL 973) is rendered more problematic by the fact that Benjamin's essay itself is—perhaps more than any other—a text that deconstructs itself, a self-ruining and hence self-criticizing operation, consigned to catastrophic history and thus exhibiting the same attraction that had drawn Benjamin to the forgotten genre of the baroque *Trauerspiel.* "Critique of Violence," on Derrida's reading, is a text dedicated to undermining and contaminating the very distinction between founding and conserving violence—and between mythic law and divine justice—that the text labors to construct. Thus Derrida's reading sets out to identify those moments of the essay in which the excluded other itself, under the sign of the perished victim, asserts its own force at the precise moment at which Benjamin attempts to determine its position. The text is "haunted in advance" (FL 973) in 1921 by the image of the total annihilation of justice. "I purposely say this text is haunted by the theme of exterminating violence because . . . it is haunted by haunting itself, by a quasi-logic of the phantom which, because it is the more forceful one, should be substituted for an ontological logic of presence, absence or representation" (FL 973). This "quasi-logic" of the ghost of memory is the only possible one for the reading of Benjamin's critique of violence and the prehaunting of the Holocaust. For Derrida, the condition for thinking the Holocaust thus becomes

> a readiness to welcome the law of the phantom, the spectral experience and the memory of the phantom, of that which is neither dead nor living, more than dead and more than living, only surviving, the law of the most commanding memory, even though it is the most effaced and the most effaceable, but for that very reason the most demanding. (FL 973)

The memory of the other haunts the text; it haunts *us.* Haunting is the beginning of the possibility of the experience of infinite responsibility. An impossible moral relation—a moral relationship with those not in exis-

tence—can only be discharged by deconstructive remembrance, by recalling the "singularity of the other," by anamnestically choosing sides.
Deconstruction's anamnestic duty becomes "never to yield on this point,
constantly to maintain the interrogation of the origin, grounds, and limits of
our conceptual, theoretical, or normative apparatus surrounding justice"
(FL 955).

Anamnestic criticism interrogates not just to lay bare the arbitrariness of the
supposedly eternal conditions of social injustice, but also to discharge an
impossible ethical relation, one that perhaps only the Holocaust could have
impressed upon the institution of social and literary criticism. Moments
when such a responsibility are met—perhaps the collective shocks, in the
Benjaminian sense, of an unwilled, politically explosive *memoire involon-
taire*—are moments that stand outside of time, moments in which the grip of
legally sanctioned forgetting is loosened. These are moments of justice:
experiences of a radical break in the fabric of legality and force.

Of course, Derrida is not willing to maintain a stable opposition between
the dominion of mythic law and heterogenous justice as the counterforce
that interrupts it. This would be too good, too messianic, too much of a
Kantian regulative idea. Imposed upon the history that stands in need of
deconstruction, such an opposition would clandestinely legitimate it by
compromising the singularity and unrepeatability of demands for justice—
memories—themselves. Derrida will insist upon deconstructing this very
opposition between law and justice, showing how the two contaminate one
another and how the specter of the undecidable, of what lies beyond all conscious calculation and decision, underlies and makes possible all those
legal calculations and decisions that comprise political life. Deconstruction
thus seeks to occupy the narrow space of undecidability between aporetic
and incalculable justice and historical law. It occupies this space in order to
radicalize it, to recall again and again what is rotten in the law.

The formula "deconstruction is justice" expresses something like this
habitation as well. It is a place where we tell each other ghost stories that are
meant to shock us awake, to keep us, for a while, from nodding off, to make
us remember. Anamnestic criticism is the response to the Holocaust that
Derrida suggests. Beyond any simplistic moral didacticism, beyond justifi-
catory discourses about vengeance and vigilance, the memory of the
Holocaust commands us to mobilize a critical violence against the array of
discourses and practices in which the Holocaust was possible.

One can only think, that is remember, the uniqueness of the final solution from a place other than this space of the mythological violence of right. . . . One cannot think the uniqueness of an event like the final solution, as extreme point of mythic and representational violence, within its *own* system. One must try to think it beginning with its other, that is to say, starting from what it tried to exclude and destroy, to exterminate radically, from that which haunted it at once from without and from within. (FL 1042)

Remembering the names of the forgotten others and deconstructing the mythic source of this forgetfulness and this violence thus become *the same* project for Derrida. The "lesson" of the Holocaust—if such a thing could still contain a moment of justice—is a radical critical program or perhaps a permanent disposition, a life, that is simultaneously "consciousness-raising" and "redemptive," to use a pair of terms that Jürgen Habermas first applied to Benjamin.[7] "We must think, know, represent for ourselves, formalize, judge the possible complicity between all these discourses and the worst (here the final solution). . . . It is this thought that the memory of the final solution seems to me to dictate" (FL 1045).

At no other point does Derrida stand closer to Habermas. Like Derrida, Jürgen Habermas has turned to a relation between justice and memory for the task of formulating a response to the ethical "meaning" of the Holocaust. It is remarkable that Habermas, widely regarded as a kind of Enlightenment dinosaur, arrives at conclusions—but more important, I suspect, generates dispositions and attitudes—concerning the task of critical remembrance that bear striking affinities with those of Derrida.

Habermas's contributions to the "Historians' Debate" in the mid-1980s, unlike Derrida's work, self-consciously continue an older, specifically West German debate, often associated with Theodor Adorno and Karl Jaspers in the 1950s, concerning the singularity of the Holocaust and the relevance of collective guilt in the formation of a distinctively West German political culture. Habermas correctly perceives neoconservative attempts toward a relativization of the Holocaust, and a concomitant lifting of the burden of collective guilt and responsibility, as political expedients. The goal of these relativizations—for example, the historian Ernst Nolte's argument that the Holocaust was a "copy" of the "more original" "Asiatic deed" of the Soviet gulag[8]—is the removal of the phenomenon of collective guilt as an ethical barrier for the reappropriation of German cultural traditions. Such prewar traditions—ethnic nationalism, particularism, "family values," the whole shopworn bundle of appeals to a specifically German experience of national identity—are thus to be artificially reattached as premodern prostheses, compensations for the fragmenting effects of social and economic modernity. The relativization of the Holocaust thus serves as the spearhead of a politically strategic instrumentalization of collective memory in the interests of an artificially enhanced political legitimation. The heart of Habermas's writings on memory and the Holocaust is a double objection to this instrumentalization. First, Habermas will argue that the artificial compensation of premodern cultural traditions is inadmissible insofar as it seeks to turn back the fragile growth of universal, postconventional value orientations that the Federal Republic had painfully nurtured in the five decades since the Nazi years. Second, and for our interests more important, Habermas objects that the instrumentalization of memory is inadmissible on *moral* grounds. But what form of moral relationship could still exist between those living and those who have perished?

Only a perspective that has definitively broken with all the traditions and cultural heritages in which the Holocaust was possible could grant itself the right to interpret such traditions without an inherently moral dimension. For contemporary German society, however, just the opposite is the case. As Habermas writes,

> Our own life is bound up with the conditions in which Auschwitz was possible—not through contingent circumstances, but inherently. Our form of life is tied to that of our parents and grandparents through an inter-woven fabric of familial, geographic, political and intellectual heritages; that is, through an historical milieu that has made us who and what we are.[9]

For this reason, the incessant criticism—or "interrogation," as Derrida would put it—of all cultural traditions is to be understood as a moral demand or as a call for justice. Like Derrida, Habermas understands that such a call for justice introduces the necessity of rethinking the operation of historical memory. Habermas insists that, if memory is to serve both as the only possible medium for the persistence of an ethical relation with vanished victims and as the catalyst for a critical interrogation of the cultural practices that inflicted violence upon these victims, then *justice* ought to be envisioned as the weak persistence of an utterly simple demand for the provision of needs, recognition, and the rights of individuals to live without fear, rather than as Derrida's wild alterity. Justice, for Habermas, is always already encoded within every syllable of everyday language.

Habermas thus extends the claim for a kind of normativity, a moral relation with the past, in which memory *continues* by virtual extension a moral life that is ingrained in everyday speech and practices. It is this act of counterfactual *extension* of moral recognition that is the special work of memory, and in this way memory constitutes a limit-concept for the possibility of ethics as such, and discourse ethics in particular.[10] There is, Habermas claims,

> the duty [*Verpflichtung*] that we in Germany have . . . to keep alive the memory of the suffering of those who have perished at German hands. These dead have above all a claim on the weak anamnestic force of a solidarity that the younger generation can only exercise in the form of a continuously self-renewing, often desperate, nevertheless obligatory remembrance. (AS 141)

And elsewhere,

> Can one continue the traditions of German culture without assuming liability for the form of life in which Auschwitz was possible? Can one take responsibility for the circumstances in which these crimes were committed—circumstances with which our own existence is historically interwoven—in any other way than through the solidaric remembrance of that which cannot be made good again, otherwise than through a reflexive, self-examining attitude over against one's own identity-building traditions? (AS 144)

Guilty memory crystallizes into the call for absolute responsibility. This responsibility can, paradoxically and incompletely, be exercised—or exorcised—only through a desperate and aporetic, nevertheless demanding, memory. Such memory establishes an "anamnestic solidarity,"[11] "the analytic power of a remembrance,"[12] a compassionate *Andenken* or *Eindenken* that in turn can be practiced only through the medium of social criticism. What are the purposes of this critical project? They are, of course, Habermasian aims. From the very beginning, the project of a theory of communicative action, the project of the salvaging of the utopian-normative content of Enlightenment, of a discourse ethic, has been propelled by the memory of absolute catastrophe. Habermasian theory was always intended to assist in the generation of a collective moral discourse about the status and value of "cultural heritages"; the formation of postconventional, that is, postnationalistic and postparticularlistic, modes of will-formations; the loosening up of institutional controls on personal and collective identities;

the critical revision of the range of functional imperatives of economic and political systems; and the recovery of the power of rational resistance and protest by marginalized cultural groups such as Greens, feminists, the handicapped, and gays and lesbians.

On Habermas's terms, then, criticism is an agency dedicated to the self-development of moral institutions and practices within everyday speech and action. It thus exhibits a dual structure, aiming not only at the revelation of the course of rational development as such, but also revealing "the traces of violence that deform repeated attempts at dialogue and recurrently close off the path to unrestrained communication."[13] This is the anamnestic, restitutive dimension of social criticism, that unity of reason and remembrance that clings not just to the unfinished project of Enlightenment, but also—and first—to the victims of its delay. "Communicative reason," like the critique that appeals to it, "operates in history as an avenging force."[14]

Justice consists precisely in a society's capacity and willingness to develop institutional vessels for universalistic value orientations and departicularized sources of selfhood. These sources must be institutionally secure enough to assure that the attribution of rights of individual autonomy is no longer tied to functional imperatives from social-political subsystems, but is instead installed within a reinvigorated public sphere. Justice—and on this reading Habermas comes, I think, far closer to a "Jewish" ideal than Derrida's *justice fou*—is the durable respect for inherently abstract understandings of rights that exceeds any dependence on particular exigencies.[15] Such justice goes hand in hand with an unconditional demand for solidarity, a demand according to which compassion, acknowledgment of difference, generosity, and care for the needs and well-being of one's neighbor assure that rights that are held abstractly extend a further claim to the validity of the material and spiritual needs of all.[16] Justice flows from the experience of duty; solidarity flows from the intertwining of shared needs. Both of them demand a communicative rationality in which individuals have an unambiguous claim to speak and to be heard, to personal freedom and recognition, to a respect that extends beyond—while arising from—particular forms of life. The claim to universality of justice is, for Habermas, always haunted by that which can never be made good again. For the dead there is no justice. Only by an anamnestic solidarity with them can the claim to universal justice be redeemed. Such a memory exceeds the limits of the morally possible, but, in doing so, traces this limit and illuminates how it arcs through the structures and patterns of everyday social existence.[17]

We need not rehearse in great detail the postmodern response to this late Enlightenment project. Derrida, understanding something about the unwillingness of meaning to confine itself to the tidy performatives on which Habermas's discourse ethic depends, is not greatly moved by these appeals to universal justice. Such a justice could only replicate the moment where universality effaces its dependence on force—illocutionary force—where reason insists that the incalculable moment of justice must conform to the dreary, shopworn logic of inside and outside, of rule and of ruled. A more compassionate whip does not make a dead horse any less dead.

Habermas—who famously describes Derrida as a Jewish mystic, and an incompetent one at that—nevertheless validly indicts deconstruction's overmannered and inchoate account of its own status as sheer inscriptions of indeterminacy itself. All the whys and wherefores of collective life dissolve into the warm swamp of *différance*. The bad faith of deconstructionist texts, for Habermas, consists precisely in the presence of powerful "normative intuitions that go beyond what they can accommodate in terms of the indirectly affirmed 'other of reason'."[18] The older, Hegelian vision of undamaged intersubjectivity, actualized in the ethical community, is gone for good. But deconstruction's "cryptonormative" strategies of resistance, like unconditional and incalculable advocacy for the indeterminate other, depends finally on the quasi-regulative intuition of a reconciled nature and persists as the motive for a totalizing critique of reason.

Derrida still pines for an inherently emancipatory ideal. Such an ideal is worse than useless, however, unless the relation between it and the critical project itself can be expressed without recourse to willfully nebulous philosophemes. From Habermas's point of view, indeed, the *total* critique that Derrida proposes as a response to the Holocaust, in which all discourses must be deconstructed to confess their collaboration with the final solution, will be all too successful. Collaborators will be found everywhere and anywhere, and critique itself will fulfill the bleak prophesy of Horkheimer and Adorno, replicating the age-old indifference of curse, crime, and guilt. In the absence of any intelligible criterion for justice apart from the avowal of sheer alterity, Derrida would merely be repeating the Schellingian blind invocation of *something else*.[19]

At best, such appeals might expand the textual possibilities open to us as we attempt to imagine the limits of our discourses and laws. At worst, however, the project of deconstruction itself, crushed under the terrific weight of memory and responsibility, reduced to the repeated intonation of a fantastically complex *kaddish*, strangely replicates the very historical conditions and political pathologies of "secular Jewish messianism" that so deeply trouble Derrida in Benjamin's case. Absolute and bottomless critique is a pendulum that describes an ever-narrowing arc between passivity and nihilistic violence.[20] Justice as the total rupture in the fabric of historical time; justice as absolute memory of *avenir*; justice as not yet, but always already over, as the illegible inscription of an impossible grammar, an "it shall not have been"; justice as the ghost stories we tell ourselves; justice as the demand for the end of the world. In the apocalyptic subjunctive, it is no wonder that Derrida must accuse Benjamin of invoking the image of a divine, uninterpretable violence—God's bloodless justice—which for Derrida serves as an "intolerable," horrifying "temptation" as a "reading" of the Holocaust itself (FL 1044).

Rightly so. Derrida's deconstructive criticism, as remembrance from a justice immune from criticism, is offered as a sort of prophylactic against this threat of a *deus ex machina*, a signification machine capable of processing even the Holocaust. But is Derrida's criticism able to withstand this temptation itself? Does not its protection against moral idiocy—against Benjamin's "messianico-marxist . . . archaeo-eschatological" gestures of transcendence (FL 1044)—come at a terribly high price, according to which the avowal of incalculable justice must move all discussions of moral catastrophe into the esoteric rites of *différance*? And if these rites serve to reinaugurate the memory-responsibility of total critique, do we not also lose the question of the historical and moral *singularity* of the Holocaust, do we not transform victims into *material* for deconstructive critical work—does not their existence in memory, as ghosts, condemn them to an afterlife *as* victims?

Perhaps, nevertheless, it is here in this impossible duty that we can discern a moment of ethical response in Derrida's deconstruction of Benjamin's "prehaunted" text of the Holocaust that Habermas's anamnestic solidarity cannot encompass. For Derrida, no "destruction" of modernity, either Benjaminian or Heideggerian, could do justice to the memory of the Holocaust. Destruction of discourse is still dialectically duplicitous with it; it still abides in an older logic of presence and absence, origin and exile, inside and outside. But ghost stories undo this logic from within. In

Derrida's "Force of Law," a response to the responsibility of memory ends with a step beyond destruction and toward a "yes" as a final signature, a "deconstructive affirmation" (FL 1045). "Yes" to what? Affirmation of catastrophe? Affirmation of impossible justice? Affirmation of the Holocaust?

The generous "yes" at the end of Derrida's text reminds itself, first of all, of the enormous difficulty that is involved in the anamnestic affirmation of the other—not the other as an accident that befalls me or as the mere embodiment of a duty to be discharged, but the other who addresses me, who asks me something, before and beyond all of my addresses.[21] The "yes" at the end of Derrida's essay is intimately related to the double "yes" of his "Ulysses Grammophone." It is the duality of the relation between memory and life. It is the shouted "yes" to the horrific, infinite, ghastly archive of mnemonic traces; the "yes" to the hypertrophied, suffocating system of memories that Nietzsche and Kierkegaard had understood as hostile to life and that Benjamin had recognized as the "allegorical way of seeing." It is the "yes" uttered by a beast of burden; in a certain sense, too, a "yes" of resistance in the face of catastrophe: "The desire for memory and the mourning of the word *yes* set in motion the anamnestic machine. And its hypermnesic overacceleration."[22]

And yet to think this "yes" is, for Derrida, always to recognize that all "yeses" are double and contain within themselves a repetition or a relation between two recollections:

> [O]ne of them comes down to the Christian assumption of one's burden, the *Ja, Ja* of the donkey overloaded as Christ was with memory and responsibility; and the other *yes, yes* that is light, airy, dancing, solar is also a *yes* of reaffirmation, of promise and of oath, a *yes* to the eternal recurrence. The difference between the two *yeses*, remains unstable, subtle, sublime. One repetition haunts the other. (UG 584)

In this haunting, perhaps we can still make out a trace of an openness to the other—a promise older than responsibility, a gift older than language, perhaps nothing more than a recollection—that makes possible all the "yeses" of language, all the fragility of resistance, all the generosity of memory. It is a trace of a "yes" that is neither seen nor heard, but synaesthetically offered in the perfumed, final, capital "Yes" of Molly Bloom; a Yes whose written initial magiscule reenacts the oldest attitude of prayer, in which the dead, the living, and the earth that is their common home are all embraced with raised and open arms. And if, in this Yes, we find the possibility of a justice that will always have been older than all the nay-saying of Ulysses, then perhaps, unlike our own point of departure, we recognize the possibility of a justice neither "in history" nor "to date." Is even this too little?

NOTES

1. Max Horkheimer and Theodor W. Adorno, *Dialectic of Enlightenment* (New York: Herder & Herder, 1972), 57.

2. Jacques Derrida, "Force of Law: The 'Mystical Foundation of Authority'," in *Deconstruction and the Possibility of Justice Cardozo Law Review* 11 (July/August 1990): 943. Hereafter referred to in the text as FL.

3. This may be too generous; at times Derrida's text comes eerily to resemble what Adorno attacked as Heidegger's "vacuous copula" in *Negative Dialektik* (Frankfurt: Suhrkamp, 1975), 107–9.

4. Jacques Derrida, *Of Grammatology*, trans. Gayatri Chakravorty Spivak (Baltimore: The Johns Hopkins University Press, 1976), 47.

5. For an excellent discussion of the varieties of aesthetic criticisms of reason in Adorno and Derrida, see Christoph Menke-Eggers, *Die Souveranität der Kunst. Äesthetische Erfahrung nach Adorno und Derrida* (Frankfurt: Athenäum, 1988), 217–52.

6. See, for example, Richard Bernstein, "Serious Play: The Ethical-Political Horizon of Jacques Derrida," *Journal of Speculative Philosophy* 1.2 (1987).

7. See Jürgen Habermas, "Walter Benjamin: Consciousness-Raising or Redemptive Critique," in *Philosophical-Political Profiles* (Cambridge, Mass.: MIT Press, 1983), 129–64.

8. Ernst Nolte, "Vergangenheit, die nicht vergehen will," in *Historikerstreit: Die Dokumentation der Kontroverse um die Einzigartigkeit der nationalsozialistischen Judenvernichtung* (Munich: Piper Verlag, 1987), 45.

9. Jürgen Habermas, "Vom öffentlichem Gebrauch der Historie," in *Eine Art Schadensabwicklung. Kleine Politische Schriften VI* (Frankfurt: Suhrkamp Verlag, 1987), 140. Referred to hereafter in the text as AS.

10. See Max Pensky, "The Use and Abuse of Memory: Habermas, 'Anamnestic Solidarity,' and the *Historikerstreit*," *Philosophy and Social Criticism* 15.4 (1989).

11. The term "anamnestic solidarity" was coined by Christian Lenhardt in "Anamnestic Solidarity: The Proletariat and its *Manes*," *Telos* 25 (1975): 133–55.

12. Habermas, "Keine Normalizierung der Vergangenheit," in AS, 13.

13. Jürgen Habermas, *Knowledge and Human Interests* (Boston: Beacon Press, 1968), 315.

14. Jürgen Habermas, "Reply to my Critics," in *Habermas: Critical Debates*, ed. John B. Thompson and David Held (Cambridge, Mass.: MIT Press, 1982), 227.

15. The attempts of Jewish rationalism to tie Jewish law to Enlightenment ideals (*haggadah* and *haskalah*) has, of course, a long and tragic history of its own. One informative moment of this history is Leo Baeck's attempts to depict the commandment of *Zedakah* directly into the traditions of rational natural law. The point where the identity breaks down is the moment where, in the face-to-face with my neighbor, I am commanded to "make his life a part of my own."

> All our duties to our neighbor come under the commandment of jus-
> tice, the domain of absolute obligation. According to the development
> of this conception in Judaism, justice is not merely the avoidance or
> prevention of interference with the rights of others. It is rather a posi-
> tive and social commandment, the sincere and willing acknowledge-
> ment of our fellow man, the realization of his equality and of the right
> of man. This claim is his inalienable right which he can never lose and
> which surpasses all other "rights," for it is his human right by virtue of
> which he may demand that we make his life a part of our own. If we
> render him this we have done justice to him, Jewish justice. [Leo
> Baeck, *The Essence of Judaism* (New York: Schocken Books, 1976),
> 194–95.]

16. See Habermas, "Morality and Ethical Life," in *Moral Consciousness and Communicative Action* (Cambridge, Mass.: MIT Press, 1990), 200.

17. See "Reply to My Critics," 247.

18. Habermas, *The Philosophical Discourse of Modernity* (Cambridge, Mass.: MIT Press, 1987), 337.

19. See Peter Dews, *Logics of Disintegration* (London: Verso, 1988), chapter 1.

20. See Anson Rabinbach, "Benjamin, Bloch, and Modern Jewish Messianism," *New German Critique* 34 (Winter 1985): 86.

21. See Peggy Kamuf, "Tele-types (Yes, Yes)," in *A Derrida Reader: Between the Blinds*, ed. Peggy Kamuf (New York: Columbia University Press, 1991), 461.

22. Jacques Derrida, "Ulysses Grammophone," in *A Derrida Reader*, 576. Hereafter referred to in the text as UG.

CHAPTER 17

Reification and the Nonidentical

*On the Problem of Nature in
Lukács and Adorno*

STEVEN VOGEL

The tradition of German Western Marxism that begins with Lukács and continues through to Habermas has struggled from the very start with a set of
problems about the status of nature that it has never really been able to
solve. Lukács famously launches the tradition by rejecting Engels's conception of a "dialectics of nature" into which social theory fits as just a part.
Lukács insists that social theory and knowledge of nature are fundamentally
and epistemologically distinct and that "orthodox Marxism" belongs
entirely to the former realm. Marxism is only a social theory and must be
carefully distinguished from any account of the natural world.[1] The irony of
course—just as famous—is that Lukács then proceeds to define the social
in such a broad (and Hegelian) manner that nature itself turns out to be
nothing but a social category. Thus the supposed restriction on Marxist theory ends up looking like a merely verbal move.[2]

   This difficulty is paradigmatic for the tradition as a whole and derives
from a fundamental tension within its epistemological views. The tradition's
sympathy for a quasi-Hegelian view emphasizing the active and social character of knowledge and the influence of the socially situated subject on the
object known stands in uneasy conflict with its equally strong (Marxist) commitment to something like "materialism" which would insist on the existence of a substrate underlying social action that makes such action possible

and is not itself constituted by it. The trouble, of course, is that if knowledge is active and social, then it is not clear how this putative substrate could itself possibly be known or, conversely, if it *could* be known, then why this would not tend to vitiate the whole force of the Western Marxist critique of scientific objectivity as "positivism."

This difficulty, which has something of the structure of an antinomy, reproduces itself both within the work of each of the thinkers who form the Western Marxist tradition and also between these thinkers as well, forming a central strand in the internal debates that have shaped that tradition's history. Lukács and Adorno will stand in this essay as representatives of the two sides of the dilemma; in Lukács, of course, it is the Hegelian theme that has the upper hand, whereas Adorno's work is clearly much more influenced by "materialism." By examining the issues that divide these two seminal Western Marxist thinkers in their accounts of nature, I hope to help to clarify the difficulty that I have suggested besets the tradition as a whole. The point here, however, is not a merely historical one. The questions about nature that I wish to examine have significant relevance to a whole set of contemporary concerns, not the least of which are those that have been raised in recent discussions of nature influenced by "environmental" or "deep ecological" thinking. I will return to this point below.

I

In *History and Class Consciousness*, Lukács reformulates Marx's account of commodity fetishism into a broad critique of "reification." According to this critique, the central ideological phenomenon of contemporary society is the failure of humans to recognize the human character of the world they inhabit—that is to say, its character of having been produced through human action. Just as in Marx's account, the exchange values of commodities, which in fact reflect the quantity of human labor necessary for their production, appear to participants in the capitalist market as independent physical properties of the objects themselves, so too, Lukács argues, does the social order as a whole appear as something independent of human action and human choice. In truth, however, it is itself only the product of such action and choice.[3]

"Bourgeois thought" thus is marked epistemologically by what Lukács calls the "contemplative attitude." This attitude takes the world of objects that it encounters to be something other than and opposed to the human subject. It sees those objects as independent of and unchangeable by that subject's acts and conceives of the world that the subject inhabits as a massive and immutable system to which she must simply adjust herself. The proletarian social revolution, Lukács argues, is above all an *epistemological* revolution: it occurs when the subjects whose practical creation the world actually is come to recognize that fact—seeing the world they inhabit not as a realm of otherness independent of them, but rather as a realm in which their own action and their own choices are explicitly reflected.

In such an account "nature" must inevitably take on a negative sign. It is precisely the appearance of the social environment as "natural"—as *not* the product of human action, as independent of human will and desire—that this account criticizes as the reification that is to be overcome. For this position, the "natural" stands for that which has *not yet* been recognized as human, and therefore for those forces that humans have put into effect but that—not yet being recognized as such—have come to take on an alien power over humans themselves. The realm of that which humans have in their practices produced but do not know as such (like the realm of the capitalist market where anarchy reigns) is described by both Marx and Lukács as a realm of *Naturwüchsigkeit*. The *Naturwüchsige* is that which grows up "by nature," like weeds, precisely in the absence of conscious human planning. Social revolution, on this view, consists in the replacement of *Naturwüchsigkeit*, of this market apparently ruled by nature, by conscious social control; it consists, that is, in the practical reassertion by humans of their own responsibility for their environment, for the world that surrounds them.[4]

"Nature" thus stands here for the realm that is to be *abolished* by the revolution and replaced by a realm of the self-consciously and explicitly social. Lukács's epistemological arguments take a radical form, for they are arguments against *any* assertion of the possibility of knowledge about realms of being independent of humans and human practices. Any such assertion appears to him to be a fall back into contemplation and reification. This is what leads him to say that "nature is a social category."[5] What is taken to be "natural" in any given society, he argues, has more of a sociological than an ontological significance, that is, it indicates the extent to which that society has come to recognize (or has failed to recognize) its own practical responsibility for the environment it inhabits.

"Nature" is not to be taken here (entirely) metaphorically. Lukács's emphasis on practice (in Marxist terms, on labor) is meant to underscore the way in which the literal physical environment that we inhabit—our "natural" surroundings, if you will—is itself almost always the product of real human activity. Marx's well-known critique of Feuerbach's nature-worshipping materialism in *The German Ideology* is important to Lukács's view here: the cherry-trees about which Feuerbach rhapsodizes as symbols of "nature" are themselves the product of much earlier labor, both agricultural and commercial, since they are by no means indigenous to northern Europe.[6] This is paradigmatic for Lukács: the tendency to see the objects that surround us, including the "natural" ones, as independent of us, and to fail to recognize the extent to which they are always already the consequences of previous human practices, is for him symptomatic of a social order marked by reification.

There are, of course, other senses in which we might speak of "nature" as meaning more than simply the immediate environment that surrounds us. "Nature" might refer to the wilderness of natural areas where humans have not yet ventured, or to the physical stuff of which we believe all objects, both "natural" and "human-made," are formed, or to the universe indefinitely extended beyond the human both in space and time. But we can see Lukács's argument as suggesting that these senses are all in some way derivative of the primary one in which nature appears as the *Umwelt*, the real world of ordinary objects (and of social institutions) by which we really are surrounded; a world, I am suggesting, that is quite literally a "construct." Yet nature is doubtlessly also social in these other senses as well, although the character of the practical acts in which it is socially "constructed" takes on less direct forms. Thus wilderness today is made possible only through complex social processes protecting legally defined regions, while "matter"—as postempiricist philosophy of science has helped to show—is in a certain sense constituted by communities of scientists in and through their communicative and laboratory practices.[7] The "nature" that extends beyond us is itself a kind of intentional object, available to us only in terms deeply imbued from the very start by social and ideological forces sedimented in imaginative traditions of myth and literature and religion and philosophy.

In all these senses, then, the critique of reification turns into a critique of nature. Lukács recapitulates arguments familiar from German idealism about the active involvement of the subject in constituting the realm of objects, and he does so at a level where the distinction between the natural and the social has not yet arisen (which is why his assertion that his is not a theory of nature sounds so lame). He then gives these arguments a twofold Marxist twist. First, he understands the "active" connection between subject and object as a *practical* one, specifically and literally as human labor. Second, he explains the difficulty that we feel in recognizing our connection to the environment that we inhabit (the fact, that is, that objects certainly *appear* to us to be independent of subjects) as itself no mere error, but rather as the expression of a social reality characterized by reification, one in which we are precisely alienated from the products of our practices. Correcting that error (which is to say, overcoming that alienation) will thus need in its turn to be a practical process, not just a philosophical one: not a new interpretation of the world, but a changing of it. But changing the world in this sense will mean *abolishing nature*, at least if "nature" is understood as meaning the illusion that the world we inhabit is independent of our own acts.

II

The Frankfurt School, despite its clear debt to Lukács's reformulation of the Hegelian basis of Marxist thought, distances itself from his position, and especially from his theory of reification, for just this reason. Adorno rejects the idealism he discerns in Lukács's argument precisely because it seems to lead toward the claim that any appeal to a world independent of acting human subjects is a fall back into "bourgeois thought." For Adorno, this claim involves a dangerous hubris, the very hubris that he and Horkheimer identify with the enlightenment project whose fatal course they trace in their *Dialectic of Enlightenment*. For them, enlightenment is marked from the start by the disenchantment of nature, in which the real otherness of nature is systematically denied and the natural world comes to be seen as a realm of meaningless matter available for human use and human purposes, and hence, as something to be dominated. But the attempt to dominate nature, on their account, is a quixotic one: for in the overcoming of external nature, the entwinement of humans themselves in the natural order, and so humans' *own* nature, must also be overcome. It was in the interest of human happiness, which cannot be separated from pleasure and from the somatic, that enlightenment was supposed to be working. Yet paradoxically, it was only through renunciation, self-abnegation, and repression of human desires that the enlightenment project could even begin to be carried through.[8]

The dream was that by separating themselves from nature humans would be able to improve their condition. But to the extent that they succeed in doing so, they must also deny their own natural character, which leaves it no longer clear *in whose name* enlightenment functions. If matter is meaningless, if no "values" can be found in nature, then humans too, as natural and material beings, seem to be emptied of meaning and value. Enlightenment—especially in the form of science and technology—now appears as an end in itself, a force above and beyond human purposes to which those purposes have become irrelevant. Its own values—truth, reason, justice, human freedom—appear as "merely beliefs" and hence as scientifically unjustifiable to a rigorous objectivism that was supposed to work in the interests of those very values. Thus ultimately enlightenment "abrogates itself," Horkheimer and Adorno write.[9] If there is any possibility at all of a countermovement to this fatal dialectic—and Horkheimer and Adorno are tentative at best as to whether there is—it would come, in their view, only in the form of a new and humble recognition by humans of their own natural character, of their entwinement in the natural world, and of their inability, even in principle, to turn everything in the world into the object of their dominative acts.

For Adorno, who in later works such as *Negative Dialectics* develops these views in the most consistent directions, Lukács's theory of reification must thus appear as just another case of "identity thinking," a thinking marked by the illusory hope that human cognition could in fact grasp the world as a whole. As we have seen, for Lukács the suggestion is that alienation would be overcome at the very moment when humans realized that the world they inhabited was indeed within their grasp and was in fact in a certain sense the product of their own activity. Against this, Adorno offers an eloquent plea for a "negative dialectics" based on the *non*identical, on that which inevitably and in every case *escapes* human action—which is also, he thinks, that which has always been left out of Western thought. The call is instead for a thought that thinks against itself, that knows its own inevitable limitation and refuses to go beyond it.[10] This is Adorno's (very sophisticated) version of materialism. It is in the necessary gap between concept and object, in the inevitable nonidentity between thought and that which it thinks, in the brute facts of physicality and the somatic that go beyond any attempt to theorize about or justify them, that Adorno puts his trust. It is just this gap, this irreducible role for *difference* and for *what is left out*, that he thinks Lukács's view hubristically fails to grasp.[11]

Here is the *other* intention within Western Marxism: the one that emphasizes that which is independent of and prior to human acts and which underlies them. It founds its social critique in a call to humans to recognize not their own power over the world, but rather its very otherness from them—which also means their otherness from themselves, their embeddedness in the material or the natural. The two critiques—Lukács's and Adorno's—are in this sense the inverse of each other. Each one's diagnosis of the cause of contemporary social crises turns out to be identical with the other's proposal for the solution to those crises. One is a critique of the illusion of human impotence before the external world, calling for us to assert explicitly and to organize self-consciously the power over the world that we already posit implicitly in our acts. The other is a critique of the very idea of such an assertion and such a power, calling instead for a humility in the face of an otherness that always and inevitably escapes human action and thought. This is just the antinomy mentioned earlier that Western Marxism constantly confronts.

Adorno's view has more in common with the standard materialism of nineteenth-century Marxism, which also saw social critique as founded on a recognition of the effects of forces beyond human choice and control ("material conditions") upon social structure and social change. But Adorno avoids the contradiction in which "scientific socialism" was perpetually getting enmeshed. Engels's dream was always of a human theory (call it "dialectical materialism") that would somehow allow us to grasp those extrahuman forces and control them and of a world-changing practice (call it "socialism") based upon that theory. He forgot that by his own account all theories and all practices were themselves already under the sway of those forces, and hence were presumably incapable of turning around to master them. Adorno sees clearly the deeply paradoxical and even tragic situation in which such a consistent materialism lands one—a situation that could only be captured by a "negative dialectics" austerely devoted to revealing the necessary failure in any attempt to grasp the world in theory (or even thoroughly to transform it in practice) and to resisting the (constant) temptation to make some such attempt itself.

Thus instead of the natural science magically exempt from the otherwise universal assertion of thought's ideological dependence on material conditions to which Engels appeals, Adorno puts his faith in art, the realm in which he thinks the paradox and the tragedy can be most perfectly (which is to say, imperfectly) expressed. Art shows that which conceptual thought cannot say—nonidentity, that in the object that is other than thought, other than practice. Art shows this not by successfully representing it, but rather, Adorno provocatively suggests, precisely and above all in its *failure.* Art's ambition to unity and homogeneity is always thwarted—by the resistance of material, by the contingencies of performance, by the inevitable upsurge of "extraneous" matter (psychological, social, accidental) into the supposedly autonomous work. The result is a set of fractures and fissures that give the lie to the pretension to perfection implicit in every artwork and that thus reveal most directly the irreducible remnant of nonidentity within every claim to identity.[12]

III

You could call this element of the nonidentical of which Adorno speaks "nature" if you wanted, but it would be misleading. He sees how deep the temptation to "identity thinking" goes: to speak of that which is left out, of the "other" of thought, as "nature," he recognizes, is to try once again to hold it, to grab it by means of a concept and thereby to overcome its otherness. We cannot theorize about, or even adequately name, the nonidentical. All we can do is show it, as in art, or try through a negative dialectic to "think against thought"—with a humble awareness, that is, of such thought's own limitations.[13] The "nonidentical" is not a thing, nor a hidden realm behind things, nor even some mystical transcendent aspect of things (which is what Adorno objects to in Heidegger's talk of Being). It is, rather, simply the persistent difference between each concept and its putative object.[14] Hence there is no particular thing to grasp or even to regret that we fail to grasp, only a series of failures or incompletenesses in each of our attempts to think. And those failures occur when we think of "nature" no less than when we think of the "human world."

Thus Lukács's point still holds, as Adorno admits: what we *call* nature is always social, always conceptual, not the Other but the Other under the sign of the Same. On this—which is central to Western Marxism's critique of Engels's "orthodox" account of nature—Adorno and Lukács do not disagree: we have no access, and can have no access, to some special realm of "nature" that not only is independent of and prior to the social processes that produce our lived environment but can actually be known, by some special ("scientific," "dialectical") method, as such. Knowledge is inevitably social, inevitably conceptual. Both Lukács and Adorno agree that knowledge of a world of "nature" independent of our practices and of our concepts is not achievable and that any assertion of such knowledge must be deconstructed to show its roots in those particular practices and those limited concepts.

Adorno, I am arguing, thus avoids (for the most part) the mistake of identifying the nonidentical, that which is left out, with "nature" as something that can be positively conceived. Much contemporary discussion of nature and environmental issues, however, which often looks back to figures such as Horkheimer and Adorno as important precursors, falls precisely into that mistake. It criticizes "anthropocentric" thought and action in the name of a "nature" that is intended to be other than the social, but that is in fact itself already marked by it.[15] The attempt here is to found what is essentially a social critique on an account of nature, without first asking how knowledge of the "nature" in whose name the critique takes place could ever be achieved at all.

Thus positions associated with "deep ecology" criticize both industries and epistemologies for attempting to "dominate" nature and reject many contemporary human practices as "violations" of the natural order; they call instead for a new human relation to the world in which we live, in "harmony" with a nature now viewed holistically and not as something to be manipulated for our own purposes.[16] Yet such a view typically does not show much interest in clarifying to itself where it gets its own concept of the "natural" or how that concept manages itself to be anything other than yet another ideological projection of social hopes and fears onto the external world (just like the contemporary science it criticizes). Deep ecology needs "objective" access to nature as it "really" is in order to determine what counts as a violation of nature and what counts as harmony with it; but its own holism and its critique of dominative epistemologies seem to render such objectivity both impossible and undesirable. Any characterization of nature that "we" offer will be merely "our" characterization, of course. To call it true of nature in itself, and to use it as the basis for social critique and social action, would seem once again to "impose" human categories and concerns upon a natural world that is supposed to be utterly other than the human—and so again would seem to be a "dominative" violation of that otherness.

Antifoundationalist arguments such as those of Adorno—not to mention some more recent postmodernist arguments as well—should rather lead us to distrust *any* appeal to immediacy, of which the deep ecological appeal to "nature" is a species. All there is is mediation, mediation by us. The mark of the human is everywhere in the world, both in the "conceptual world" where we think of nature in terms that are inevitably always our own (and not "nature's," whatever that would mean) and also in the "real" physical world which, as I have suggested, is always one that we have already shaped and built. The dream is that if we think hard enough, or work hard enough, or perhaps listen well enough to our bodies, we will finally break through to some ultimate hard-edged lowest level of immediacy on which and out of which everything is built, one that was here before us and that could be known by us as it is in itself (and with which we could live in harmony). But the vertigo to which a thorough-going deconstructionism leads us is the vertigo of realizing that it is mediations all the way down—that there is no such foundation that we could ever reach, nor any reason to think that one exists.

Thus "Nature" cannot serve, any more than can "absolute thought" or "*ego cogito*" or "sense-experience" or "God," as the indubitable basis on which we may build our account of the world and justify our criticisms of the errors, theoretical or practical, of others. Whatever we take to be "natural" is always already a construction, the product of social mediations. But this means that we have no access to a nature-in-itself being "harmed" by contemporary technology that might found our critique of environmental depredations, just as we have no access to an "inner nature" whose harm could be the foundation of our critical social theory. Proponents of deep ecology would protest here that we are thereby left without any critique at all; if we reject the notion of nature as an absolute first that could ground our criticisms of technologies as "violations" of nature, it is no longer clear why indeed they ought to be criticized, and we seem to be left without any means for rationally choosing among various ways that society might want to interact with its physical environment. If the world we live in is fundamentally shaped by our practices, and if the same is even true of ourselves, then it becomes uncertain how or on what basis a critique of those practices would be possible: in whose name would it be raised?

Adorno's (and postmodernism's) view seems to fall here into a relativism that leads to critical impotence, one that he only rhetorically overcomes in his self-consciously paradoxical formulations. He too, finally, wants to base his social critique on something other than the human: *his* critique is in the name of nonidentity. Adorno's problem is to reconcile such a critique, inevitably conceptual in form, with the assertion that nonidentity cannot be conceptually grasped. The danger is that the critique will turn out to have no content, dribbling off rather into appeals to the ineffable. This is why something like nature inevitably returns, functioning as the concept of the non-conceptual. In the *Aesthetic Theory*, for instance, Adorno calls nature "the mediated plenipotentiary [*Statthalter*] of immediacy,"[17] trying thereby to acknowledge the mediated and social character of what we take as nature while still assigning to its concept a special role as somehow *standing for* immediacy. Elsewhere, showing the influence of Benjamin and Bloch, he speaks of natural beauty as an "anamnesis of something that is more than just for-other,"[18] and of nature as the "cipher of the not-yet [*des noch nicht Seienden*], of the possible"[19]; he calls nature "the trace of non-identity in things under the spell of universal identity."[20]

Yet despite the evocative character of all these formulations, they finally are unsatisfactory. That which nature "stands for," "recalls," "promises," "traces" must itself somehow be thought of as known and as present if it is to be the basis for a critique of the technological world's failure to acknowledge it, but it is just this knowledge and this presence that the notions of the nonidentical and of a negative dialectics were supposed to rule out. The result is an antinomy at the heart of the account, since it gets its (substantial) emotional impact from the very kind of nostalgic appeal to a lost immediacy to which its own argument knows it has no right. We are pining for something that the theory itself shows is not there and could not be known if it were; no amount of paradox-mongering can erase that contradiction. Adorno at his best recognizes this, of course, which accounts for the heartbreaking despair so characteristic of his style.[21]

IV

Thus Adorno's argument is led into a cul-de-sac. The attempt to offer a critique in the name of the nonidentical, where the latter is described precisely as that which can never be conceptually grasped, ends as Horkheimer and Adorno said enlightenment did. It abrogates itself, unable to say anything conceptual about what it is that contemporary practices—including those that influence the "environment"—fail to do justice to, and therefore why they are to be criticized at all. The danger, as I have suggested, is relativism. If the nonidentical in nature cannot be grasped and so what we do "to" it cannot be coherently criticized, then—once the remnant of romanticism and sentimental nostalgia is removed from Adorno's view—we seem set free to do anything we wish, which is just the hubristic conclusion Adorno wanted to avoid.

At this point we are perhaps directed back to Lukács's view, especially to the very critique of reification we saw Adorno reject. Lukács is more consistent, recognizing that if all there are are mediations (which is the real import of the claim that "nature is a social category"), then social critique simply *cannot* base itself on an appeal to immediacy, even one as sophisticated as Adorno's appeal to the nonidentical. But this only seems to threaten relativism if one is still secretly mourning immediacy's loss. Lukács's suggestion instead is to look for the basis for critique within mediation itself. The recognition of the always already mediated or constructed character of the world that we inhabit itself offers a basis for distinguishing among the practices in which that mediation takes place: practices that *know themselves* as responsible for the world they construct have a higher status than those in which the actors are systematically misled about what it is they are doing.

This is the core of the theory of reification: it criticizes the practices of contemporary society precisely because those practices are not self-conscious in this sense and so produce a world of social institutions and social objects that appear as natural and as independent of our will. Lukács's critique of capitalism—unlike that of most other Marxists—does not depend on arguing that capitalism dehumanizes people, or that it is economically irrational, or that it destroys external nature. He thinks that such arguments will not work (and indeed that they reveal their own entanglement in reification) because they would require the kind of external and "objective" knowledge of human or economic or natural essences independent of our social practices that his epistemological account suggests is impossible. The critique is thus not in the name of anything immediate or independent of the social, but rather is *in the name of mediation itself*: of world-constructing practices that know themselves as such and that take their responsibility seriously.

Thus the objection that social constructionist views of nature lead to a relativism that renders environmentally oriented social critique impossible is one that can be answered, but only in the context of something like a theory of reification. The answer involves pointing out that although it remains true that "nature" is always a social construction, so that we cannot appeal back to "nature in itself" to decide which relations to nature are the "right" ones, this does not entail that all relations are equally right. Rather it entails precisely that those that recognize the constructed character of what we take as natural possess an advantage over those that remain under the delusion that nature is independent of us. On this view (which deep ecologists might find unrecognizable, but which I think in fact supports many of their best instincts), it is our social failure to recognize our responsibility to choose what kind of environment we want, and to put that choice into effect, that leads us to live in the ominous world of potential environmental catastrophe that we now inhabit. Incapable of recognizing the enormous consequences of our own transformative practices on the world that surrounds us, and incapable also of organizing those practices on the basis of rational processes of dialogue and democratic choice, we allow them to be dictated instead by a capitalist "market" that functions toward us in exactly the way that we think "nature" does—as an external and independent force that we are unable to control. The solution is not to "live in harmony" with that market or that force, but rather to recognize that it is *not* independent of us; instead it is exactly the form that our practices take when we fail to acknowledge them as our own. The call, then, is for a new relation to the environment based on a new set of practices—not practices that try to avoid transforming the world we live in (which is in any case an impossibility), but ones that know their own responsibility for that world and that take that responsibility in earnest.

V

But what of the hubris and idealism that Adorno so roundly criticizes in the theory of reification? Any account that so unhesitatingly speaks of the world, including the natural world, as "socially constructed" seems immediately to fall prey to just such a critique. It fails to grasp the nonidentical, the inevitable gap between what we plan and what we do, the brute reality and thereness of the world. Yet I think the view I have been defending in the last pages can survive this critique, because I think that the critique fails to understand the central role in that view of what I have been calling *practice*.

The nonidentity thesis—like its most recent formulation as a thesis about *différance*—has something important and right about it. Against an idealism and a foundationalism that still believe in the possibility of deducing a priori a system that would grasp and explain everything there is in the world, it insists rather on the simple realness of the world, on its hardness and resistance to us, and on the limitations of our knowledge and the fallibility of our acts. But its real objection, it seems to me, is to what might be called the *theoreticism* of such an idealism, and it misunderstands itself when it thinks there is more to its critique. To say that the world cannot be grasped as a whole, or cannot be grasped by pure thought, is not to say that it is not graspable at all; rather it is to say that "grasping" is primarily a matter of *practice* and not of theory. In our practices—and first of all in our laboring practices—we *do* grasp the world. We do so not by getting some correct "view" of it into our "minds," but by transforming it—a transformation, to be sure, that is never complete, never infallible, and certainly never easy.

Adorno in *Negative Dialectics* praises classical German idealism for identifying spirit with activity, and he then correctly points out that this identification leads to the *Aufhebung* of idealism itself since activity necessarily involves a moment of resistance that is inevitably extramental.[22] But he interprets this moment only negatively, as pointing to the existence of some substrate or realm of the nonidentical entirely other than the humans

266   *Steven Vogel*

who engage in the activity, and this does not follow from the argument. To say that our activity in the world must be real and not just theoretical activity, and that it therefore is difficult, involves planning, and sometimes fails, does not by itself show the world to be "ontologically independent of the subject" unless the subject is taken to be merely a *thinking* subject—which is exactly the mistake of traditional idealism. German idealism's arguments, from Kant on, against the notion of a "substrate" "upon" which activity works continue to be valid ones; what considerations like those introduced by Adorno show is that this activity cannot be thought of as the mysterious act of a disembodied *Geist*, but rather as the real concrete practices of living human beings.

What I am suggesting is that, correctly understood, *practice already contains within itself the moment of what Adorno calls "nonidentity."* Indeed, it is just this that distinguishes it from "theory": unlike thinking about the world, changing the world is difficult, is fallible, encounters resistance, and so forth. This is not because "thought never fully comprehends its object" or "concepts do not correspond with things," although both those statements are true; real practice is precisely *not* a matter of "thought" or "concepts" being "applied" to some external reality independent of it. And it is also not because the world is "other" than us, unless the "us" referred to is the pure (mental) subject of classical idealist metaphysics. We are always already in the world, which means that we are also always already acting upon it and changing it in our practices. It is in this sense *not* other than us, but always already formed and transformed by us. The world we live in is the world we have created, and are creating, through our practices—which is not to deny that it is a world that sometimes looks quite different from the one we "thought" we were creating, or from one where our practices never fail.

My claim, then, is that the concept of practice—rather than that of nature or the nonidentical—allows one to reject the theoreticism and idealism that Adorno quite rightly wants to overcome, and that he sees as associated with the catastrophe of enlightenment, without having to accept the materialism, naive or sophisticated, whose aporia Lukács develops and criticizes. One can say, as I just have, that it is part of what it is to be a practice that it is difficult, fallible, encounters resistance, without at the same time positing a static "nature" independent of us that produces the difficulty, that causes the failures, that does the resisting. The unquestioned metaphysical assumptions that prevent us from seeing that, leading us to believe that practice requires some "substrate" that is other than us and upon which we must act—or, in the deep ecological version, which we ought not to violate—are precisely the contemplative ones identified by Lukács and associated by him with a world marked by reification. This by itself is not a decisive argument that those assumptions are false, of course, but it does suggest that they are neither so self-evident nor so trivial as they might at first appear.

NOTES

1. Georg Lukács, *History and Class Consciousness*, trans. Rodney Livingstone (Cambridge, Mass.: MIT Press, 1971), 24n.6.

2. See ibid., 130, 234.

3. Ibid., 83–110.

4. See Steven Vogel, "Marx and Alienation from Nature," *Social Theory and Practice* 14 (Fall 1988): 367–87.

5. Lukács, *History and Class Consciousness*, 234.

6. Karl Marx and Frederick Engels, *Collected Works*, vol. 5 (New York: International Publishers, 1976), 39.

7. See, for example, Bruno Latour, *Science in Action* (Cambridge, Mass.: Harvard University Press, 1987).

8. See Max Horkheimer and Theodor Adorno, *Dialectic of Enlightenment*, trans. John Cumming (New York: Seabury Press, 1972), 3–42.

9. Ibid., 93.

10. See Theodor Adorno, *Negative Dialectics*, trans. E. B. Ashton (New York: Continuum Press, 1973), 141.

11. For Adorno's critique of Lukács, see Adorno, *Negative Dialectics*, 189–92, 374–75.

12. Theodor Adorno, *Aesthetic Theory*, trans. C. Lenhardt (London: Routledge and Kegan Paul, 1984), 80–81.

13. See Adorno, *Negative Dialectics*, 136.

14. See ibid., 106.

15. Indeed, I would argue that *Dialectic of Enlightenment* also falls prey to this mistake on occasion, employing as it does some fundamentally naturalistic lines of argument; it is only in Adorno's later work that he gives up "nature" and turns to the nonidentical as the locus of his critique. But even there he sometimes slips—as does Marcuse, whose naturalism is much more evident than Adorno's. On the latter, see Steven Vogel, "New Science, New Nature: The Habermas-Marcuse Debate Revisited," *Research in Philosophy and Technology* 11 (1991): 157–78.

16. See, for example, Arne Naess, *Ecology, Community, and Lifestyle*, trans. and ed. David Rothenberg (Cambridge: Cambridge University Press, 1989), or Bill Devall and George Sessions, *Deep Ecology: Living as if Nature Mattered* (Salt Lake City: Peregrine Smith Books, 1985).

17. Adorno, *Aesthetic Theory*, 91. See Theodor Adorno, *Aesthetische Theorie* (Frankfurt: Suhrkamp, 1970), 98.

18. Adorno, *Aesthetic Theory*, 110.

19. Ibid., 109. Translation altered slightly; see Adorno, *Aesthetische Theorie*, 115.

20. Adorno, *Aesthetische Theorie*, 114; my translation. See Adorno, *Aesthetic Theory*, 108.

21. In *Minima Moralia* this contradiction forms the central topic and even the central structural principle of the work.

22. Adorno, *Negative Dialectics*, 200–201.

CHAPTER 18

Nature

A Theme for Finite Philosophical Thinking?

UTE GUZZONI

The reflections I would like to share with you have been arranged in seven parts. The first four sections could be entitled "Nature and Finite Thinking," the last three "Finite Thinking and the Relation between Nature and Second Nature."

I

If we put it in a shortened way, the question underlying the reflections that follow is whether or not *nature* can be or even should be a theme in today's philosophy. If we ask whether it *can* be, this seems to be a strange question. We feel inclined to say: "Of course, why not?" Nature has been a major theme for reflection since the very beginning of Western philosophy or, more likely, since human beings started thinking about themselves and their world at all. If we ask if nature *should* be an important theme for philosophy today, one might ask whether there really exists a criterion to decide what is and what is not worthy of philosophical thought. Everything that appears curious and questionable to thinking seems to be a possible matter for philosophy.

But this is precisely the point: *is* nature today something that calls forth our questioning? Does it still have anything to do with us? Are we forced to ask questions about it?

Today, nature often seems to be questioned primarily in the form of doubting its very existence. To the question "Is there still such a thing as 'nature'?" the sociologist Ulrich Beck, for example, responds negatively in his book "*Gegengifte.*"[1] He speaks of the "invalidated opposition between nature and society" (p. 16) and reproaches the ecology movement for reacting and acting "in the name of a nature that doesn't exist anymore" (p. 18).

We could cite Blumenberg too, who tells us that although originally "the metaphysical exclusivity of the concept of nature . . . left no place for the legitimate margin of authentic human work," "at the end of the violent counter-move . . . the validity of nature itself was contested by the absolute claims of work in technology and art."[2]

Or, to mention still another very different voice: Critical Theory, too, has become skeptical in the face of nature. This skepticism belongs to the basic theme of *The Dialectic of Enlightenment.*[3] Because of the necessary dominance that Mind holds over Nature, nature nowadays has changed into "mere objectivity" and, thereby, has become lost in itself.

In those places and situations in which we still do come in contact with nature today, it has become almost entirely "unnatural," that is, artificial, dressed up by society. Wherever nature becomes either the object of aesthetic enjoyment or a mere means to recreation, it itself is withdrawing and appears to exist only at the margin of social reality. "With a branch of chestnut upon the piano, nature enters the scene" says an ironic line of Gottfried Benn's poem "Notturno."[4] The picture charms us precisely in the artificiality of its introduction of nature.

Nature—a theme for philosophical thinking? Let us try a poem, a draft belonging to the second part of the "Sonnets to Orpheus" by Rilke:

> My answer—I don't yet know
> the time, I'll say it.
> But, listen, a rake which is already at work.
> Up there, alone in the vineyard talks
> a man already with the earth.[5]

I will allow myself to relate these lines to our context. Can and should nature be a theme for philosophical thinking? Does it still exist? Let us leave the answer to these questions open. "My answer—I still don't know the time, I'll give it," perhaps as well as the time I'll be able to give it. Perhaps even whether I'll be able to give it at all. "But, listen." Precisely by way of this leaving open, by way of this *Gelassenheit*, something becomes audible. The tensed yet calm attentiveness meets with the sound of "the rake which is already at work." As Rilke says in the twenty-fifth sonnet to which this draft belongs, we listen to "the human beat in the restrained silence of the strong early-spring earth."[6]

That which comes to be heard is the working rake, in the words of the sonnet: "the first rake's work." The sound is a human beat; a man is talking with the earth. He is alone up in the vineyard, but yet he talks—neither with himself nor with others, he talks with the earth.

Then is he the one who, incidentally perhaps, gives the sought-after answer? Surely he is not talking about the earth, but he is talking with the earth. He is doing so by way of the working of the rake. He abandons himself to the "rake's work." It is precisely in this active and mutual communication of man and earth that earth herself is real—that nature is real.

Nevertheless, this evidence does not suffice to establish nature as a relevant subject of philosophical reflection. For example, one might raise the objection that these verses were written sixty-nine years ago; too much has happened between then and now that might refute modern attempts to rely still on their experiences. Besides that, even if—in spite of all mechanization and industrialization—the significance that nature has for agriculture will never completely disappear, this significance does not allow us to deduce any sort of universal social importance of nature. Further, in this poem nature is something with which man communicates by *work*, not by *thought*. Finally and above all, we are used to thinking that poetic evidences could not serve as a valuable proof, neither of the reality nor of the actual importance of anything; it is said to be the poet's privilege to treat fictions like realities.

II

So how may we advance? To begin with, it may be time to explain what I mean by "Nature" and how it is understood when we ask whether it is or is not a valid theme for philosophical thinking.

There are two main uses of the word nature within everyday understanding. First, nature is the sum of all that occurs or is simply there by itself on earth and in heaven and is not caused by human beings. Within this usage, a further distinction between three nuances of meaning may be drawn. In the first place, nature refers to that which is given in the form of a natural material to human beings, to their intellect, and, above all, to their technological activity. In this sense, nature is the unobtrusive condition and presupposition, as well as the universal matter, for human acting and being in the world.

Aside from this immediate relatedness to human making and doing, nature at the same time is seen and treated as the untouched, as the "naturally occuring," as that which by itself is different from and alien to human beings. The so-called forces of nature seem—or, better yet, seemed—to pose a threat to the human race and its self-preservation. Yet it is precisely nature in this sense that barely exists anymore, inasmuch as today everything that occurs or might occur seems to exist only within the clutches of human beings who incorporate everything into their plans and change it into what Heidegger calls a *"Bestand,"* into a factor to be reckoned with and manipulated. But all the same, in our everyday consciousness nature continues to be an actuality, at least as an alien factor or even as an opponent that remains intrinsically unknown.

Finally, in a third nuance of the first sense, nature is the "nature within us," our own naturalness: the fact that we are born and will die; that we breathe, eat, and sleep; that we see with our eyes and hear with our ears; that we feel and love. Of course, this nature is essentially a human nature, our way of seeing with our eyes has been formed and altered by the historical and social activities of former generations. But in spite of this alteration or humanization, it has not ceased to be nature.

The various facets of the first sense of nature agree that in one way or another nature can be regarded as the opposite of mind and intellect. In the second sense—I confine myself to just mentioning it—this opposition is of no relevance whatsoever. According to this second sense, nature equals essence; thus when we talk about the "essence or nature of a thing," we mean its "idea" or even its spirit.

The specific denotation of the word "nature" as I use it falls within the context of the first sense mentioned above. What I am concerned with is the concrete nature that we talk about in our ordinary everyday language, what—to a certain extent—could equally be called "earth." "Up there, alone in the vineyard talks a man already with the earth." It is not only the stony ground in which the vines take root that is meant in these lines. What the man is talking with might just as well be the chill of the spring morning and the song of the birds taking flight; he talks with the first pale rays of the sun climbing up the opposite slope and with the promise of growing ripeness and of harvest that lies waiting within the earth. Nature is what we call the world of natural things. We experience it as something that exists by itself and that is different from us, as well as something to which we ourselves belong and in which we participate by way of our own naturalness.

These concrete natural things—may they as such be a theme for philosophical thinking? But philosophical thought, even when it has renounced the major metanarrations and the inquiry into being as a whole and as such, still concerns itself with the universal; and it has to do so if it does not want to become subjective and arbitrary. If we speak of "mountain," then it seemingly cannot be the mountains in the sense of those particular mountains I came to know in the last month; if we speak of "bird," then it cannot be the bird in the sense of that particular blackbird singing on the roof of the house next door. Nature in the sense of particular mountains and particular birds seems to be in no way a theme for philosophical thought. The fact that early in the morning and up in the vineyard a lonely man is talking with the earth is a theme for poetry, but not for philosophy. Even less is it itself philosophy.

III

At the beginning of this essay I intentionally introduced my title question in an abbreviated form. I now have to discuss what that hitherto neglected element is about. What is the meaning of *finite* philosophical thinking?

Nothing, not even the work in the concept and meaning of language, has become so decisive for philosophy in the past one and a half centuries as the tendency towards philosophy's self-contemplation. Philosophy has become insecure about its right to exist after the sciences claimed a good part of what was previously considered to be philosophical problems and inquiries. Moreover, after the final metaphysical stage of German Idealism, the firm belief in the eternal and absolute character of philosophical subjects has become old and brittle. One of the firmest presuppositions in its understanding of itself, the identity of thinking and being, has implicitly become questionable.

Since its very beginning, Western philosophical thinking had attempted to comprehend the world in some unique and unified thought, in an all-encompassing view. Although historically differing in its contents and forms, it always proceeded from one or more first principles that were estimated as everlasting and universally valid. Throughout all epochs of history, philosophical thinking has been an *infinite* thinking.

So what about philosophical thinking today? In what way can philosophy think, when it has realized that it is no longer an inquiry into sources and origins, into identity and unity, into principles and causes? When it deserts the vantage point of the Grand Theory, it must begin to behave and to think just according to the specific situation and constellation that it encounters. It may look around attentively in the different directions and parts of the world and tell about whatever appears or disappears. In going and continuing its way through the various and colorful landscapes of the world and mingling with the variety of the manifold beings, it can neither lose sight of the world nor of the act of looking at it. Yet the perspectives and aspects keep varying as it wanders along; the views change. When it names the world, when it tells about the things it sees and discovers, here and there, now and then, before, in the meanwhile, and afterwards, then it no longer has a central perspective with a central vanishing point according to which it might classify and subdivide the diversity and multitude of all those things that it observes and to which it listens. Just like a stranger in a foreign land, it relies entirely upon its own seeing and learning. In other words, it lets itself be finite in a finite world, it is a finite thinking.

Another way to express this would be to say that thinking today should deny what used to be the highest claims of traditional philosophy, namely, its claim to reliability, to universal validity, and even to truth—this latter denial appearing as the utmost in scandalous philosophical behavior. In doing so it does not decay in a dizzying and groundless "anything goes." On the contrary, this finite thinking finds itself for the first time really on a ground and foundation, that is, on the ground of the world; it comes to be situated within an actual weft or texture of all that is finite, it realizes itself to be a part of the community of all that is and is not, of what is experienced by this one and that one, as well as what they say to each other.

Being amidst things and among others is an essential characteristic of finite thinking. He who thinks is a part of the things that seem to occur in front of his eyes, yet not without his eyes. He is taken prisoner by the experiences that engage him for or against something. He has to include his current time and his current place, his body and his history, in the activity of his thinking or, as Adorno would say, in his thinking as a comportment. All his experiences and all his relationships mutually encounter, cross, affirm, or question each other; they all vary and differ in time and place and mode. They result in changing situations and constellations and do not correspond to any pre-given structure or law.

By the term "finite philosophical thinking" I therefore have in mind a thinking by which finite, that is, mortal, human beings understand themselves in accordance to their finitude, to their sensual and intellectual sensibility, to their "natality" as Sloterdijk calls it, and to their mortality. Of course, the insight into finitude and mortality seems to belong to the *"condition humaine"* as such; it is even traditional metaphysical thinking itself that starts with the experience of finitude—in order, however, to sublimate it or to compensate for it. What finite thinking is concerned with is facing and accepting the fact of finitude as such, in the same way that we accept the fact of heaven and earth, of day and night, of ourselves and others. We face and accept it not as a deficiency or as a curse, but rather as a fact of our being-in-the-world that lies beyond or before any curse or praise. To acknowledge finitude means to relate to it in a mode of open consent.

Yet can a finite philosophy in this sense actually be imagined? Is there or could there be a kind of philosophical thinking that proceeds from and consents to its own mortal sensibility and sensuality and, therefore, comports itself mortally and sensually? Is not philosophy, on the contrary, the kind of comportment by which, ever since Parmenides and Heraclitus, the "thinking man" has left behind the intellectual blindness and deafness of those who rely on their senses?

IV

Strangely enough, it seems to be so easy and so familiar to abandon the experiences of the sensible world of the mortals in favor of a thinking that is infinite and that, in the act of an absolute perceiving, becomes identical with its object. And yet, it also seems to be so difficult to resign oneself to infinite thinking in favor of an insistence on the here and now, in favor of a finite thinking. In order to increase the evidence for this latter possibility, I will present some reflections on today's philosophical thinking insofar as it no longer claims to be absolute and infinite.

Let us take, for example, the concept of "aesthetic thinking" that is introduced by Welsch.[7] Far from being restricted to the realm of art, this concept designates an *"aisthētic"* thinking in the Greek sense—as I myself would say, a sensual thinking—for which perception by the senses, as well as sensitive seeing and feeling of sense and meaning, has shown to be of the utmost importance. "You just could say that today's thinkers mobilize their senses, that they practice a thinking that uses senses and makes sense by senses" (p. 47). In sensual thinking, the senses that experience the world and that sensually perceive and feel the sense and meaning of things together with their moods, atmospheres, and situations are no longer left behind as merely providing the material for rational molding and formation. Rather, aesthetic thinking moves within the realm of sense and senses; it tries to mediate between them and recognizes them as its own powers. Its "exact phantasy" (as Adorno calls it), its colorful dreams and fancies, its attentive glances into something unseen, and its intense listening to something unheard are no longer mere preliminaries or impulses to further proceedings, but rather their very own ways and paths.

Aesthetic thinking excludes neither abstract concepts nor logical and argumentative elements. But these, being only a part of it, depend upon whatever the way of thinking demands and do not build its decisive telos. Welsch is correct in emphasizing the necessity that the scheme of an opposition between "sensation, feeling, emotion and the like," on the one hand, and "reflection, thought, concept," on the other hand, "should no longer be complied with" (p. 55).

That the situation of thinking has fundamentally changed and that a new understanding is looked for becomes evident too in the revaluation of the relationship between activity and passivity, which we find, for example, in Lyotard and Sloterdijk, and earlier in Heidegger and Adorno. Doing and letting be, activity and passivity, spontaneity and receptivity, speaking and hearing, changing and tolerating—these are all pairs of concepts that have continued throughout our history to color and to determine our understanding of life and world. They are expressions of life views and patterns of behavior that characterize the complementary sides of the relationship between the contemporary human being and the reality before him or her.

But their meaning and especially the relevance of their oppositional character has begun to change. They no longer can be separated from each other. And it is no longer possible to ascribe them to mind, culture, and technology, on the one hand, and to nature and sensuality, on the other. Activity, spontaneity, initiative, work—nowadays there is far more than this. It is because of our insight into the negative consequences that accompany technology, science, and the continual progression of achievement and accumulation that the opposite attitudes, that is, waiting and receptive behavior patterns, appear in a new light. They no longer have to be understood in terms of doing nothing or of disinterestedly letting things go. On the contrary, they accompany, take part in, and attend to the things for which they care. Thus their posture is active as well as passive, giving as well as taking, spontaneous as well as receptive. I think that, at least in general opinion, the ability to listen, to be patient and attentive, is beginning to take the place of the will to command, to organize, and to master.

A contributing factor in this change is the perception that human possibilities are not without limits, neither the possibilities for manipulating other people, nor those for the exploitation of the earth. Nowadays the will to dominate and to master is discovering its boundaries and limits. One can no longer pretend that its consequences are constructive and preserving; instead of contributing to self-preservation and self-enhancement, they rather create isolation, loneliness, and devastation. Thus, this will might reexamine itself. It might make way for attentiveness and listening. The tendency to a more and more active mastery might turn into an attempt to learn a passive attitude of releasement and letting go, of *"Gelassenheit."*

As is well known, *"Gelassenheit"* has been discussed by Heidegger in, among other texts, his *"Feldweggespräch über das Denken,"* under the very title *"Zur Erörterung der Gelassenheit."*[8] The term *"Gelassenheit"* does not mark a stoic pattern of comportment, but rather denotes a way of thinking in which activity and passivity have become one or at least act together, or, in the words of Heidegger, even lie "outside the differentiation between activity and passivity."[9] *"Gelassenheit"* means a calm attentiveness, a receptive openness, and a patient letting happen toward that which is to be thought or done; it means waiting for the other to turn toward one and to speak, knowing that such a speaking in itself needs to be waited for.

What speaks is that which is individual, peculiar, and different; that which changes; that which is accidental and incidental. Thinking *différance*, especially characteristic of contemporary French philosophers, is, in itself, a finite thinking. That which differentiates itself, which becomes or is different, is exactly that which resists the unity and unification of the universal *genos* while it asserts its own colorful and ambiguous peculiarity and singularity as well as its being accidental and its nothingness.

Parmenides, defending against the finite thinking of ordinary mortals, characterizes opinions, which he considers to be only empty names, as "the fluctuation of luminous color."[10] Colorfulness indeed might be the most important and—together with smell—the most sensual mark of difference in the sense of individuality and peculiarity of special things. Colors are various as well as varying. They convey atmospheres and moods. They may be subdued and gloomy, but they may also be garish and loud. They may harmonize or kill each other, may be convenient or inadequate, cheering or saddening. Colors are the most visible of all visible things.

Finite thinking is thus a sensual thinking. Using sense and senses, it is released and open, it listens to the other as to something that is different; it might as well be called a colorful thinking. Finite thinking is, according to circumstances and situations, a slow or a hasty thinking, belligerent or loving, smiling or mournful, disturbing or comforting, weak (in the sense of Vattimo's *pensiero debole*) or sometimes even strong.

Finite thinking speaks of that which is; it talks about the earth and the world, that is, about those things among which it happens to be. It is a thinking on the earth—precisely because we, the thinking mortal beings, instead of finding ourselves in some sort of abstract vacuum of pure thought, live upon the earth and under the sky, that is, in a world where specific mountains and specific birds are to be found. To think finitely means to start from and to move toward the specific situation in which we find ourselves here and today, understanding ourselves as natural and finite, as mortal beings among others who are natural, finite, and mortal like we are.

V

When we say that we want to think "in a worldly way" about the earth and upon the earth, then it seems as if nature were indeed the first and central theme of thinking, as if the main concern were to think the evening and the morning, land and sea, mountains and birds, ourselves and the others, seeing and hearing and feeling. Yet what is left out of this list—and not accidentally, of course—is precisely the majority of those thing that we usually deal with in our everyday life: apartment buildings and factories, cars and computers, nonnatural clothing, and nonnatural food. Is it not rather *these* things and facts that matter to our situation here on earth? Do not they determine us more decidedly and thoroughly than such facts as the times of the day and of the year? Must not finite thinking, therefore, be concerned primarily with human-made things and social conditions, rather than with nature, especially if it really wants to emphasize the fact that we live upon the earth?

Or is there something wrong with this alternative, at least with its exclusiveness? This difference between things that come forward in their own right and those with which we ourselves populate and change the world, is it really as decisive as we were always convinced it was? Perhaps it has taken on a different character in the meantime, one that should encourage us to consider anew the relations maintained by both sides to each other and to ourselves. Could nature—and now I am returning to my leading question— could nature become a new and unavoidable theme for philosophy just because it itself as well as our relation to it might equally illuminate our relation to human-made things? It is indeed this latter presumption that is suggested by the thoughts that follow. I propose that a finite reflection on

nature and on our comportment to nature could also bring about a transformed or even an actively transforming relation to our everyday, mainly
technologically determined world.

It can certainly no longer be the concern of a philosophical reflection on
nature to say and to define *what nature is*, that is, to assert any persisting
nature of nature. The "what is?" questions have to become suspect in a
world of accepted finitude. Instead, we find ourselves involved in "*how* is
it?" questions. We know that nature exists because we, the finite and sensual beings, experience it within us and around us. But we know equally that
it plays an ever-diminishing role for our everyday world. Neither outer nor
inner nature still has to be encountered as an adversary or as a threat from
which we have to protect and preserve ourselves. Instead, it has nearly
fallen out of view and, at the same time, it has become something like a sensitive ward that we have to defend, especially against ourselves. It itself—
once again outer as well as inner nature—has become exposed to a deadly
threat caused precisely by human beings, by their intellect and their overwhelming will to dominate, by their science and their technology.

Today, the need to ask questions about possibilities, ways, or alternatives
that might be able to help us to find a new relationship between nature and
technology is becoming urgent because, to twist the Hegelian dictum, "there
is an Untruth," and we are living in circumstances that have become dominated by force and alienation. Yet, at the same time, since this situation has
been created by humans, it should not be taken as an unchangeable situation that remains without alternatives. It, instead, might lead us to a transformed attitude toward the world and toward our being in the world.

Let us consider, for the sake of example, the transformations in the world
of working that have been brought about by information technology. The
transformation of work and of our way of life now occurring may lead to an
absolute triumph of external regulation and reckless consumerism, to the
loss of all individuality, and to radical isolation. *Or* the possibilities inherent
in this transformation may at last be recognized, namely, the increasing
opportunities for participation and communication based on shared and
mutual knowledge. We either will continue to be bewitched by what Adorno
calls the "spell of identity" or we will succeed in breaking up the fabric of
uniformity and one-dimensionality and in countering the barely functioning
passivity by means of specific activities, for example, by the participation
and communication I just mentioned.

As was mentioned above, a new valuation of passivity in the sense of an attentive and intentional becoming involved in the realm and the matters of the Other might obstruct the modern ideology of activity. Adorno says: "Passivity hides within the heart of activity, the I extending itself to the Non-I." He also evokes a thinking that moves itself close up to things and a "long and non-violent look at the object."[11]

These attitudes imply a complementary move as well, namely, the emergence of a new significance of activity, self-reliant comportment, and responsibility. The emphasis upon an activity to be awakened and unfolded in a positive way begins with the realization that today's technologically determined world, with its social mechanisms of compulsion and pressure, has led us into an attitude of mere acceptance and of powerless letting things go. Just as this unproductive passivity differs from an attitude of getting involved with and close to the matter, so too the new activity is fundamentally different from the overbearing power that modern subjects exert over their objects. Rather, it acts out of mutuality and out of a behavior that keeps listening to things and to their situation.

Thus, the attitude I am talking about is at the same time active and passive, doing and letting happen, giving and receiving. Those who attend to this attitude do not allow their opposite to scare them or to subjugate them as mere objects. Nor do they insist on managing and determining the world according to their own interests and profits, according to their own will to power. An essential characteristic of their behavior is that they see their opposite as something alien, something other and therefore astonishing, that comes forth toward them on its own. Only where the coming forth by itself and the otherness of the Other are taken seriously and are preserved, there and only there can the prearranged identities and so-called "objective necessities" lose their almighty power. The joining of passivity and activity, the involving of oneself in the realm of the different and the unfamiliar, and the emphasis upon one's own peculiarity might be one way by which we could reach a transformed relationship to technology and to technical things.

VI

The attitude and behavior of active passivity and receptive spontaneity derive from and participate in what I think are the two characteristic features of *nature* today, that is, its otherness and its coming forth by and from itself. What is the exact meaning of this formula: coming forth by and from itself?

First of all, it implies not coming forth from different or other ones, more succinctly, not coming forth from humans, not being generated by them or subjugated to their wills and actions. Moreover, that which is and emerges from and by itself somehow carries within itself a proper impulse of its being and its movement. This impulse, this inner impetus of nature, is a kind of letting be and letting happen, a kind of easing itself and the natural things to themselves, letting them take their course. It opens the way for them, releasing them at the same time to set off on their own.

For Aristotle, to come forth from and by itself is the distinguishing characteristic of nature, for he considers entities from the aspect of their being caused and generated; he can thus draw a neat distinction between that which has its origin and principle in itself and that which is brought about by the hands and intellect of humans. For us, however, the ontological character of being generated or caused has lost its fundamental strength of conviction. The fact that nature has the origin and principle of its movement within itself nowadays can only mean that it begins in itself and with itself, that it is a rising and revealing of and to itself (as in the Greek word *phyein*). The beginning can no longer be thought of as the determining anticipation of the end, the principle is no longer the telos—or maybe it is so only in the sense that it is a directed beginning, directed at and to itself, a beginning that fulfills itself in itself, going forth from itself toward itself.

This characteristic, that something is solely from and by itself, is it today still a characteristic only of natural things? Might it not also apply to things brought about by human hands and mind, as long as they are not primarily seen as being brought about and produced? If we recall the work of art and, for example, the sentence of Mörike, "that which is beautiful blissfully appears in itself,"[12] then we will immediately answer this question with a *yes*. But what about the other *techne onta*? Why not accept this feature as a characteristic not only of a stone and a flower and a child, but also of a house and even of a city? In many situations, indeed, we experience our technological world as something that has detached itself from us and that now speaks to us from itself and moves by itself—toward us or away from us.

It is generally considered to be a common feature of modern technology and social affairs that their products and results become increasingly emancipated and independent from their human creators. To an alarming extent, we even get subdued by them, placed at the mercy of their powerful dominance and control. We are no longer sure and certain of our self-made surroundings. The widely understood phenomenon of *alienation* is an expression of the fact that human subjects, on the one hand, and objective facts and affairs produced and constructed by human beings, on the other, have become fundamentally independent from each other. Because of this tendency to emancipation and alienation, the world of technological and social entities has been called a *second nature*. I cite Sloterdijk, one voice among many, who says: "We have surrounded ourselves with an epi-nature made of consequences of our actions that have slipped out of our history-making praxis."[13]

Of course, that which has slipped away is still a *techne on* in the Aristotelian sense, that is, something brought about by somebody other than itself, made out of some material, according to a definite plan and for a premeditated end. It is the *poioumenon* of an *episteme technike*. Nevertheless, at the same time it does slip away from our praxis and out of the realm of our productivity and so becomes a second nature; the fact that it is brought about by its human creator becomes irrelevant. In order to understand the intrinsic meaning of this development, we can recall the difference that exists, for example, between a truck and the traffic, a personal computer and information technology, a high-rise building and the city, an evening dress and the textile industry. We could, of course, designate both as technology or rather as technological products. But it is only of the second item in each of those pairs that we can say that it has emancipated itself and become independent from its producer and thereby has taken on that uncanny character of something that has slipped away and become self-reliant. The rationality invested in those "products"—such as traffic, industry, technology—to some extent has loosened itself from its original, purely instrumental context; it thus has acquired a certain autonomy, a "life" of its own—a life including the concrete things mentioned above such as trucks or computers, which now become functions and functionaries of these "concrete abstractions."

The mode of being that is peculiar to the concrete abstractions may no longer be thought of within the traditional duality of thinking and being, of subjectivity and objectivity. Hegel spoke of the "objective mind," a formula that, within our special context, we should take up in its complete contradictory tension, so that, surely against Hegel, it is no longer understood as a stage in the mind's self-positing, but as technology shifted into nature, as something brought about by human activity, yet grown out of its producer's realm of control. To these emancipated powers evidently belong things like family, civil society, and state, or trade, traffic, and social organization. But equally belong things like the city, a chain of stores, any administration, or even a social trend. They all seem to develop their own rules and behavior patterns and no longer are wholly controllable by those who produced them and put them into action. They emancipate themselves into a second nature.

How can we come to know the meaning and the importance of this "second nature"? Do we have to interpret it in the way of the *Dialectic of Enlightenment* of Horkheimer and Adorno, that is, in view of the fact that, within and through dominance and enlightenment, myth and nature are triumphant, along with such features as repetition, blind necessity, or pure objectivity? Must we listen to the *Negative Dialectic*, where Adorno says: "the second nature remains the negative of that which might be thought of as the first nature"?[14]

Or might this conviction itelf—that emancipation and becoming independent in the case of objects and objectivities are wholly *negative* phenomena—be a presupposition that still belongs to the modern claim of power and domination, which in no way is willing to release anything out of the realm of its authority? Could not the ultimate origin of the thesis of the "spell of identity" and the totality of alienation still be a perspective of the modern subject that is preprogrammed for appropriation? I think we would be mistaken in assuming that the comparative link between the "first" and the second nature lies only in the totality of violence and dominance, that is, in the supremacy of a general power over each individual.

VII

Social affairs or technological rules and conditions appear as a second nature because and insofar as they emancipate themselves from their being brought about by humans. They acquire otherness and an essence of their own. I think this grants them the character of nearly natural beings with which we can try to establish an attentive, communicative, and participative interaction. Thus, by means of a new relation to these "second natural" beings, we might even step out of the mere passivity and powerlessness that we have experienced in the face of technology and society until today. If that which had been generated by humans is now losing its correspondent character of being something already known and intended, then, like a person who has grown up, it steps out into a world of immediateness and otherness, in which relations and familiarities must and can be built, a world in which it may take part and be involved, either positively or negatively.

The relation to and behavior toward social facts and technological objects no longer implies an unconditional surrender. One could even ask whether, in a definite sense and in definite contexts, the alienated things and affairs might cease to be alienated and in the future might be simply alien in the sense of different and "other"; they thus might provoke a new relation, an inter-relation. What seemed to be of our own property would reveal itself to be something other and differing from us, speaking to us from itself. Things to whom we seemingly had loaned our language would actually speak to us with their own words.

By this change of view, I intend neither to disclaim nor to demolish the differences between the natural and the social-technological. Surely concrete abstractions do not change into exactly nature's mode of being by and from itself. Decisive differences do remain and ought to be worked out from a new point of view. Yet those differences are no longer criteria for delimiting and defining the one, nor are they legitimations for discriminating, subjugating, and dominating the other. The contrasts between the natural and the technological do not suddenly become inapplicable, rather they become widely irrelevant. They cease to be unambigous and they lose their capacity of explaining anything. I think it is no longer so important whether something is of human or of natural origin; there are questions far more important, such as whether a certain thing or fact is life-supporting or extremely dangerous, whether it brings people together or drives them apart, and whether or not it allows a released intimacy with itself.

In the same way that we cannot deny the differences between nature and technology, we ought not to deny differences within the realm of technological and social objects and contexts. And there remains the important question of if and how the various exploitive and destructive forces that the Occident with its unchecked craving for dominance and control has set forth into the world might be tamed and somehow called back into a realm within which fruitful conversation and open communication with those forces could become possible.

I think that only then would a decisive, contradicting "No" also get a chance. For recognition is not the same as approval. When we first have learned to recognize and to respect a thing or a fact, only then may we also turn away from it, fight it, or try to change it. When we accept that the technical and social facts exist and that they exist by and from themselves and, on the other side, when we cease to understand ourselves as somehow programmed into the course of their operation, then we can be challenged to enter into a free discussion and to cooperate with them—or to fight against them.

Today, the possibilities of intruding into the context of the technological world seem to be restricted and limited because, among other reasons, technology has slipped out of our control. We feel powerless in the face of its supremacy because there seems to exist a dialectical alternative between its dominance and ours. Second nature, however, in the sense I intend, says that we might experience the technological world neither as pure objectivity nor as an overwhelming supersubject, but rather as the specific reality that it is and with which we must learn to interact. Seeing technology as an independent being by and from itself means disclaiming any relationship of dominance between us. It means adopting a relationship of free mutuality that for the first time enables a genuine and somehow equal communication between both of us.

In view of the emergence of a second nature, we have to redefine what human activity is and what the relations that have evolved between human beings and reality are, in order to revise and review our former adjustment to and outlook upon the world. The process in which human artifacts emancipated themselves and thus became a second nature is not simply an additional factor in the modern subject's project and tendency to master and, eventually, to destroy nature. On the contrary, it is the necessary consequence of this project, which, at the same time, it fundamentally and vigorously calls into question. The emergence of a second nature undermines the basis and logic of our reality. The self-assured grip that the acting subject had over all entities, and with which it tried to guarantee truth and certainty, is lost if the action of subsuming and subjugating sets itself free from the acting subject or even hits back at it.

The subject does not simply cease being the subject; rather, it becomes evident that it never could have been one. The modern individual had been mistaken about his possibilities. According to this delusion, facts have evolved that must be adjusted to, looked for, and criticized in a wholly new way. Yet we have to adjust to *these* new and different facts and not to any that are only to be found in obsolete categories—such as in those of the opposition of *physis* and *techne*, or even of nature and mind.

In conclusion, I return to Rilke:

My answer—I don't yet know
the time, I'll say it.
But, listen, a rake which is already at work.
Up there, alone in the vineyard talks
a man already with the earth.

What might it be that they are talking about? The evening and the morning, land and sea, mountains and birds and people, seeing and hearing and feeling? Perhaps. Yet also—and I think that this would be the more important talk—about human dwelling upon the earth. About what it is today and might be tomorrow. What it means to live in a city nowadays. What significance it has, that work is changing. How to encounter the fact that opinions increase and diversify, yet become uniform at the same time. And so on.

So why quote the man who talks with the earth, alone up in the vineyard? Not because of what Heidegger called "the inexhaustible force of the simple."[15] In any case, not only because of this. Rather, because our reflection on the talk with the earth might render visible in a new way the often quoted "communication of the different."[16] Recognizing and preserving qualities like being in and of itself and otherness might bring about a finite and, in a new sense, "natural" communication with things and facts, whether those belong to the "first" or to the "second" nature.

NOTES

1. Ulrich Beck, *Gegengifte. Die organisierte Unverantwortlichkeit* (Frankfurt Am Main: Suhrkamp, 1988).

2. Hans Blumenberg, "Nachahmung der Natur," *Zur Vorgeschichte der Idee des Schöpferischen Menschen, Studium Generale* 10 (1957): 270.

3. Max Horkheimer and Theodor Adorno, *Dialektik der Aufklarung: philosophische Fragmente* (Frankfurt Am Main: Suhrkamp, 1981).

4. Gottfried Benn, *Gesammelte Werke*, Band 3: *Gedichte* (Wiesbaden: Limes Verlag, 1960), 256.

5. Rainer Maria Rilke, *Sämtliche Werke*, Zweiter Band: *Gedichte*, Zweiter Teil (Weisbaden: Insel Verlag, 1956), 473.

6. Rainer Maria Rilke, *Sämtliche Werke*, Erster Band: *Gedichte*, Ester Teil (Weisbaden: Insel Verlag, 1955), 767.

7. Wolfgang Welsch, *Äesthetisches Denken* (Stuttgart: P. Reclam, 1990).

8. Martin Heidegger, *Gelassenheit* (Pfullingen: Neske, 1959).

9. Ibid., 35.

10. Parmenides, *Peri Physeos*, frg.8,41.

11. Theodor W. Adorno, *Gesammelte Schriften*, Band 10.2: *Stichworte* (Frankfurt Am Main: Suhrkamp, 1977), "Anmerkungen zum philosophischen Denken," 601, 602.

12. See Martin Heidegger, *Gesamtausgabe*, Band 13: *Aus der Erfahrung des Denkens* (Frankfurt Am Main: V. Klostermann, 1983), "Zu einem Vers von Mörike," 93.

13. Peter Sloterdijk *Eurotaoismus. Zur Kritik der politischen Kinetik* (Frankfurt Am Main: Suhrkamp, 1989), 24.

14. Theodor W. Adorno, *Negative Dialektik* (Frankfurt Am Main: Suhrkamp, 1966), 349.

15. Martin Heidegger, *Gesamtausgabe*, Band 13: "Der Feldweg," 90.

16. Theodor W. Adorno, *Gesammelte Schriften*, Band 10.2: *Stichworte. Dialektische Epilegomena*, "Zu Subjekt und Objekt," 743.

Index

absence, 3–15; absolute, 42; in Husserl, xv
accessibility: of alienworld, 75–76
activity: and passivity, 276–77, 280
Adorno, Theodor, xx; compared to Derrida, 240; rejection of idealism, 257; agreement with Lukács, 260; materialism, 258–59; and the nonidentical, 260, 263; and relativism, 262
aesthetic: experience, 275–77; sense, 58
Aesthetic Theory, 262
affirmation: and deconstruction, 249
agonistics: of reason and power, xiv
agricultural life: for Hegel, 105
aletheia, 162; and truth, 160, 166; as openness, 170
alien: and familiar, 167
alienation, 257–58, 279, 282, 283, 284
alienworld. *See* homeworld
Alltäglichkeit, 127
alterity, xiv
analogy, viii
anamnestic criticism, 242
anarcho-communist tradition, 132
anthropocentrism, 260
antinomy, 263; of Western Marxism, xix, 254, 259
apology, xviii; and judgment, 200, 201; in Levinas, 203, 204
apperception, 83; of alien body, 87–90; as judgment, 85–86; and transcendent community, 96–98; of the world, 20
appresentation: nature of, 85
appropriation: of one's will, 198
Arendt, Hannah, xviii; and conscience, 201–02; and judgment, 195, 196, 197; and political discourse, 204; representation, 134
Aristotle, viii, 281; and Gadamer, xviii, 181–82; and Heidegger, 29, 30, 32, 34, 42, 47; and justice, 231; as inspiration for phenomenology, xi; speaker and hearer, 152
art: for Adorno, 259; and truth, 160, 168–69; presentational character, 163

asymmetry: axiological, 76
authentic: moral life, 139
authority: legitimacy of, ix, 146–47; critical theory and, 146

beautiful, the: and language, 165; metaphysics of, 160, 161–62; and metaphysics of light, 180; and mimesis, xviii
Beck, Ulrich, 270
Being and Time, xv, 176; origins of, 29–49; and phenomenology, 52; as a text, 32–34
being: experience of, xv; for Gadamer, 165; -in-itself and language, 178; -in-the-world, 59; question of, 29–30; temporal apriori of, 33. *See also* Dasein
Benjamin, Walter: and Derrida, 241
Bernstein, Richard, 160, 184
Blumenberg, Hans, 270
body: flesh of, 59; constituted by forces, 226; of the other, 87–90
Brentano, Franz, 10–11

call, the, 102, 109. *See also* destiny
Caputo, John, 186–87; and Gadamer, 175
Cartesian Meditations, vii, viii, 95; fifth Cartesian Meditation, 22, 68, 71, 72, 74, 77, 83, 84
chiasm, 58–59
circulation: state limits on, 101–11
civil society: for Hegel, 102–07, 116; for Heidegger, 102
commodities: Hegel's analysis of, 103–04
communication: and community, x; constitutive role of, 66; and analysis of social world, 77
community: and agriculture, 105; of communication, x; as fundamental concept, 83–84; and conflict, 208; and consensus, 186; and culture, 96–98; danger of, ix; and deferred identity, 215–17; interpretive, 160, 211; loss of sense of, xix, 214; nature of, xviii, 92–93, 109, 207; and normalization, 73–74; and others, xvi, 90–99; and philosophy, 274; political, xvii;

289

emancipatory ideal, 247
empathy, vii, viii, x, xi, xii, xii n. 21, xiii
enlightening. *See einleuchtende*
Enlightenment, 263; Adorno's critique of,
    257–58; critique of authority, 146; ideology,
    149; narratives, 207
environment, xix, 265
epistemology: as domination, 261; in Lukács's
    thought, 255; Marxist, 253
epoché: 53; and the other, 85; more than method-
    ological tool, 56; residuum after, 67; and solip-
    sism, 84, 95
ereignis: 32, 35, 40, 48, 103, 108; being's with-
    drawal in, 109; and meaning, 102
essence: phenomenology as study of, 52; plural-
    ity, 168
ethics: of deconstruction, 239
event, the, 45; communicative, 165; instituting,
    228, 229; of truth, 165; of understanding, 155;
    the word as, 154
evidence, xviii; and foundation, 67; in Husserl,
    182–83; as consistent verifiability, 86
evil: as willed chaos, 203
existentialism: in *Being and Time*, 33–34
Experience and Judgment, xiii, 24
experience: basic level of, 18–19; of body, 89;
    environmental, 44–45, 46; of experience, 46;
    immanent, 55; immediate, 46, 47, 48; liminal,
    74; original, 45; reduction of, 84–85; structure
    of, 76

facticity, 32; as an event, 45; hermeneutics of,
    36–39; and phenomenology, 52; problem of, 68
falsifiability: in hermeneutics, 168, 169
feminine: potency of matter, 43
finite philosophy, 273–75, 277–78
finitude: 110, 210, 211; as Christian idea,
    152–53; experience of, 275; and language,
    154; ontological, 108; philosophy of, 60; and
    tradition, 148, 149
flux, 4, 6, 43, 187; absolute, 13–15; of
    appearances, 161; and invariance, 54; of the
    Sachen, 186; of sensations, 38, 41
"Force and Signification," 222, 224
"Force of Law: The 'Mystical Foundation of
    Authority',", xix, 226, 228, 249
force: in Derrida, xix; field of, 224–26; Hegel's
    law of, 223; and law, 221, 222; and sense,
    226–27

form: judgment of, 107
Formal and Transcendental Logic, viii, ix, 17,
    182
foundation: 65, in Husserl, 66–68
freedom, xvi; and circulation, 106–07; for Hegel,
    122; Idea of, 196; and modernity, 101; and
    political critique, 117; from prejudice, 155;
    and the state, 120; and tradition, 148–50

Gadamer, Hans-Georg, xiii, xvii, xviii; and
    Derrida, 165–66; and Habermas, 122; and
    Heidegger, 170; and image, 162–67; and tradi-
    tion, 145–56; and truth, 159–60, 161–67, 175
gaze, the, 46, 121
gelassenheit, 277
generosity, 200
gestalt switch: and enlightening, 185
gestell, 101, 103, 104, 109, 111
givenness, 75–77
grundschicht, 18, 19–26
guilt, 203

Habermas, Jürgen, xvii; and critique, 118, 119;
    and Derrida, 243, 247–50; and Gadamer,
    175–75; and Hegel, 115–24; and justice,
    243–47; and Lyotard, 215, 216
Hegel, G. F.W., xii, xiv, xvi, xvii, xix; and agricul-
    tural life, 105; and book of nature, 221–23; and
    civil society, 102–07, 116; analysis of
    commodities, 103–04; and constitution, 124;
    and corporation, 105–06; abandonment of cri-
    tique, 123; and Heidegger, 101–11; and judg-
    ment, 196; objective mind, 282; political
    philosophy, 115–124; reversal, 152
Heidegger, Martin, viii, ix, xi, xv, xvi, xx; and
    Being and Time, 29–49; and civil society, 102;
    critique of metaphysics, 150; early and late
    thought, 35–36; and Gadamer, 160, 170; com-
    pared with Hegel, 101–11; and hermeneutic
    understanding, 176; and phenomenology, 52
Held, Klaus, 73
Henry, Michel, 55
hermeneutics, xiii; experience, 167, 170;
    phenomenological, 38; and phronesis, 181; and
    political conservatism, 145–46; and particular-
    ity, 122; and prejudice, 177; structure of, 162;
    and truth, xviii, 166, 175–77
hierarchy: and *différance*, 227; and the general
    text, 226